FOR BADIOU

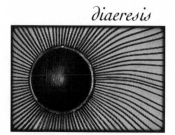

*diaeresis*

# FOR BADIOU

## Idealism without Idealism

Frank Ruda

Preface by Slavoj Žižek

Northwestern University Press
Evanston, Illinois

Northwestern University Press
www.nupress.northwestern.edu

Printed in the United States of America

10  9  8  7  6  5  4  3  2  1

**Library of Congress Cataloging-in-Publication Data**

Ruda, Frank, author.
    For Badiou : idealism without idealism / Frank Ruda ; preface by Slavoj
Žižek.
        pages cm. — (Diaeresis)
    Includes bibliographical references and index.
    ISBN 978-0-8101-3087-6 (cloth : alk. paper) — ISBN 978-0-8101-3097-5
(pbk. : alk. paper) — ISBN 978-0-8101-3088-3 (ebook)
    1. Badiou, Alain. 2. Materialism.  I. Žižek, Slavoj, writer of preface. II. Title.
III. Series: Diaeresis.
    B2430.B274R83 2015
    194—dc23
                                                                    2015004439

And *remember* also him who is forgetful whither the way leads . . .
  —Heraclitus

# Contents

# Preface: The Book We Are All Waiting For

Slavoj Žižek

With regard to materialism, we are today witnessing a paradoxical reversal. In the standard pre-critical metaphysics, "finitude" was associated with materialist empiricism ("only material finite objects really exist"), while "infinity" was the domain of idealist spiritualism. In an unexpected paradoxical reversal, today, the main argument for spiritualism, against radical materialism, relies on the irreducibility of human finitude as the unsurpassable horizon of our existence, while it is today's forms of radical scientific materialism which keep the spirit of infinity alive. The standard line of argumentation is: we should not forget that the technological dream of the total mastery over nature and our lives is a dream that we, humans, remain forever grounded in our finite life-world with its un-fathomable background—it is this finitude, this very limitation of our horizon, which opens up the space for proper spirituality. All of today's predominant forms of spirituality thus paradoxically emphasize that we, humans, are not free-floating spirits but irreducibly embodied in a material life-world; they all preach respect for this limitation and warn against the "idealist" hubris of radical materialism—exemplary is here the case of ecology. In contrast to this spiritualist attitude of limitation, the radical scientific attitude which reduces man to a biological mechanism sustains the promise of the full technological control over human life, its artificial re-creation, its biogenetic and biochemical regulation, ultimately its immortality in the guise of the reduction of our inner Self to a software program that can be copied from one to another hardware.

It is as if, with this shift, the old materialist insight of Spinoza according to which terms like "God" are false terms with no positive meanings, just terms which provide a deceiving positive form for the domain of what we do *not* know, gets its final confirmation: the religious dimension is explicitly linked to the limitation of our comprehension, that is, this dimension is not the intimation of a "higher" knowledge, but the inverted assertion of its limitation. Which is why religious thinkers like so much (what appears as) the limits of our knowledge: don't try to understand the biogenetic foundations of our mind, the result may be the loss of soul; don't try to reach beyond the Big Bang, this is the point where God directly intervened into material reality . . . It was already Kant who said that he limited the space of knowledge to create the space for faith.

These two sides of the same coin are clearly discernible in the work of Andrei Tarkovsky: what pervades Tarkovsky's films is the heavy gravity of Earth, which seems to exert its pressure on time itself, generating an effect of temporal anamorphosis, extending the dragging of time well beyond what we perceive as justified by the requirements of narrative movement (one should confer here on the term "Earth" all the resonance it acquired in late Heidegger)—perhaps Tarkovsky is the clearest example of what Deleuze called the time-image replacing the movement-image. This time of the Real is neither the symbolic time of the diegetic space nor the time of the reality of our (the spectator's) viewing the film, but an intermediate domain whose visual equivalent is perhaps the protracted stains which "are" the yellow sky in late van Gogh or the water or grass in Munch: this uncanny "massiveness" pertains neither to the direct materiality of the color stains nor to the materiality of the depicted objects—it dwells in a kind of intermediate spectral domain of what Schelling called *geistige Koerperlichkeit*, the spiritual corporeality. In our standard ideological tradition, the approach to Spirit is perceived as Elevation, as getting rid of the burden of weight, of the gravitating force which binds us to earth, as cutting links with material inertia and starting to "float freely"; in contrast to this, in Tarkovsky's universe, we enter the spiritual dimension only via intense direct physical contact with the humid heaviness of earth (or stale water)—the ultimate Tarkovskian spiritual experience takes place when a subject is lying stretched on the earth's surface, half submerged in stale water; Tarkovsky's heroes do not pray on their knees, with the head turned upwards, towards heaven, but while intensely listening to the silent palpitation of the humid earth . . . One can see, now, why Stanislaw Lem's novel *Solaris* had to exert such an attraction on Tarkovsky: the planet Solaris seems to provide the ultimate embodiment of the Tarkovskian notion of a heavy humid stuff (earth) which, far from functioning as the opposite of spirituality, serves as its very medium; this gigantic "material Thing which thinks" literally gives body to the direct coincidence of Matter and Spirit. A consequent materialism has to break with both these features: to get rid of Spirit, it gladly sacrifices matter itself in its inert density.

The fundamental premise of today's advocates of the finitude of our existence is thus: we are thrown into a world which preexists us, which we did not create, and so cannot ever fully grasp, control, or dominate; whatever we do, even in our most radically autonomous act, we have to rely on the opaque background of inherited traditions and the socio-symbolic texture which predetermine the scope of our acts. Hans-Georg Gadamer made this point in very plastic terms: the time has come to turn around Hegel's famous formula on the becoming-subject of Substance, of the subjective-reflexive appropriation of all our substantial presuppositions, and accomplish the same journey backwards, from the subject to its substantial presuppositions. In the same mode, the lesson the predominant ecological ideology is constantly hammering is our finitude: we are not Cartesian subjects extracted from reality, we are finite beings embedded in a biosphere which vastly transgresses our horizon. In our exploitation of natural resources, we are borrowing from the future, so one should treat our Earth with respect, as something ultimately Sacred, something that should not be unveiled totally, that should and will forever remain a Mystery, a power we should trust, not dominate.

Who, then, *is* a materialist today? Many orientations claim to be materialist: scientific materialism (Darwinism, brain sciences), "discursive" materialism (ideology as the result of material discursive practices), what Alain Badiou calls "democratic materialism" (the spontaneous egalitarian hedonism) . . . Some of these materialisms are mutually exclusive: for "discursive" materialists, it is scientific materialism which, in its allegedly "naive" direct assertion of external reality, is "idealist" in the sense that it does not take into account the role of "material" symbolic practice in constituting what appears to us as reality; for scientific materialism, "discursive" materialism is an obscurantist muddle not to be taken seriously. Discursive materialism and scientific materialism are, in their very antagonism, the front and the obverse of the same coin, one standing for radical culturalization (everything, inclusive of our notions of nature, is a contingent discursive formation), and the other for radical naturalization (everything, inclusive of our culture, can be accounted for in the terms of natural biological evolution).

The basic premise of discursive materialism was to conceive language itself as a mode of production, and to apply to it Marx's logic of commodity fetishism. So, in the same way that, for Marx, the sphere of exchange obliterates (renders invisible) its process of production, the linguistic exchange also obliterates the textual process that engenders meaning: in a spontaneous fetishist misperception, we experience the meaning of a word or act as something that is a direct property of the designated thing or process, that is, we overlook the complex field of discursive practices which produces this meaning. What one should focus on here is the fundamental ambiguity of this notion of linguistic fetishism: is the idea that, in the good old modern way, we should distinguish between "objective" properties of things and our projections of meanings onto things; or are we dealing with the more radical linguistic version of transcendental constitution, for which the very idea of "objective reality," of "things existing out there, independently of our mind," is a "fetishist illusion" which is blind to how our symbolic activity ontologically constitutes the very reality to which it "refers" or which it designates? Neither of these two options is the correct one—what one should drop is their underlying shared premise, the (crude, abstract-universal) homology between discursive "production" and material production.

This "discursive materialism" relies on the so-called linguistic turn in philosophy which emphasizes how language is not a neutral medium of designation, but a practice embedded in a life-world: we do things with it, accomplish specific acts . . . Is it not the time to turn this cliché around: who *is* it that, today, claims that language is a neutral medium of designation? So, perhaps, one should emphasize how language is not a mere moment of life-world, a practice within it: the true miracle of language is that it can *also* serve as a neutral medium which just designates a conceptual/ideal content. In other words, the true task is not to locate language as a neutral medium within a life-world practice, but to show how, within this life world, a neutral medium of designation can emerge.

How, then, are we to orientate ourselves in this mess? The best starting point is Lenin's thesis that every great scientific breakthrough changes the very definition of materialism. Today, *the* scientific discovery which needs philosophical rethinking is quantum physics—how are we to interpret its ontological implications while avoiding the double trap of superficial pragmatic empiricism ("the only thing that matters is that calculations based on the theory work; who cares about ontology?") and obscurantist idealism ("mind creates reality")? Quantum physics compels us to turn against Lenin himself and drop the assertion of "fully existing external reality" as the basic premise of materialism—on the contrary, the premise of today's materialism is the "non-All" of reality, its ontological incompleteness. (Recall Lenin's deadlock when, in *Materialism and Empiriocriticism*, he proposes as a minimal philosophical definition of materialism the assertion of an objective reality which exists independently of human mind, without any further qualifications: in this sense, Plato himself is a materialist!)

Today's materialism also has nothing to do with any positive determination of content, like "matter" versus "spirit," that is, with the substantialization of Matter into the only Absolute (Hegel's critique is here fully justified: "matter" in its abstraction is a pure *Gedankending*). One should thus not be afraid of the much-decried "dissolution of matter in a field of energies" in modern physics: a true materialist should fully embrace it. Materialism has nothing to do with the assertion of the inert density of matter; it is, on the contrary, a position which accepts the ultimate Void of reality—the consequence of its central thesis on the primordial multiplicity is that there is no "substantial reality," that the only "substance" of the multiplicity is Void. This is why the opposite of true materialism is not so much a consequent idealism but, rather, the vulgar-idealist "materialism" of someone like David Chalmers who proposes to account for the "hard problem of consciousness" by postulating "self-awareness" as an additional fundamental force of nature, together with gravity, magnetism, and so on—as, literally, its "quintessence" (the fifth essence). The temptation to "see" thought as an additional component of natural/ material reality itself is the ultimate vulgarity.

The minimal definition of today's materialism hinges on the admission of a gap between what Schelling called Existence and the Ground of Existence: prior to fully existent reality, there is a chaotic non-All proto-reality, a pre-ontological virtual fluctuation of a not-yet fully constituted real. This pre-ontological real is what Badiou calls pure multiplicity, in contrast to the level of appearances, which is the level of reality constituted by the transcendental horizon of a world. It is here that, in order to specify the meaning of materialism, one should apply Lacan's formulas of sexuation: there is a fundamental difference between the assertion "everything is matter" (which relies on its constitutive exception—in the case of Lenin who, in his *Materialism and Empiriocriticism*, falls into this trap, the very position of enunciation of the subject whose mind "reflects" matter) and the assertion "there is nothing which is not matter" (which, with its other side, "not-All is matter," opens up the space for the account of immaterial phenomena). What this means is that a truly radical materialism is by definition non-reductionist: far from claiming that "everything is matter," it confers upon the "immaterial" phenomena a specific positive non-being.

When, in his argument against the reductive explanation of consciousness, Chalmers writes that "even if we knew every last detail about the physics of the universe—the configuration, causation, and evolution among all the fields and particles in the spatiotemporal manifold—*that* information would not lead us to postulate the existence of conscious experience,"[1] he commits the standard Kantian mistake: such a total knowledge is strictly nonsensical, epistemologically *and* ontologically. It is the obverse of the vulgar determinist notion, articulated, in Marxism, by Nikolai Bukharin, when he wrote that, if we were to know the entire physical reality, we would also be able to predict precisely the emergence of a revolution. This line of reasoning—consciousness as an excess, surplus, over the physical totality—is misleading, since it has to evoke a meaningless hyperbole: when we imagine the Whole of reality, there is no longer any place for consciousness (and subjectivity). There are two options here: either subjectivity is an illusion, or reality is *in itself* (not only epistemologically) not-All.

One should thus, from the radically materialist standpoint, fearlessly think through the consequences of *rejecting* "objective reality": reality dissolves in "subjective" fragments, *but these fragments themselves fall back into anonymous Being, losing their subjective consistency.* Fred Jameson drew attention to the paradox of the postmodern rejection of consistent Self—its ultimate result is that we lose its opposite, objective reality itself, which gets transformed into a set of contingent subjective constructions. A true materialist should do the opposite: refuse to accept "objective reality" in order to undermine consistent subjectivity. This ontological openness of the one-less multiplicity also allows us to approach in a new way Kant's second antinomy of pure reason whose thesis is: "Every composite substance in the world consists of simple parts; and there exists nothing that is not either itself simple, or composed of simple parts."[2] Here is Kant's proof:

> For, grant that composite substances do not consist of simple parts; in this case, if all combination or composition were annihilated in thought, no composite part, and (as, by the supposition, there do not exist simple parts) no simple part would exist. Consequently, no substance; consequently, nothing would exist. Either, then, it is impossible to annihilate composition in thought; or, after such annihilation, there must remain something that subsists without composition, that is, something that is simple. But in the former case the composite could not itself consist of substances, because with substances composition is merely a contingent relation, apart from which they must still exist as self-subsistent beings. Now, as this case contradicts the supposition, the second must contain the truth—that the substantial composite in the world consists of simple parts.
>
> It follows, as an immediate inference, that the things in the world are all, without exception, simple beings—that composition is merely an external condition pertaining to them—and that, although we never can separate and isolate the elementary substances from the state of composition, reason must cogitate these as the primary subjects of all composition, and consequently, as prior thereto—and as simple substances.[3]

What, however, if we accept the conclusion that, ultimately, "nothing exists" (a conclusion which, incidentally, is exactly the same as the conclusion of Plato's *Parmenides*: "Then may we not sum up the argument in a word and say truly: If one is not, then nothing is?")? Such a move, although rejected by Kant as obvious nonsense, is not as un-Kantian as it may appear: it is here that one should apply yet again the Kantian distinction between negative and infinite judgment. The statement "material reality is all there is" can be negated in two ways: in the form of "material reality *isn't all there is*" and "material reality *is non-all*." The first negation (of a predicate) leads to the standard metaphysics: material reality isn't everything, there is another, higher, spiritual reality . . . As such, this negation is, in accordance with Lacan's formulas of sexuation, inherent to the positive statement "material reality is all there is": as its constitutive exception, it grounds its universality. If, however, we assert a non-predicate and say "material reality *is non-all*," this merely asserts the non-All of reality without implying any exception—paradoxically, one should thus claim that "material reality *is non-all*," *not* "material reality is all there is," is the true formula of materialism.

How is such a position possible, thinkable even? Let us begin with the surprising fact that Badiou does not identify as the "principal contradiction," the predominant antagonism, of today's ideological situation the struggle between idealism and materialism, but the struggle between two forms of materialism (democratic and dialectical): since materialism *is* the hegemonic ideology today, the struggle is *within* materialism. Plus, to add insult to injury, "democratic materialism" stands for the reduction of all there is to the historical reality of bodies and languages (the twins of Darwinism, brain sciences, etc., and of discursive historicism), while "materialist dialectics" adds the "Platonic" ("idealist") dimension of "eternal" Truths. However, to anyone acquainted with the dialectics of history, there should be no surprise in it.

In his *Logiques des mondes*, Badiou provides a succinct definition of "democratic materialism" and its opposite, "materialist dialectics": the axiom which condenses the first one is "*There is nothing but bodies and languages . . . ,*" to which materialist dialectics adds "*. . . with the exception of truths.*"[4] This opposition is not so much the opposition of two ideologies or philosophies as the opposition between non-reflected presuppositions/beliefs into which we are "thrown" insofar as we are immersed into our life-world, and the reflective attitude of thought proper which enables us to subtract ourselves from this immersion, to "unplug" ourselves, as Morpheus would have put it in *The Matrix*, a film much appreciated by Badiou, the film in which one also finds a precise account of the need, evoked by Badiou, to control oneself (when Morpheus explains to Neo the lot of ordinary people totally caught ["plugged"] in the Matrix, he says: "Everyone who is not unplugged is a potential agent"). This is why Badiou's axiom of "democratic materialism" is his answer to the question of our spontaneous (non-reflexive) ideological beliefs: "What do I think when I am outside my own control? Or, rather, which is our (my) spontaneous belief?" Furthermore, this opposition is immediately linked to what (once) one called "class struggle in philosophy," the orientation most identified by the names of Lenin, Mao Zedong, and Althusser—here is Mao's succinct formulation: "It is only when there is class struggle that there can be philosophy." The ruling class (whose ideas are the ruling ideas) is represented by the spontaneous ideology, while the dominated class has to fight its way through intense conceptual work, which is why, for Badiou, the key reference is here Plato—not the caricaturized Plato, the anti-democratic philosopher of the aristocratic reaction to Athenian democracy, but the Plato who was the first to clearly assert the field of rationality freed from inherited beliefs.

Furthermore, one should bear in mind the Platonic, properly metaphysical, thrust of Badiou's distinction between democratic materialism and materialist dialectics: *prima facie*, it cannot but appear as a proto-idealist gesture to assert that material reality is not all that there is, that there is also another level of incorporeal truths. Badiou performs here the paradoxical philosophical gesture of defending, *as a materialist*, the autonomy of the "immaterial" order of Truth. As a materialist, and in order to be thoroughly materialist, Badiou focuses on the *idealist* topos *par excellence*: how can a human animal forsake its animality and put its life in the service of a transcendent Truth? How can the "transubstantiation" from the pleasure-oriented life of an *individual* to the life of a *subject* dedicated to a Cause occur? In other words, how is a free act possible? How can one break (out of) the network of the causal connections of positive reality and conceive an act that begins by and in itself? Again, Badiou *repeats within the materialist frame the elementary gesture of idealist anti-reductionism*: human Reason cannot be reduced to the result of evolutionary adaptation; art is not just a heightened procedure of providing sensual pleasures, but a medium of Truth; and so on.

This, then, is our basic *philosophico-political choice (decision)* today: either repeat in a materialist vein Plato's assertion of the meta-physical dimension of "eternal Ideas," or continue to dwell in the postmodern universe of "democratic-materialist" historicist relativism, caught in the vicious cycle of the eternal struggle with "premodern" fundamentalisms. The key concept which enables us to think Plato's "Ideas" in a materialist vein is the concept of Event. *The* three contemporary philosophers—Heidegger, Deleuze, Badiou—are philosophers of the Event: in Heidegger, it is the Event as the epochal disclosure of a configuration of Being; in Deleuze, it is the Event as the de-substantialized pure becom-

ing of Sense; in Badiou, it is the Event as the reference which grounds
a Truth-process. For all three of them, Event is irreducible to the order
of being (in the sense of positive reality), to the set of its material (pre)-
conditions. But, in contrast to Heidegger, Deleuze and Badiou both perform the same paradoxical philosophical gesture of defending, *as materialists*, the autonomy of the "immaterial" order of the Event. Additionally,
against the false appearance that this gesture is also aimed at psychoanalysis (is not the point of the notion of "sublimation" that the allegedly "higher" human activities are just a roundabout "sublimated" way
to realize a "lower" goal?), therein resides already the significant achieve-
ment of psychoanalysis: its claim is that sexuality itself, sexual drives per-
taining to the human animal, cannot be accounted for in evolutionary
terms.

This makes clear the true stakes of Badiou's gesture: in order for
materialism to truly win over idealism, it is not enough to succeed in the
"reductionist" approach and demonstrate how mind, consciousness, and
so on can nonetheless somehow be accounted for within the evolutionary-
positivist frame of materialism. On the contrary, the materialist claim
should be much stronger: it is *only* materialism that can accurately explain the very phenomena of mind, consciousness, and so on; and, con-
versely, it is idealism that is "vulgar," that always already "reifies" these
phenomena.

This paradox is what Frank Ruda aims at with his wonderful qualification of Badiou's thought as "idealism without idealism." His *For Badiou:
Idealism without Idealism* is not only the best book on Badiou, it is a book
which addresses *the* question of today's philosophy: how can we break out
of what Quentin Meillassoux calls "transcendental correlationism" and
assert a materialist position without regressing to a new version of pre-
transcendental realism (as Lenin did)? This is why his book is the book
we were all waiting for: a book which cannot be ignored since it changes
the entire field. Even if one doesn't agree with its premises, one's disagreement has to be formulated *within* the field opened up by this book.
*For Badiou: Idealism without Idealism* is a proof—against all postmodern
historicist temptations—that genuine philosophical thinking is not only
possible, but urgently needed.

# Acknowledgments

Samuel Beckett once spoke of "the time taken to be proved true." My sincere hope is that the time this book took to materialize will have been a time taken to be proved solid, rigid, and consistent. However, this very time would not even have existed without Eva Heubach—Alain Badiou, Ray Brassier, Lorenzo Chiesa, Rebecca Comay, Joan Copjec, Christoph Menke, Mladen Dolar, Simon Hajdini, Peter Hallward, Agon Hamza, Hugo Heubach, Adrian Johnston, Mark Potocnik, Ozren Pupovac, Rado Riha, Anneliese Ruda, Gerd and Manuela Ruda, Cornelia and Ralf Schmidt, Aaron Schuster, Lidija Sumah, Jelica Sumic-Riha, Catherine Toal, Jan Völker, Slavoj Žižek, and Alenka Zupančič.

# Abbreviations

For all works of Alain Badiou and other authors I cite frequently I use the following abbreviations within the text. All other references are indicated in the bibliography. Any translation of a text that was not available in English has been prepared by the author.

## Badiou

| | |
|---|---|
| *BBE* | Badiou, Alain. 2005b. *Being and Event*. London: Continuum. |
| *BC* | Badiou, Alain. 2008a. *Conditions*. London: Continuum. |
| *BCH* | Badiou, Alain. 2010a. *The Communist Hypothesis*. London: Continuum. |
| "BCP" | Badiou, Alain. 2010f. "The Courage of the Present." http://www.scribd.com/doc/52646249/Badiou-The-Courage-of-the-Present. |
| *BE* | Badiou, Alain. 2001. *Ethics: An Essay on the Understanding of Evil*. London: Verso. |
| *BIT* | Badiou, Alain. 2003a. *Infinite Thought: Truth and the Return of Philosophy*. London: Continuum. |
| "BITP I" | Badiou, Alain. 2001–2002. "Séminaire: Image du temps présent I." http://www.entretemps.asso.fr/Badiou/01–02.3.htm. |
| "BITP II" | Badiou, Alain. 2002–2003a. "Séminaire : Image du temps présent II." http://www.entretemps.asso.fr/Badiou/02–03.3.htm. |
| "BIV" | Badiou, Alain. 2012–2013. "Séminaire: L'immanence des vérités." http://www.entretemps.asso.fr/Badiou/12–13.htm. |
| "BLO" | Badiou, Alain. 2012b. "Logology Against Ontology." In *The Adventure of French Philosophy* by Alain Badiou, 309–20. London: Verso. |

| | |
|---|---|
| *BLoW* | Badiou, Alain. 2009a. *Logics of Worlds: Being and Event, 2.* London: Continuum. |
| *BMP* | Badiou, Alain. 2005c. *Metapolitics.* London: Verso. |
| "BMPH" | Badiou, Alain. 2000. "Metaphysics and the Critique of Metaphysics." *Pli* 10: 174–90. |
| *BMPHI* | Badiou, Alain. 1999. *Manifesto for Philosophy.* Albany: SUNY Press. |
| *BMS* | Badiou, Alain. 2008b. *The Meaning of Sarkozy.* London: Verso. |
| "BN" | Badiou, Alain. 2001–2002. "Séminaire: Image du temps présent I." http://www.entretemps.asso.fr/ Badiou/01–02.3.htm. |
| *BNN* | Badiou, Alain. 2008c. *Number and Numbers.* Cambridge, Eng.: Polity. |
| *BOD* | Badiou, Alain. 2009b. *Of an Obscure Disaster/On the End of State-Truth.* Maastricht: Jan van Eyck. |
| "BPAP" | Badiou, Alain. 2011–2012. "Séminaire pour aujourd'hui: Platon!" http://www.entretemps.asso.fr/Badiou/07–08.htm. |
| "BPCR" | Badiou, Alain. 2007a. "Philosophy as Creative Repetition." *The Symptom: Online Journal for Lacan.com* 8 (Winter). http://www .lacan.com/badrepeat.html. |
| *BPP* | Badiou, Alain. 1985b. *Peut-on penser la politique?.* Paris: Seuil. |
| "BQM" | Badiou, Alain. 2010–2011. "Séminaire : Que signifie 'changer le monde'?" http://www.entretemps.asso.fr/Badiou/10–11 .htm. |
| *BRH* | Badiou, Alain. 2012f. *The Rebirth of History: Times of Riots and Uprisings.* London: Verso. |
| *BRK* | Badiou et al. 2011b. *The Rational Kernel of the Hegelian Dialectic.* Melbourne: re.press. |
| *BRL* | Badiou, Alain, and Élisabeth Roudineso. 2012. *Lacan, passé present: Dialogue.* Paris: Seuil. |
| *BRP* | Badiou, Alain. 2013b. *Plato's Republic: A Dialogue in 16 Chapters.* Cambridge, Eng.: Polity. |
| *BSMP* | Badiou, Alain. 2011c. *Second Manifesto for Philosophy.* Cambridge, Eng.: Polity. |
| "BSP I" | Badiou, Alain. 2004–2005. "Séminaire : S'orienter dans la pensée, s'orienter dans l'existence I." http://www.entretemps. asso.fr/Badiou/04–05.2.htm. |

"BSP II"    Badiou, Alain. 2005–2006. "Séminaire : S'orienter dans la pensée, s'orienter dans l'existence II." http://www.entretemps.asso.fr/Badiou/05–06.2.htm.

"BSP III"    Badiou, Alain. 2006–2007. "Séminaire : S'orienter dans la pensée, s'orienter dans l'existence III." http://www.entretemps.asso.fr/Badiou/06–07.2.htm.

*BSPQ*    Badiou, Alain. 2012d. *Sarkozy: Pire que prévu, les autres: Prévoir le pire.* Circonstances, 7. Paris: Lignes.

*BSPU*    Badiou, Alain. 2003c. *Saint Paul: The Foundation of Universalism.* Stanford, Calif.: Stanford University Press.

"BTN"    Badiou, Alain. 2008d. "The Three Negations." *Cardozo Law Review* 29, no. 5: 1877–83.

*BTS*    Badiou, Alain. 2009c. *Theory of the Subject.* London: Continuum.

Others

"APRW"    Althusser, Louis. 1971b. "Philosophy as Revolutionary Weapon (February 1968)." In *Lenin and Philosophy and Other Essays*, 11–12. New York: Monthly Review Press.

*DM*    Descartes, René. 2000b. *Discourse on the Method for Conducting One's Reason Well and for Seeking the Truth in the Sciences (1637).* In *Philosophical Essays and Correspondence*, by René Descartes, 46–83. Indianapolis, Ind.: Hackett.

*DMFP*    Descartes, René. 2000a. *Meditations on First Philosophy (1641).* In *Philosophical Essays and Correspondence*, by René Descartes, 97–142. Indianapolis, Ind.: Hackett.

"FRRW"    Freud, Sigmund. 1964. "Remembering, Repeating, Working Through. (Further Recommendations on the Technique of Psycho-Analysis II)." In *The Standard Edition of the Psychological Works of Sigmund Freud*, 12: 145–56. New York: Norton and Norton.

*HOP*    Hegel, G. W. F. 2008. *Outlines of the Philosophy of Right.* Oxford: Oxford University Press.

*HSL*    Hegel, G. W. F. 1969. *Science of Logic.* New York: Humanity Books.

*LAN*    Lazarus, Sylvain. 1996. *Anthropologie du nom.* Paris: Seuil.

*PPP*    Pasolini, Pier Paolo. 2007. *Der heilige Paulus.* Schüren: Marburg.

"SCF"     Sartre, Jean-Paul. 1967. "Cartesian Freedom." In *Literary Philosophical Essays*, by Jean-Paul Sartre, 180–97. Vancouver: Collier Books.

*SLU*     Lavine, Shaughan. 1998. *Understanding the Infinite*. Cambridge, Mass.: Harvard University Press.

*ZID*     Žižek, Slavoj. 2008. *In Defense of Lost Causes*, London / New York: Verso.

*ZLE*     Žižek, Slavoj. 2010a. *Living in the End Times*. London: Verso.

*ZLN*     Žižek, Slavoj. 2012. *Less Than Nothing: Hegel and the Shadow of Dialectical Materialism*. London: Verso.

"ZPV"     Žižek, Slavoj. 2006b. "Philosophy, the 'Unknown Knowns,' and the Public Use of Reason." *Topoi* 2: 137–42.

*ZR*      Žižek, Slavoj. 2002b. *Die Revolution steht bevor: Dreizehn Versuche über Lenin*. Frankfurt am Main: Suhrkamp.

*ZST*     Žižek, Slavoj. 2001. *Did Somebody Say Totalitarianism? Five Interventions on the (Mis)Use of a Notion*. London: Verso.

*ZTF*     Žižek, Slavoj. 2009b. *First as Tragedy, Then as Farce*. London: Verso.

*ZV*      Žižek, Slavoj. 2008a. *Violence: Six Sideways Reflections*. New York: Picador.

FOR BADIOU

# Introduction

## I, Philosophy, Speak

"*Dialectic* is one of those ancient sciences that have been most
misunderstood in the metaphysics of the moderns, as well as by
popular philosophy in general, ancient and modern alike."
—*HSL*, 831

In 1914 Sigmund Freud published a remarkable text. In it he for the
first time introduced the concept of the compulsion to repeat, of the
transference neurosis, and of working through.[1] Freud begins it by periodizing (and analyzing) the history of psychoanalytic technique. As he
reconstructs its history, psychoanalysis first sought to make the analysands
remember and abreact (often if not mostly in hypnosis) the psychic processes of those situations that were deemed constitutive for the symptom
formation of the patient. This was supposed to allow them to then be put
under the guidance of conscious activity. In its second phase and after re-
nouncing hypnosis as an essential element of its practice, psychoanalysis
focused on deciphering from the free associations of the patient precisely
those elements that he was unable to consciously recall. These resistances
provided the basis of the analyst's interpretation with which he then confronted the patient. These confrontations aimed at eluding these very
resistances and were supposed to enable the patient to remember what
previously he could not remember. In these two stages, analysis assumed
that behind the formed symptoms there lie (objective) situations that if
remembered would dissolve the symptoms of the patient. But whereas the
first stage of psychoanalytic technique linked the dissolving of symptoms
to something akin to the Aristotelian catharsis (by letting the patient work
out how to work off what he previously, in the original situation, was unable to abreact), the second stage sought to rather use the very amount
of labor the patient had to come up with "in being obliged to overcome
his criticism of his free association" ("FRRW," 147). The first stage recon-

3

structed the situation, in which the symptom was formed for the sake of generating a different psychic response to it; the second already asserted that it is more crucial to deal with the patient's resistances against remembering the situation in question and thereby implied the insight that the patient's resistance counts a great deal—yet its focus was still on finding access to an objective situation behind and at the ground of the symptom(s). "Finally there was evolved the consistent technique used, in which the analyst gives up the attempt to bring a particular moment or problem into focus. He contents himself with studying the respective surface of the patient's mind" ("FRRW," 147).

The final stage of psychoanalytic technique still aimed at filling "in gaps in memory" and overcoming "resistances due to repression" ("FRRW," 148) as the others did before, but it is the first to fully assume that the only thing that truly counts are the resistances of the patient (and not an objective situation behind it). Only the last stage of psychoanalysis was able to adopt the radical insight that the only thing that counts is what the patient is actually saying and also "what the subject is not saying."[2] To assume that one needs to get around resistances because they hinder the access to an objective condition of the patient also implied an assumption that there is something behind the surface of what the patient is articulating. That is to say that the first stages of psychoanalysis still involved a resistance of psychoanalysis against the fact that it is nothing but a talking cure and therefore there is nothing of greater relevance than things actually spoken and unspoken. Only in the last and for Freud final stage was psychoanalysis able to affirm on the level of its technique and practice that the reality it has to deal with is not the material reality of a factual and objective situation but rather the psychical reality of its subject, that "his illness" is "not an event of the past, but a present-day force" ("FRRW," 151). This implies that only then was it possible to accept that "in psychoanalytic anamnesis, what is at stake is not reality, but truth";[3] not a deeper and hidden objective material truth of the symptom but a subjective truth of a speaking subject. Only then did analysis finally become ready to assert that there is nothing but resistance and now it is the subject who is finally in question.

To reach this insight, as one may say, it seemed necessary to "apply [the] psychoanalytic method to the collectivity that sustains it."[4] But if psychoanalysis had itself to go through an analysis—a self-analysis—to reach an adequate understanding of itself (and this analysis went through the different stages Freud depicts), if analysis has to be analyzed, this implies that it cannot rely on external or objective norms; there is no transcendental horizon for psychoanalysis. And therefore it will even remain unclear when it is finished and it reaches its final stage. With the insight into this paradox, namely that psychoanalysis itself needed an analysis to become what it is, psychoanalysis discovered for the second time that there is an unconscious (even an unconscious of psychoanalysis itself). Psychoanalysis hence reached its last stage, according to Freud, when it "'remembered' what could never have been 'forgotten' because it was never at any time noticed—was never conscious" ("FRRW," 149), namely the unconscious itself. It "repeat[ed]" its discovery of the unconscious "without, of course, knowing that" it was "repeating it" ("FRRW," 150). The history of psychoanalysis according to Freud is hence the time it took to realize what psychoanalysis is all about, the time taken to be proved true. The history of the unfolding of its technique itself thereby embodies what happens in an analysis.[5] But should analysis not have known this from the very beginning? Could passing through all the stages not have been prevented?

Freud, after periodizing and analyzing the unfolding of psychoanalytic technique, refers to problems that keep occurring in analysis even in its third stage. If forgetting would be the only appearance of resistance against analysis, analysis would only have to deal with phenomena of people shutting themselves off from memories, with the functioning of screen memory that lays itself over and is even able to retroactively constitute past experiences and with the peculiar phenomenon that certain things can have an effect on people that never have entered their consciousness. But Freud argues that "under the new technique very little, and often nothing is left of this delightful smooth course of things" ("FRRW," 149), since there are cases in which the patient simply does not remember anything but acts out and repeats instead of remembering;[6] this leads to the fact that "in the end we understand that this is his way of remembering" ("FRRW," 150). That is to say for some things to be remembered, repetition is needed. Such may hence also be the case with regard to psychoanalysis. But at the very end of his text, Freud reports of further difficulties psychoanalysis was confronted with. "I have often been asked to advise upon cases in which the doctor complained that he had pointed out the resistance to the patient and that nevertheless no change has set in; indeed the resistance had become all the stronger, and the whole situation was more obscure than ever. The treatment seemed to make no headway" ("FRRW," 155).

Here one encounters a peculiar phenomenon, namely that an analyst, a doctor, complains and not a patient. It is a "doctor, who suffers, an analyst, who needs an analyst."[7] It is precisely in this context that Freud introduces the third term after remembering and repeating: working through: "The treatment was as a rule progressing most satisfactorily. The analyst had merely forgotten that giving the resistance a name could not result in its immediate cessation. One must allow the patient time to become more conversant with this resistance with which he has now become acquainted [*sich . . . zu vertiefen*], to *work through* it, to overcome it, by continuing, in defiance of it, the analytic work according to the fundamental rule of analysis . . . The doctor has nothing else to do than to wait and let things take their course, a course which cannot be avoided nor always hastened. If he holds fast to this conviction he will often be spared the illusion of having failed when in fact he is conducting the treatment on the right lines. This working-through of the resistances may in practice turn out to be an arduous task for the subject of the analysis and a trial of patience for the analyst" ("FRRW," 155). Again, it is the analyst, not the patient, who has forgotten something this time. But what needs to be done is "to wait and let things take their course," although this may seem like a failure at first. The analyst needs to hand himself over to the course of things, he has to let things be and become part of the movement of analysis itself. The seemingly stable roles and functioning of the analytic setting (the roles and functioning that were assumed by the complaining analyst) prove themselves to be destabilized: one is neither left with an active and interpreting analyst and a passive (reactively resisting) patient, nor with an active talking patient and a passive listening analyst. In analysis things do not follow any foreseeable course. Working through is linked to the insight that there is a path, which cannot be avoided, but also not be hastened. It is linked to the insight that one has to hand oneself over to the movement of analysis and that *id takes time*. And this also implies that another category involved in analysis is also not objective, as one could presume, but subjective, namely time. In another text Freud links the operation of working through to what he calls "the *resistance of the unconscious*."[8] Not only—as one may have presumed previously—is the ego resisting, and any resistance is of the ego; the unconscious also resists. In an abbreviated manner one may state that one type of its resistance is embodied in the assumption that the unconscious is an agency separated from the ego, playing its own game on another level, a game that from time to time interferes with the ego's proceedings.

What Freud ultimately suggests is that the very unfolding of psychoanalytic technique was itself a working through, a letting things be, letting them run their course, which the analyst could not hasten, because it was the time needed for psychoanalysis to be properly subjectivized. This is why Freud ends his 1914 text with the remark that from "a theoretical point of view" working through "correlate[s] with the 'abreacting' of the quotas of affect strangulated by repression—an abreaction without which hypnotic treatment remained ineffective" ("FRRW," 156). With the operation of working through, with the operation only accessible from within the third stage of psychoanalytic technique, something returns that from a theoretical point of view has already been immediately present in its first stage. But obviously this is neither simply a repetition—hypnosis was renounced as an element of the psychoanalytic technique—nor is one here dealing with a way of simply remembering an insight. Rather, in working through, something is remembered in a completely changed situation and with new means—it is the same but totally different. This is why one may say that the very relation between the three elements present in the title of Freud's text—remembering, repeating, working through—is (over-)determined by its last element.[9] Slavoj Žižek once suggested that the famous Lacanian triad of the Real, the Symbolic, and the Imaginary has to be read such that each term is related to all the others (following a distributive principle).[10] One has to account for the real Real, the symbolic Real, the imaginary Real, and so on. To properly grasp the relation between the triad of Freud's text, one should apply the same principle: there is a remembered remembering, a repeated remembering, a worked through remembering; a remembered repetition, a repeated repetition, and a worked through repetition, and there is a remembered working through, a repeated working through, and a worked through working through.

But why begin a book on Badiou with a reference to Freud, the history of psychoanalytic technique, and the complications of remembering, repeating, and working through? Firstly, could one not, a hundred years after Freud and his depiction of the unfolding of psychoanalytic technique, state something similar to this depiction with regard to the history of philosophy? Because it was once argued that the whole history of philosophy is nothing but a series of footnotes to Plato, one can legitimately assume that in the beginning of philosophy there was Plato. He—think of the infamous cave allegory—accounted for the constitution of the world and of any subject by recourse to the realm of ideas, which then afterwards was immediately to be read as entailing a two-world theory (there is the level of appearances and then there is the level of the ideas). After Plato there was Descartes, who asserted that the most crucial thing is not the constitution of the world as such, but the subject from whose existence the world depends as far as it can be reconstituted from it. And then there was Hegel, who claimed that what first has to be accomplished for the substance also needs to be realized as subject. And as a committed Hegelian could argue—though there are not that many today—it is true that the whole history of philosophy is nothing but footnotes to Plato, but this is only true up to Hegel. After Hegel even Plato will have been a footnote to Hegel. But in Hegel Plato's theory of the idea is remembered and repeated in a totally different context (as absolute idea) and hence there is a repetition of the immediate in the result. And if today Badiou proclaims a return to Plato, seeks to revamp the very idea of the idea and proposes a new theory of the subject, could one not be tempted to read this gesture as a peculiar way of remembering Plato, of repeating Descartes's gesture and hence of working through Hegel and the history of philosophy? The present book assumes that this reading can be validated. This is also why its very structure follows the triad of remembering, repeating, and working through.

Secondly, Badiou has been frequently attacked for defending a position that claims what one needs to do today is to wait for something unforeseeable to happen (say an event in politics that will change everything). Thereby, as a standard version of the attack runs, his position is doomed to delegitimize the smaller transformations possible in today's world and devalues what can directly be done by hoping for some gigantic and muscular eventual transformation. The claim to wait then turns into a way of obfuscating the fact of the incapacity of one's own position, of the lack of plan, and ultimately endorses nothing but a generalized skepticism, hopelessness, and passivity. Against such an assessment the present book assumes that Badiou's way of working through philosophy (and its conditions, namely politics, art, science, and love) is "part of the work which effects the greatest change . . . and which distinguishes analytic treatment from any kind of treatment by suggestion" ("FRRW," 155–56). This is to say that I take Badiou's position to be far more radical than all the self-proclaimed philosophers who complain about it and suggest (easy) alternatives. This is among many things because Badiou's position starts from a fundamental affirmation of philosophy. But because for him philosophy is conditioned by non-philosophical practices (that he refers to as conditions), this very affirmation of philosophy from within philosophy also implies an affirmation of the very practices that philosophy is based upon (because they are what constitutes philosophy's peculiar "object"). Hence to affirm philosophy constitutively implies to affirm the very existence of politics, art, love, and science. The present book will delineate how such an affirmation of the conditions of philosophy through the self-affirmation of philosophy may work—a finally objectless philosophy.[11] It does so not only by frequently resorting to questions of political practice, but also by investigating some of the most fundamental coordinates of political action and the history of the politics of emancipation. The present book fully endorses the idea of a necessary self-affirmation of philosophy and is hence a book for philosophy—a book that seeks to remember, repeat, and work through Badiou's gesture and is precisely for this reason "for Badiou."

Thirdly, Badiou once stated that "a modern philosophy is a philosophy that is able to stand up to Lacan."[12] He also asserted that Lacan—with his infamous return to Freud—is "our Hegel" (*BTS*, 132).[13] Philosophy is properly modern when it is able to stand up to the idea of returning to Freud's final stage of psychoanalysis. What is this supposed to mean? It means that philosophy has to be on the same level as psychoanalytic technique, a technique that fundamentally is about remembering, repeating, and working through. But if Lacan is "our Hegel" this also means that he also allows for a return to philosophy, a return to Plato and Descartes. With this return one also attains a modern manner of accounting for philosophy's history, its unfolding from Plato onwards. Therefore Lacan's proposed return to Freud—"a return to Freud" that "is a return to Freud's meaning"[14]—is not only a return performed within psychoanalysis but of high value for philosophy; one may say philosophy has to repeat Lacan's gesture and insist that the meaning of a return to philosophy is a return to the meaning of philosophy. That is to say, one needs to remember, repeat, and work through what is the meaning (and significance) of philosophy. But Lacan also indicates an opening of philosophy for non-philosophical forms of thought; it is via Lacan that the history of philosophy can be read in a different way, namely in a way that affirms the existence of non-philosophical practices that condition philosophy.

Modern philosophy has to stand up to Lacan by assuming that the meaning of philosophy can only be articulated today by opening philosophy to practices outside of it—and hence to rewrite philosophical history. A book "for Badiou" is hence a book that affirms philosophy and affirms political emancipation, true artistic practice, that science thinks, and ultimately psychoanalysis. It also affirms that with and through Badiou the history of philosophy will have been a different one; he makes it possible to conceive of a new Plato, a new Descartes and—without any doubt—of a new Hegel, because he also contends like Hegel did that "nothing is real except the Idea" (HOP, 14).[15] "For Badiou" does thus not mean a return to Plato, Descartes, or Hegel as such, but a return to philosophy. This return has to take into account what Lacan once rightly remarked, namely that any "recourse to the idea of matter is but naive, [an] outmoded form of authentic materialism."[16] With this he implicitly affirmed a materialism without matter. If modern philosophy has to stand up to Lacan and he is our Hegel, could one here not be reminded of Hegel stating that "in the lovers there is no matter"[17] and of the fact that philosophers are precisely the lovers of wisdom? As much as there is no other way to begin a love relationship than by declaring one's love, there is no other way to properly philosophize than by a declaration, by taking a stance for the love of wisdom, for the idea of an idea. That is why this book contends that one needs to affirm that any recourse to the idea of the idea is not naive, an outmoded form of authentic idealism, but precisely what needs to be defended at all costs.

   To return to the meaning of philosophy is to return to the meaning of the idea of the idea; without any naive conception of it. One
hence needs to remember, repeat, and work through the idea of the
idea and propose a new form of idealism. An idealism that does not fall
back into naive conceptions of the idea, of the subject, of philosophical
practice—an idealism that is able to stand up to Lacan, in short, what the
present book coins as idealism without idealism and proposes as a way
of reading Badiou's philosophical endeavor. It is therefore precisely not
simply a book on Badiou, but rather one that seeks to unfold what any
Badiousian stance in philosophy has to entail: a dialectic of dialectic and
non-dialectic and an understanding of the concatenation of remembering, repeating, and working through that it addresses under the name of
philosophy as meta-critical anamnesis. To end and finally begin: in 1977
Badiou wrote a text called "The Current Situation on the Philosophical
Front," which begins with the following words: "Philosophy as partisanship" and continues to assume that "there is only one great philosopher
of our time: Mao Zedong. And this is not a name, not even a body of
work, but time itself."[18] "For Badiou" assumes that indeed philosophy
is partisanship and that there is one great philosopher of our time; it is
not the individual born in Rabat, Morocco, in 1937, author of numerous
books and articles, playwright, novelist, mathematician, political activist,
and so on. It rather assumes that any book of the philosopher "Badiou"
should be read according to the following directive: I, philosophy, speak.

# Remember

## Idealism without Idealism

> Philosophy can only complete its abstract, rigorous and system-
> atic theoretical work on condition that it fights . . . about very
> "scholarly" words (concept, theory, dialectic, alienation, etc.).
> —"APRW"

> This propensity to pathologize metaphysics and to prescribe a
> brutal therapy to deal with its most acute cases has been hugely
> popular, to the present day. One can no longer count the physi-
> cians crowding the bedside of the man either sick with meta-
> physics, or sick from the sickness of metaphysics itself.
> —"BMPH," 176

### Idealism and Materialism after the Death
### of Idealism

God is dead and idealism died on the very same day.[1] Our time is one which can therefore be designated as coming "after the death of idealism." Today, these not only seem to be quite self-evident statements, they also derive their evidence, following Badiou, in a large part from the fact that they have historically been proven by Georg Cantor[2] among others. As he claimed: the development within and thus the history of philosophy itself can be understood in accordance with an operation that he called "creative repetition" ("BPCR"). There is always something unchanging in the form of the philosophical gesture (say philosophers make claims about truth, that it does exist or not, etc.), but there is also a transfor-mation inside philosophy due to "the pressure of some events and their consequences" that bring along the "necessity [of] transforming some as-pects of the philosophical gesture" (ibid.) Philosophical practice remains one and the same, yet it cannot be done in one and the same way in all historical circumstances. This is why one can state that as soon as one of the conditions of philosophy,[3] namely science (with Cantor), offers a new intellectual creation that provides a proof for the inexistence of God or of an all-encompassing totality—by irrefutably showing that there cannot be a set of all sets[4]—the old ideological battle, to echo Louis Althusser, between idealism and materialism that always will have determined and always will determine philosophy reaches a new phase.[5] The split that separated idealism from materialism, a split that leads right into the heart of all debates about the role and stance philosophical thought takes in view of a world to which it seeks to be contemporary, this very split after the disappearance of idealism reappears within materialism.

This is as yet a still overly abstract but nonetheless possible rendering of how one might historically situate the distinction between democratic materialism and materialist dialectics that is famously introduced on the very first pages of Badiou's *Logics of Worlds*. If idealism becomes impossible, the only viable and thinkable option is materialism, and if materialism still has the status of being an "ideological atmosphere" (*BLoW*, 11), one could assume at first sight that the repetition of the distinction of idealism and materialism inside materialism brings forth an *idealist materialism*, a "bad one," and a "good and proper" *materialist materialism.* However, the contemporary inscription of the distinction between idealism and materialism into the domain of materialism itself should be understood in a different and profoundly more dialectical way. To cut a long story short and immediately lay my cards on the table: the main idea behind the subsequent reflections is an attempt to claim that one can and ought to differentiate between two different forms of materialism but that the inscription of the distinction of idealism and materialism into materialism also—and necessarily—contains a moment of reversal. Therefore I will contend that democratic materialism can be understood as being a *materialism without idea, a materialism without idealism,* and that a materialist dialectics providing the groundwork for any contemporary, true philosophical enterprise rather needs to be conceived of as what I call an *idealism without idealism.*[6] The elaboration of this very concept thus also entails the elaboration of what I take to be the most fundamental coordinates of the philosophical position of Alain Badiou. So I take Badiou to be a peculiar kind of idealist and I will demonstrate that—maybe paradoxically—such a type of idealism provides the coordinates for what one then might justifiably refer to as a contemporary version of materialism (with emphasis on both, the contemporaneity and on materialism). Although it seems rather easy to agree with the often articulated criticism that the very distinction between idealism and materialism is itself an idealist invention (since the two terms of the distinction themselves can never be attained in a pure manner, because there is always something idealist about materialist claims and always some dimension of materialism within idealism), there are also some good reasons why one should not simply withdraw from this distinction. One would be that this might come with the overly obvious temptation to simply get rid of idealism and directly affirm materialism (and thereby leave this distinction behind). To my mind, what Badiou depicts with his distinction of democratic materialism and materialist dialectic is precisely what might follow from such a too swift abandonment of the allegedly idealist distinction. I thus will start the following investigations in this chapter from the distinction between materialism and idealism, because I contend that only through the very act of first choosing something that seems to be idealist (the distinction between idealism and materialism) can one attain the necessary elements for something materialist to appear (an idealism without idealism), which does not again fall back onto the side of idealism (a materialism that is in no need of anything else but itself)—one first needs idealism and materialism as two sides and one then has to subtract idealism (one of the two sides) to get the empty remainder, the empty place left by idealism precisely as that which makes materialism properly materialist (and thus one subtracts the very distinction one first assumes), by introducing a dialectical twist into it.

So what is at stake in what follows is nothing less than a possible answer to the question of what today a true materialist position (in philosophy) might look like, and the answer to this question is what Alain Badiou's oeuvre sought and seeks to give. To put it differently and in a more fundamental manner: what is at stake here is an answer to the question what today the signifier "materialism" might mean at all. To address these questions and the implications of the above mentioned *historically specific* creative transformation of philosophy (death of idealism) might seem at first to be overly discussed and thus old hat. Yet, this strange and peculiar old hat became the *slogan* of any self-proclaimed materialist stance within the last two centuries, therefore it nonetheless appears to be an adequate starting point. It is the 11th thesis on Feuerbach written by Karl Marx, which famously reads: "The philosophers have only *interpreted* the world, in various ways; the point is to *change* it."[7] So, one might rephrase the questions above in a very simple manner: What is to be done with this thesis—in a very simple manner: how to read it?—when materialism has become the dominant ideological atmosphere of our contemporary time? What does it mean to read it, when the idealism of mere interpretation has disappeared and everyone is a materialist today (ready to or already practically involved in changing the world)?

Taking into account the historical coordinates mentioned (the death of idealism due to the impact of new inventions in one of the conditions of philosophy), one can substantiate the claim about the reversed repetition of the split between idealism and materialism inside materialism by reconstructing in a rather general manner three different but nonetheless paradigmatic readings of Marx's 11th thesis on Feuerbach, as will be demonstrated subsequently. These readings all center on the theme of how the task of philosophy should be understood in relation to the notion of change and on the question of what this change means. Since it is precisely one implication of the *materialist slogan*—the 11th thesis—that materialist thought has to insist on change. But then the question arises with regard to this very slogan: What to do with philosophy? Must philosophy also change? Or must it simply change its conception of change? Or does it have to change its practice *tout court*? What is its position or role after the disappearance of idealism? These questions obviously lead into the kernel of Badiou's own thought, even more so because he returned to very similar questions in seminars that he gave from 2010 onwards under the paradigmatic title which apparently echoes Marx: "What does it mean to change the world?"[8]

The three paradigmatic readings that will be evoked in the following will help to delineate three different answers to this question. Against this background one will then be able to show how, starting from the philosophical systematic Alain Badiou provides that one can and one today even should draw a diagonal across these three readings (to offer a consistent account of a materialist philosophical position). After elaborating the crucial cornerstones of such a diagonal, the third argumentative step this chapter undertakes will start from a discussion of statements by Badiou that are not only in themselves instructive but will be employed to construct the first coordinates for a renewed materialist stance in and of philosophy today. This obviously will also delineate how Badiou himself stands with regard to the materialist question, the question of materialism. The task this chapter thereby sets itself is the following: how to read Marx's 11th thesis from a Badiousian perspective if what is at stake with it is precisely what materialism in philosophy might mean today. It will therefore conclude by proposing a number of elements that necessarily have to be taken into consideration for a Badiousian, and this is to say: contemporary materialist dialectical, that is, an actualized reading of the 11th thesis. Ultimately, the chapter will end by proposing from such a materialist perspective at least one consistent rephrasing of it that might be said to be valid for our times. Thus all the above questions condense into a shorter one: How to read Marx's 11th thesis today?

## Change the World, Change Interpretations, Changing Interpretations

Some cognitive mapping to begin with: what followed the first publication of the Marxian theses on Feuerbach are many different attempts to present original and coherent reconstructions of Marx's thesis 11, a text which is, as George Labica put it, aside from the fragments of the pre-Socratics "the shortest document of our occidental philosophical tradition."[9] But notwithstanding its conciseness, what is clear is that the relevance and validity of the thesis as such never was put into question by anyone who considered himself a materialist. The 11th thesis has been read as containing "much more than the ingenious germ of the new world-view [Weltanschauung]," as Karl Korsch formulated, that "hammers to the ground all joists of the hitherto bourgeois philosophy."[10] The German Marxist Wolfgang Fritz Haug insisted that the theses in general and the 11th thesis in particular are "discursive events that become more and more significant from greater distance."[11] With little effort one can formally distinguish at least three different paradigmatic ways of how to (traditionally) read Marx's 11th Feuerbach-thesis. Each one became quite influential historically, although these three readings are not always and in all their contours sharply distinguishable from one another.

The first and maybe *the* most classical reading of this thesis emphasizes the necessary transition from the *interpretation* of the world *to changing* it. This first way of reading thesis 11 I call the *transformative reading*. Its decisive features lie in the insistence that interpretation as such is nothing but a mere form of contemplation *ante rem* and thus should be replaced by a practice—also by a philosophical practice of cognition—*in rem*. Exemplary for such a reading is Ernst Bloch's *Principle of Hope* in which he extensively argues that against the hitherto contemplative idealist (this is to say: pseudo-)philosophical interpretations of the world, the 11th thesis invokes to "set sail" and arrive at "a new, . . . an active philosophy, one which, in order to achieve change, is as inevitable as it is suitable."[12] The *transformative reading* thereby in no way necessarily implies the dissolution of philosophy *tout court*. It rather insists on the need to develop a new, a different philosophy: a *philosophy of practice*[13] that is capable of revolutionizing the world. A practical philosophy *in rem* against the (idealist) philosophies of interpretation *ante rem*. Therefore it sides with Engels's introduction of a "but" as a logical-syntactical connection of the two sentences. The 11th thesis thus becomes: The philosophers have only *interpreted* the world, in various ways; *but* the point is to *change* it.

In this sense it is read as an axiom of any true philosophical practice to come. One first has to change the very notion of change—*from mere and ineffective abstract interpretation of the world to active practical intervention into the world*—and this shift of viewpoints will consequently and necessarily also produce a transformation of philosophy. Philosophy has to leave behind the interpreting "donkeys of induction,"[14] as Engels once put it, assume its proletarian-revolutionary task, and replace the empty discourse of ever-changing interpretations with real and true change. But there will be no real change as long, as Bloch puts it, as there is no "philosophical change according to the stipulations of the analyzed situation, of dialectical tendency, the objective laws, of real possibility."[15] Only by becoming a philosophy of practice, this transformative reading insists, can real change occur. This change will realize the task of philosophy by sublating the proletariat and sublate the proletariat by realizing the task of philosophy, to borrow this expression from Marx. Philosophy itself, by becoming practical, by introducing real change and not only changing interpretations within itself, can relate to, or more precisely, can itself be and become actual truth by replacing the absence of any true change with the primacy of actual change. This first reading can therefore be rendered in the following formula: replace any speculation that wants to reduce the world to a unifying principle, engage with the necessary dialectical laws of history, thereby analyze change properly, and thus change what change (philosophically) means, then you will not only change philosophy but you will also change the world.

In competition and opposition with this *transformative reading* of the 11th thesis, one can find a second one that I will call *reversing reading*. This second reading starts off from a different angle: it starts with emphasizing, to put it in the words of Günther Anders's—who among others is a paradigmatic exponent of this reading—*Outdatedness of Human Beings*: "It does not suffice to change the world. We do that anyway. And to a large extent this is what happens even without our involvement. In addition we have to interpret this change."[16] While the first reading insisted upon the necessity of a transformative replacing of the absence of change with the primacy of real change, this second reading insists on the already present actuality of ongoing change. The world is constantly changing and one thus urgently needs renewed and adequate interpretations which keep pace with this very change. Although there seems to appear a slightly conservative subtext to this rendering of the Marxian thesis 11, this reading, at least to some extent, refers to a possible rendering of the Hegelian model of philosophy, which like the owl of Minerva has to begin its flight when the day turns to dusk. Philosophy has to change because the world itself has changed, and since it keeps on changing, philosophy's task is not only to keep up with the change already happening but to render it comprehensible. As again Theodor W. Adorno put it in one of his posthumously published *Lectures on the Negative Dialectics*: "To interpret means to elucidate, not necessarily recognize. My thesis: Interpretation is criticism. Without interpretation there is no true practice."[17]

This second reading therefore explicitly agrees with the first one with respect to the view that it is necessary to change philosophy. But it disagrees with it concerning the idea of what philosophy should be or should become. This is because, as again Adorno put it, "this vantage point from which philosophy appears to be obsolete has itself today become obsolete in the meantime. And it would be ideological in its turn, namely dogmatic, if we were not to concede this."[18] The *reversing reading* upholds the claim for a necessary change of philosophy but only because it can already be considered to be an actual truth of the world that it is changing, this is to say in the last instance that truth is change as such (and thus there is truth in the world, which needs to be grasped). This means that the change taking place under given (historical) conditions (of the world) has thus initially to be reinterpreted to keep up with what is (already) happening in the world. The world is nothing but a changing world, due to the multiplicities of practices, technologies, and modes of production and so forth that are always already affecting it. Therefore philosophy has to change, but the way it can and should change is related to its proper medium, namely to interpretation, which has to reflect on that which permanently happens in and with the world. As Elias Canetti once put it: "The reality has changed to such an enormous degree that a first presentiment of it puts us in the state of perplexity . . . Therefore we need interpretation."[19] If the central motive of the first reading was the realization of philosophy as real practice, the leitmotif of the second reading is that one first has to understand the change already happening, and it therefore declares necessary a primacy of interpretation.[20]

Now, one can find another, a third reading that neither insists on the claim that philosophy itself has to change *for* the world to change, as the *transformative reading* of the 11th thesis does, nor does it insist on the fact that philosophy and its interpretations of the world have to change *because* the world itself has changed as the *reversing reading* does. The third reading, which I call an *exaggerating reading*, produces another twist in the rendering of Marx's thesis. As for example Slavoj Žižek, to whom I would attribute among others this approach, claims: "The past is never known 'as such,' it can become known only in the process of its transformation, since the interpretation itself intervenes in its object and changes it."[21] This reading, as one might derive, sees the task formulated in the 11th thesis also, as the first reading does, as a task of philosophy, and it shares with the second reading that change has to be related to interpretation. But the essential punch line put forward by this take on Marx is that only via the exertion of exaggerated interpretation will the world actually change. This can again be somehow related to a dictum by Adorno, namely the claim that psychoanalysis is only true in its exaggerations.[22] Only exaggerated interpretations can break with the one-sidedness and seemingly natural order of the world and produce true and actual change in it.

As again Žižek put it: "*the excess of 'exaggeration' is the truth which undermines the falsity of the balanced totality*"[23] of the world, and this excess is brought about precisely by interpreting and thereby intervening in it. In this way philosophy can only act upon the world and truly change it via its interpretation. This is also why this *exaggerating reading* demands that it is right now precisely not the task to change the world because this merely would come down to remaining stuck in the ideological coordinates of the world that prevent any real change. As again Žižek claims strictly:

> The first task today is precisely not to succumb to the temptation to act, to directly intervene and change things, but to question the hegemonic ideological coordinates . . . If, today, one follows a direct call to act . . . it will be an act within the hegemonic ideological coordinates . . . The kind of activity provides the perfect example . . . of doing things not to achieve something, but to PREVENT something from really happening, really changing. . . . It fits the formula of "Let's go on changing something all the time so that, globally, things will remain the same.[24]

Not to fall for the spontaneous temptations to act but precisely to interpret this temptation (and the world within which it takes place); this is the true task of philosophy, since this is the precondition for, maybe, true change taking place. It is only via interpretations that the world can change because it is only via interpretation that philosophy is relating to that which will have been possible in the past, and this past will shed its proper light on the contemporary world. Exaggeration does not only condense certain elements of the existing world to the utmost, it also displaces the focus from certain worldly momentums to others. It therefore stretches the sense of what "world" means via its interpretation of it and thereby claims to already have transformed it (by performing and also depicting a shift of perspective on the world as it is). The world is then a transformed world, for it is related to a past that was never present (even if this sounds exaggerated); this is to say: the present world is changed by overemphasizing a forgotten past that lies at its ground. By over-accentuating that the past is itself a matter of struggle—a struggle of interpretation—the present world already changed (a bit) since there is a transformation of its genealogy and thereby "exaggeration reveals uncomfortable features of experience [of the world] that would otherwise be invisible."[25]

To resume: either philosophy changes the world by becoming itself actively and practically engaging in the process of changing the world (this is the *transformative reading* that is oriented towards the *future realization of philosophy*), or interpretations have to change because the world always does (this is the *reversing reading* that is oriented towards the *actuality of change in the present*), or finally only exaggerated interpretations are able to change the seemingly stable coordinates of the given world (this is the *exaggerating reading* that is oriented towards that *which will have been foreclosed from the past*).

This obviously sketchy, and not at all exhaustive, list of these different possible readings of Marx's thesis 11 provides the groundwork for constructing a diagonal within the framework these three readings present. I will call the result of this diagonal construction a *materialist dialectical reading*, materialist dialectical in the precise sense that Alain Badiou ascribed to this label.[26] It is precisely because one can find passages, quotes, and claims in the work of Badiou that could be easily assigned to any one of these different readings, that it is necessary to reconstruct their internal relation and precisely construct a diagonal.[27] Starting from some coordinates that Badiou's system offers for such a *materialist dialectical reading*, I will therefore not claim as the *transformative reading* does that philosophy should be realized in a way that it then would be able to itself practically intervene in the world and thereby would be capable of directly changing it. Nor will I claim as the *reversing reading* does that the only task of philosophy is to offer always renewed different interpretations of the change (always already) occurring in the world. Finally, I will also not claim with the *exaggerating reading* that it is only via interpretations that the world itself and its past can be changed. In what follows I will rather try to show that starting from Badiou's conception of philosophy, reading the 11th thesis can mean that (1) philosophy has to change and that it has to perform an active gesture, an act that is properly philosophical, yet it cannot be rendered in terms of interpretation; (2) that in the contemporary situation this act is directly related to the world or better: its absence; (3) that one can conceive of this philosophical act in a way that is different from the *transformative* and *reversing reading* of the 11th thesis, since it is neither critical nor determined by the change always already taking place in the world; and (4) that one can take up the *exaggerated reading* in a different and renewed way by insisting that this philosophical act can help to avoid the hegemonic ideological coordinates by somehow returning to a seemingly obsolete moment from the past, namely to idealism.

## The Philosophical Act between Change and Interpretation

An investigation into how such a diagonal can be constructed might be begun by assembling some rather complex yet concise statements that can be found in the works of Alain Badiou. These statements will be instructive, when systematically combined, for the aim of constructing a diagonal, rendering intelligible some central coordinates of a renewed materialist stance in philosophy, which as I want to argue, can be incorporated in a Badiousian reading of the 11th thesis (a reading which up till now has not been undertaken).

The first statement by Badiou is from a text already mentioned above, *Philosophy as Creative Repetition*, and it reads: "The philosophical act is always in the form of a decision, a separation, a clear distinction" and it therefore "always has a normative dimension. The division is also a hierarchy" ("BPCR"). Philosophy is an act; an act of inscription, or better: an active incision of a line of demarcation that distinguishes two sides and implements a hierarchy between them (the demarcated space is thus a hierarchical space). One can for example easily think of the Platonic hierarchy between knowledge and opinion, the Cartesian hierarchy between soul and body, the Hegelian hierarchy between philosophy as science and philosophy as historicism, and ultimately, of course, of the Badiousian hierarchy between living under an idea and living without it.[28] Such a philosophical act can already be seen at work in the very founding gesture of Badiou's *Logics of Worlds* where he distinguishes two different axioms of a materialist conviction, or more precisely: two different *axioms* of two different materialist ideologies. The first one is that there are only bodies and languages—the axiom of "democratic materialism"[29]—and the second one, the axiom of the materialist dialectics is that "there are only bodies and languages, except that there are truths" (*BLoW*, 4). What remains stable in the very structure of philosophy's practice is this active inscription of a distinction. This is to say, philosophy for Badiou always entails a decision and introduces a hierarchy (it may also be the distinction between idealism and materialism or the one between two different forms of materialism). The first element which thus becomes crucial for a contemporary reading of the 11th thesis from a Badiousian perspective is what here has been called a philosophical act which testifies to any true philosophy's decisive gesture.

The second quotation I take from the 2007 book *The Meaning of Sarkozy* in which Badiou claims the following: "Why am I justified in saying that the real axiom of the dominant politics is that the unified world does not exist? Because the world that is declared to exist and that supposedly has to be imposed on everyone, the world of globalization, is uniquely a world of objects and monetary signs, a world of the free circulation of products and financial flows. . . . In their crushing majority, the women and men of the supposed 'world' . . . have no access at all to this world" (*BMS*, 55). This quotation implies a form of concrete analysis of the ideology within the contemporary historical situation (I will subsequently develop this further). The act of incision in which the decisive action of philosophy (point 1) consists thus has to be grasped and situated in the precise historical coordinates it takes place in. And this concrete contemporary situation can be described as followed: (1) it is governed by the "phallic name of our present,"[30] which is, as Badiou put it repeatedly in his seminars and also in a recent book: democracy;[31] (2) after the historical withering away of idealism, it is sustained by a form of materialist conviction that represents the contemporary ideological form of capitalism, namely by democratic materialism; (3) the two first elements relate to an even broader category that Badiou names *contemporary nihilism*.[32]

The contemporary form of nihilism *on the one hand* implies a reduction of human being to its own animal substructure:[33] If for democratic materialism there are only bodies and languages, consequently any individual is ultimately nothing but a finite body. Such a body is endowed with a specific potential to enjoy that can and should be realized in a particular manner, hence in a particular language and in a particular cultural form (of practice) translatable and exchangeable. Thereby human beings are essentially reduced to their individual and culturally mediated interests, their needs, small private fetishisms, since what they are is as what they appear (i.e., as their bodies). This is why today the nihilism implied in and produced by democratic materialist ideology manifests itself in the two different versions of hedonism: the libertarian and the liberal one.[34] If libertarian hedonism proclaims enjoyment without boundaries, liberal hedonism differs only slightly from it by the presupposition that on its most fundamental level enjoyment itself can (and should) be bought. This is why there is for example no contradiction in principle being at the same time a liberal libertarian hedonist and a democratic materialist. For democratic materialism in general holds that it is the (temporal) instant that counts, the instant in which the body enjoys (this is what Badiou called "the prostitutional element"[35] ["BSP II"]) in and of democratic materialism because under its reign everybody is reduced to the commercial capacities of their very bodies. Against this background it is not hard to see why for Badiou—as already for Marx—the fundamental framework needed for this (nihilist) materialism to be sustained is perfectly well provided by contemporary capitalism; a framework that fully takes into account that man is (also) an animal.

This is to say: under capitalism man is treated as an animal whose passions are solely oriented towards objects and since it is precisely overly present consumable objects that are endlessly circulating, this implies that in the current situation (the capitalist *doxa* claims that) there cannot be any passion without an object towards which it would be oriented. In fact it is in this precise sense that Badiou defines capitalism as "the only regime which absolutizes the idea that man is an animal."[36] It thereby produces a very specific animalist conception of life,[37] which amounts to equating life with survival. This generates a kind of life that Badiou in his seminars also calls, flirting with Agamben's terminology, an "empty life" ("BSP II").

*On the other hand*, if the contemporary historical situation due to the hegemonic democratic materialist coordinates and the nihilism generated and perpetuated by capitalism is determined by the absence of a common world, this means that even the most elementary symbolic places are abolished. The supposed common world is constitutively structured by a split, a division between the included and the "excluded." "Excluded is the name for all those who are not in the real world" (*BMS*, 56), as Badiou put it, or even more rigidly in an earlier variant of the same claim: "Excluded is the sole name for those who have no name, just as 'market' is the name of a world which is not a world" (*BIT*, 162). Therefore, *on one side* there is a radical reduction of human beings to their animality whose passions are centered on the circulating objects, and this position needs to totalize itself (i.e., to claim that the state it proclaims is all there is: there is nothing but bodies and languages).[38] The general equivalence of circulating objects thereby relates to the general equivalence of human animals and their passions, desires, and needs that themselves circle around these objects. This type of nihilism is thus in its very constitution self-reflexive.

*On the other side*, the given historical situation is one in which the supposed symbolic coordinates do not construct the transcendental of a common world. This seems to be in contradiction with what is proclaimed everywhere. This contradiction results from the fact that the alleged equivalence of all different languages and bodies, individuals and communities is based on an antecedent and more fundamental split that separates the "pleasures of the wealth from the desires of the poor" (*BMS*, 56) and thus imposes that the transcendental of the world of globalization is in fact only thinkable under the persisting premise of separating two different worlds. There is one world, yet it has exclusive membership conditions. And this fundamental split—that is to say in a more technical manner: two radically separate degrees of existence[39]—separates those who are more different than the others, that is, those who do not share the same norms, namely those of circulating objects and animals. The situation in which the philosophical act has to take place today is thus for Badiou one of the very absence of a world. Contemporary nihilism hence simply means wordlessness.[40] The second element that therefore is relevant for a reading of the 11th thesis from a Badiousian perspective is *the concrete analysis of concrete situations*[41] that relates philosophy to the present "world."

The third quotation is also taken from *The Meaning of Sarkozy* and it reads: "We must assert right at the start the existence of a single world, as an axiom and a principle" (*BMS*, 60). And the internal consequences are inevitably political actions based on the indifference of differences, which means: politics is an operator for the consolidation of what is universal in identities (ibid., 66). To assert therefore that "there is only one world" is a principle of action, "a political imperative" (ibid., 68). Faced with the wordlessness of given capitalist conditions and their democratic materialist ideology, this delineates a very *precise point of affirmation*. Embedded into specific historical circumstances, the affirmation of the existence of one and only one world is a very precise counter-affirmation against the given coordinates. I will call such an affirmation, by pure reference to its formal structure, a *determinate affirmation*. One can therefore read the *determinate affirmation* that there exists one and only one world as a philosophical act, a decisive philosophical gesture which first and foremost affirms the hierarchy of the universal over particular identities by affirming the indifference of differences. It thereby inscribes a decisive hierarchy between universality and particularity. One should additionally remark here that the quote does not only characterize the act of philosophy as a determinate affirmation but it also depicts such a determinate affirmative act as introducing a principle of orientation that can guide (inter alia political) action. Such a philosophical determinate affirmation can offer a point of orientation, that is to say a decisive or even *forced cognitive mapping*, as one might say with reference to Fredric Jameson,[42] by affirming a concrete point that can be upheld no matter what. This point of orientation challenges just as much as the determinate affirmative act of philosophy does the given (ideological) hegemonic coordinates. Here and now, today a philosophical act of determinate affirmation thus concerns the very existence of a world. Such an affirmation can become a starting imperative for a political organization which then consequently attempts to conduct any of its actions in accordance with this self-imposed imperative to which it commits. A determinate affirmation thereby is in its formal structure always a determination of a point.[43] It is not only the inscription of a line of demarcation or the introduction of a hierarchy of the two terms that are demarcated, but it also contains the *concrete affir-*

*mation of a concrete point*, that in this case is the pointed affirmation of an existence, the existence of one world. The third element that is relevant for a Badiousian reading of the 11th thesis is the determinate affirmation, the *concrete affirmation of a concrete point* whose existence can in no sense be derived, inferred, or deduced from the given ideological coordinates.

The fourth statement that can be combined with the previous ones is Badiou's 15th point from his *Manifesto for Affirmationism*, in which he writes the following: "It is better to do nothing than to work officially in the visibility of what the West declares to exist."[44] This quotation might at first seem to form an inadequate, maybe even inconsistent concatenation with the first three. Nonetheless, it strongly resonates with them. Not only is the name to which Badiou here refers, "the West," the signifier that introduces the fundamental split in the "world," which turns it into a non-world or, more precisely, it splits its transcendental. Moreover, to do nothing is not simply to stop acting, but it rather means not to follow anymore the given coordinates of what a meaningful action is or of what may count as an action at all. This statement therefore can be read as a counter-affirmation, that is, again as a determinate affirmation: it does not only claim that one should resist the temptation to act but rather that one should do nothing. This nothing can only be properly understood in relation to the "visibility of that which the West declares to exist." What exists for democratic materialism is primarily circulating objects and floating animals, bodies and languages or again: individuals and communities. What Badiou emphasizes here is that doing nothing should rather be understood in an active way, to *do no-thing*:[45] To do nothing then means to not produce or to not reproduce objects (some things) that are declared to exist and circulate on the market.

Doing nothing therefore here also means to produce something which has neither an objective exchange value nor an objective use-value precisely because it is not an object and cannot be immediately reified. Doing no-thing is thus an entirely subjective practice (a practice of another kind), an end in and for itself, a *causa sui*, and implies a different kind of causality that is not reducible to the causality at play in body-language-games of democratic materialism.[46] To do nothing in this precise sense then can for example mean to do something which does not seem useful, relevant, or maybe even seems futile if one assumes the perspective of the given declarations of existence. To do nothing means to do something that subtracts itself even from the use-value category, since in this sense it can counter the objective abstraction of equivalence exchanges and the real abstraction that reduces human beings to their animality. Yet, what is not useful has to be conceived of in historically specific terms. In any given situation something seems not to be useful, it may take the form of a utopian project, it might seem idiotic or maybe even suspicious. Nonetheless, what exactly seems to be not useful—it might be an abstract mathematical investigation, a philosophical enterprise, the childish language of a loving couple, and so on—changes due to the historical specificity of the situation. To account for this very specificity one therefore can ask one simple question: what is it that today is considered to be not useful, idiotic, a waste of time invested in an absurd activity? A first tentative answer could then be with regard to the contemporary situation: what seems not to be useful today is everything that challenges the reality principle and the naturalized evidence of the democratic materialist ideology. The fourth element that is thus relevant for a reading of the 11th thesis from a Badiousian perspective is the element of a *counter-affirmation*, an action that engages in a seemingly useless, futile, maybe even allegedly dull activity that at the same time from the perspective of the given situation seems to be indistinguishable from doing nothing.

To resume: the (at least) four elements that play a crucial role in a possible Badiousian reading of the 11th thesis are (1) a *philosophical act*, that is, an inscription of a hierarchical distinction; (2) an element of *concrete analysis of the concrete contemporary situations* and hegemonic ideological coordinates that relate philosophy to the present world; (3) a *determinate affirmation* that cannot be deduced from the given ideological coordinates; and (4) an *active form of doing nothing*, a historically specific way of doing no-thing. So, what is the relation between these four elements? What is the peculiar relation between 3 and 4 (determinate affirmation and counter-affirmation)? I will demonstrate that it is precisely the last of the four elements that gives the diagonal to the three readings presented above its consistency. Because one thing that seems to definitely not comply with the axiom and the consequences of democratic materialism and that therefore seems completely obsolete, absurd, useless, and to be worth nothing today, precisely because it seemed to have died a long time ago, in the same ages that God did, is exactly to engage in reworking, thinking through, and affirming (something of) idealism.

## Materialist Dialectic, or Idealism without Idealism

In his seminars Badiou remarks that faced with desperate or even disastrous times, what is often needed is "a new renaissance" that "rephrases the most fundamental questions of existence which today do not seem to have any sense anymore" ("BITP I"). He elaborates this thought further by critically remarking the following: "has idealism become the support of the emancipatory path today? This temptation always exists . . . but I consider it to be vain and without future and this because idealism is an *effectively* dead configuration" (ibid.). Idealism is in fact a dead configuration no matter what, as science has forever falsified its basic axioms.[47] But any renaissance, if it is indeed quite literally a true rebirth also might imply a resurrection of the dead; a resurrection of something (maybe long) gone, which cannot be a simple return to the dead, since it necessarily has to take place and be conceived of from within the precise coordinates of the contemporary present. In this context one should remark something quite obvious with regard to Badiou's work. His main philosophical references–namely Plato and Hegel and to some extent Descartes[48]— would be considered by most people (at least in philosophy) today as arch-idealists. I am thus not ultimately suggesting that Badiou simply returns to idealism but rather that his work can nonetheless be understood as an attempt to *renew idealism.* Badiou's renaissance can consistently be read as a *renaissance of idealism.* Yet, the question remains, how and why should that be? What form does such a renaissance take?

In his *Communist Hypothesis* Badiou characterized the contemporary situation as follows: "Just as around 1840, today we are faced with an utterly cynical capitalism, which is certain that it is the only possible option for a rational organization of society" (*BCH,* 258–59). And he continues by comparing the present situation to the situation "Marx and his friends" (ibid.) were facing at their time. Does this not seem to contain, besides the explicit declaration of Badiou's own aim, namely a return to and a re-actualization of Plato,[49] another implication? The comparison between Marx's situation of the 1840s and our present situation remains faithful to a claim that can be found in early Badiou, namely in his *Can Politics Be Thought? (Peut-on penser la politique?),* with which he suggests that "we have to redo the [Communist] Manifesto" (*BPP,* 60). What seems to be necessary for its preparation—and perfectly fits the historical Marxian chronology—is thus also a redoing of Marx's theses on Feuerbach, obviously including the 11th. So, the starting point of this chapter, the recourse to Marx's 11th thesis for accounting for a renewed materialist stance in philosophy, is far from arbitrary, but is itself systematically anchored in Badiou's philosophical operation itself. This becomes even more evident when one recalls his claim that the contemporary situation is not only structured by the absence of a common transcendental of a world, which means that the non-world is structured by a fundamental split and a perpetuated separation, but the peculiar contemporary unwordliness is reinforced by the complete practical absence of any active political truth procedures, that is to say by the absence of collectively organized practices that are an end to themselves and thereby are also able to transform the netherworld into a real world; this absence is replenished with reactive and obscure subjects everywhere.[50] But if this also and necessarily implies for Badiou that there is an absence of any proper ethical orientation (only within movements of free causality there can be true subjective orientation), the only thing philosophy can possibly do (not being politics, art, science, or love) is to propose what Badiou calls with reference to René Descartes a "morale provisoire,"[51] a provisory moral. And this is what today a necessary gesture of such a provisory moral might look like: as Badiou's own project indicates, one needs to rework the Marxian theses on Feuerbach under present conditions, maybe today especially the 11th.

Marx criticized—as George Labica and Pierre Macherey have shown in great detail[52]—Feuerbach in his criticism of idealism for not overcoming the old and problematic conceptions of materialism: Feuerbach, as to Marx, rightly criticized Hegel for his idealist conception of actualization/realization, but somehow he threw out the baby with the bath water. Yet, if in the 1840s the bath water was idealism and the baby dialectics, somehow under present conditions, this gesture has to be repeated. If after the death of idealism any materialist thought has to agree, at least following Badiou, with the axiom of democratic materialism—that there are only bodies and languages—what has to be avoided again in the present situation is a repetition of the Feuerbachian mistake of throwing out the dialectical baby with the idealist bath water. This means materialist thought has to avoid getting rid of the dialectic. Materialism and dialectics have to be thought together, otherwise vulgar materialism prevails. For, to overemphasize this maybe slightly cheesy image: this baby will develop (and maybe even become a giant). It is precisely necessary *to throw out idealism (as dead configuration)*, but it is as necessary *to keep dialectics*. This is the first necessary step to take if one wants to repeat and renew the Marxian gesture implied in the Feuerbach theses under present conditions. This is to say: *one should redo the theses on Feuerbach, since Feuerbach is everywhere.* This is supposed to say that contemporary materialism did not only throw out the idealist bath water but also the seemingly idealist baby that came under the name of dialectics. For, one might say that under the present conditions the famous Engelsian slogan from *Ludwig Feuerbach and the End of Classical German Philosophy* might be repeated in a different form: "Enthusiasm was general; we all become at once Feuerbachians."[53] Today this slogan may take the following form: "Enthusiasm is general; we all become at once democratic materialists." Feuerbach was for Marx an unavoidable transition, not to get forever away from but precisely to be able to return more rigorously to Hegel.[54] And it is such a return to

Hegel that the present book seeks to defend, to defend as something that is fully consistent with Badiou's own philosophical position.

Hegel needs to become again today the main point of reference as he has already been for Marx.[55] Already in Marx the return to alleged idealism—against Feuerbach and against the old materialism of Democritus and Epicure—was essentially a return to dialectical thought *tout court.* Already Marx turned again to Hegel, to renew Hegel *after* Feuerbach and thus Feuerbach was something like the "necessary correction"[56] that made it possible (once again) to be *a Hegelian without being an idealist,* or in short: to remain faithful to dialectics in a non-idealist but in a materialist way. This is why it is no accident that Badiou maps his own theory again to the systematic of Hegel in *Logics of Worlds (BLoW,* 141–52). This bears the marks of the attempt to renew, to redo dialectics at a time in which the "night of non-dialectical thinking came over us" (*BPP,* 19) and in a time which is structured by the very death of idealism, its axioms and its consequences. Turning back to Hegel and thereby repeating the Marxian move to be Hegelian without being an idealist leads to what Badiou himself refers to be a renewal of the dialectic[57]—a renewal that, precisely because idealism is dead, succumbs to a completely new dialectical matrix that replaces determinate negation as the motor of dialectical thinking with determinate affirmation and replaces Hegelian sublation with a practice of subtraction.[58]

If traditional renderings of Hegel's idealism entailed the necessary and axiomatic affirmation that the One exists as a Whole, which then is (or becomes) its own self-exposure as temporal extension in the form of multiplicities, it is interesting to see how Badiou relates his very own systematic to the one of Hegel. If Hegel's One can only become a Whole by repeating itself in the tension of being immediate and becoming immediate-as-the-result (this very process generates a multiplicities of figures), any dialectic after the death of idealism has to do away with the idealist kernel of this move without losing the proper dialectical gist of it. Badiou claims that the Hegelian fourfoldness, the quadruplicity of his dialectical construction,[59] is outlined as follows: "the beginning (the Whole as the pure edge of thought), the patience (the negative of internalization), the result (the Whole in and for itself)" plus the additional "Whole itself, as immediacy-of-the-result, [which] still lies beyond its own dialectical construction" (*BLoW,* 144). Badiou's own renewed rendering of this idealist dialectics is the following: "indifferent multiplicities, or ontological unbinding; worlds of appearing, or the logical link; truth-procedure, or subjective eternity" plus the additional "vanishing cause, which is the exact opposite of the Whole . . . the event" (ibid.). If Marx in his theses on Feuerbach tried to put forward *a dialectics without an idealist*

*Hegel*, Badiou's renaissance of idealism can be characterized in terms of a formula that he himself once used to describe his own enterprise. In a text called *"Metaphysics and the Critique of Metaphysics"* Badiou refers to his own philosophy as being a paradoxical "metaphysics without metaphysics" ("BMPH," 190). This self-proclamation offers a good depiction of how to read Badiou's renaissance of idealism, namely the philosophical act by which he reinscribes the very distinction of idealism and materialism into materialism. And one might put this in the following manner: his materialist dialectics is an *idealism without idealism*.[60]

But why does any contemporary materialism, as Badiou conceives of it, take the form of an idealism without idealism? Because, as the subsequent elaborations will demonstrate in greater detail, to directly choose materialism today leads precisely to the opposite of what one wants to choose; it is the repetition of Feuerbach's mistake in a new guise. As we are all spontaneously materialist—and materialism is today the very spontaneous ideology of anyone[61]—one first needs to make "the wrong choice," for "the true speculative meaning emerges only through the repeated reading, as the after-effect (or by-product) of the first 'wrong' reading" (*ZLE*, 26). In this context this means that if one were to directly choose materialism the results would be hence nothing but democratic materialist. Another way of putting this is to claim that democratic materialism by abolishing dialectic is spontaneous materialism, directly opted for. Thus to insist on a *materialism of exception* one first consciously has to make the wrong choice[62]—insist on the relevance of idealism today, accentuate that which is obviously dead and a dead end—to affirm, determinately affirm an exception to what there is. To continue the work of renewing materialist dialectics today—and present a dialectics which is apt to oppose the hegemony of democratic materialism, the obscuring insistence on the limitedness and finitude of our bodies, languages, and capacities and the reduction of human beings to animals that makes them dwell in their needs, petite fetishisms, and lets them endlessly enjoy their own pathological constitution—in the singular historical circumstances that we are in, means to materialistically reverse materialism itself. It means not to simply continue with, say, the Marxian critique of political economy and endorse an even more historicist version of historical materialism, or even worse historicism without materialism, but to precisely turn to thinkers who are usually blamed to be and branded as being the worst idealists. What fundamentally is at stake in this overall project could in a certain sense also be called a *materialist reversal of materialism itself*—of a materialism that is not materialist enough. Today as a dialectical materialist one is in a situation after the death of God, to again articulate this in somewhat Nietzschean terms, this is to say, *after* the emergence of the insight that an all-encompassing whole is unthinkable, after the insight that a set of all sets does not exist and in a situation where one has material proof of this, provided by the famous Cantorian continuum hypothesis, whose mathematical preconditions have clearly and indisputably demonstrated that there are different sizes of infinity and that there cannot be just one all-encompassing totality, which then could be called the infinity.

After the death of God and after the former modes of dialectical thought seem overcome,[63] any true materialist dialectics attempts to start from and thinks the exception from what there is, from what seems to be evident, necessary, and therefore unchangeable. It hence has to start with something which stands in a relation of exception not only to democratic materialism and its hypostatization of finitude, its organization of indifference that surrounds anyone every day. But it also has to start with an exception to (at least the traditional understanding of) idealism itself. In this sense, it is some sort of barred or double exception. The first exception to democratic materialism leads then to a take on what is an exception to (at least traditional) idealism.

For anyone attempting to think, say, *after* Hegel, he or she has to start from these singular points in which Hegel was not Hegelian enough, precisely with regard to his own dialectical matrix. One has to start thinking from the exception to democratic materialism, which is a nowadays suppressed idealism. This implies also that one has to embrace the notions of the absolute, the eternal, of truth, and at the same time one has to start conceiving of this first exception (to democratic materialism) by relating it to a second exception to what has been said to be the idealist dialectical schema. And so, materialism to be a proper materialism has to insist upon that which seems to be a wrong choice.[64] This is why Badiou resurrects idealism in a manner that is not idealist, but properly materialist, idealist without being idealist.[65] Put differently: to be a true materialist today means to turn to Hegel or Plato in order to remember, repeat, and work through them. It was Lenin who also articulated this idea in a very brief but beautiful text published in 1922 under the title "On the Significance of Militant Materialism."[66] Therein Lenin declares what the journal that he founded together with Trotsky and others, *Pod Zmamen Marksizma—Under the Banner of Marxism*—should be about. In this article Lenin, after explaining that the journal should propagate atheism, attack bourgeois reactionaries and revisionists, and endorse an alliance of natural scientists and communists, uses a beautiful image of how the collective of authors and editors of the journal should conceive of themselves. They should be like, as he puts it, a society of materialist friends of Hegel's dialectics. Lenin thus points out that the simple endorsement of materialism is not enough. One should also assert that one needs idealists like Hegel (or Plato and Descartes). Thus I suggest it is legitimate to claim: without an idealism without idealism no contemporary materialism; no materialism without necessary reference to idealism (without idealism) today.

To conclude this first chapter it is possible to draw one consequence of what has been presented thus far and offer at least one possible direct rendering of what a Badiousian reading of the 11th thesis might look like. The basic maneuver of this reading is founded upon the following move: it is not the opposition between interpretation and change, their relation, or interdependence that one today needs to be focused on. It is rather that to which the two of them are constitutively related in the 11th thesis, namely to the world. To read the 11th thesis today from a Badiousian perspective implies thus initially an affirmation of the existence of a (common) world before addressing the question of how to change it. In all previous models the world has been assumed to exist and then the question of change appeared to be central. From a Badiousian perspective and under present conditions, one can rather read the 11th thesis in the following manner: *The philosophers have only interpreted the world, in various ways; the point is to affirm it.* Or to give a longer version of this reformulation: *The philosophers have only interpreted the world, in various ways; the point is to affirm its existence.*

# 2

# Remember to Remember

## Materialism of the Idea

> Socrates . . . inaugurated the new being-in-the-world that I here
> call a subjectivity.
> —J. Lacan

> The better part of our memory exists outside of ourselves.
> —M. Proust

### Against Oblivion

Philosophy makes things endlessly more difficult. One reason for this is that philosophy in its very practice opposes forms of oblivion that make certain ways of life possible to begin with. It might be argued that one of the last thinkers to make this the center and kernel of his overall philosophical writings has been Martin Heidegger. He infamously proposed that the complete (Western) history (of being and consequentially also of humanity) can be conceived of as a history of forgetting one of the most important distinctions: the distinction between being and beings.[1] For him this type of forgetting was precisely the defining kernel of the totality of metaphysics. Metaphysics is the most influential mechanism of oblivion as it takes the distinction between being and beings and interprets it by reinscribing it into one of the two sides of this very distinction, namely into that of beings. This then ultimately leads to the consequence that there is no longer any distinction between being and beings—all there is are beings—but there is at the same time a remainder of this distinction, something like a return of the repressed, which is articulated in the assumption of a hierarchical structure within the realm of beings. This hierarchy of beings simply implies that there can be a highest being (traditionally this being goes under the name of God, but, as Heidegger continues to argue, it structurally defines the place of the "subject" in terms of that which is the underlying ground to everything, i.e., as *sub-jectum*).[2] This move—taking the distinction and inscribing it into the sides of the distinctions—is what makes metaphysics structurally onto-theological (it takes being as being the highest being) and implements a fundamental forgetting that for the first time in the history of philosophy for Heidegger occurred with Plato. He put the truth of being (*aletheia*) under the "yoke of the idea"[3] and thereby reduced "being" to the very presence that is implied in the concept of being "a being." This very onto-theological maneuver has not only led to consequences of the most catastrophic effects (mostly inaugurated by different means of subjective empowerments under the heading of "technique");[4] it also came along with a forgetting of the very act of forgetting.

In this sense the totality of, at least, Western history is a history of forgetful oblivion. True contemporary philosophical thought for Heidegger therefore has to be up to the task of countering this forgetful forgetting (i.e., metaphysics) by returning to the beginning, to its origin and its advent. It can remind us that there once has been a thought that was not yet forgetful (even of its own forgetfulness). Only in this way can philosophy oppose or overcome (more precisely: *verwinden* in German) the forgetful state we are in. Yet, the proper medium in which such a non-forgetful thought can be located is not in itself philosophical. Why that is can also become clear when the crucial coordinates of forgetfulness are taken into account. For what needs to be recalled cannot simply be "a being" (a somehow present memory, something experienced yet forgotten, etc.). What needs to be recalled is a distinction (between being and beings), which thus can never take the form of an object (i.e., of a being). Philosophy can point us to the fact that the remembering of this distinction is the most crucial thing to do, yet the proper medium of this recollection is not philosophy but it is that which Plato—who is the truly bad guy in Heidegger's scenario—did despise quite a lot: poetry. It is within poetry—the poetic thought before and up to a certain extent after Plato—in which there is something that can be used to fight the forgetful oblivion, which became in an increasingly inferior manner the structuring principle of our contemporary world. The difficult task of philosophy then is to point us to this reminder, demonstrate that there is something which we need to recall; and it can help us in understanding what has been lost by forgetting that we forgot. Philosophy is—although directed against Plato with whom began the tragedy of western forgetfulness—for Heidegger in this precise sense an anamnectical practice. However, this is a quite difficult task, as there are few things more difficult than to not be forgetful—and this is what the poets know best.

Alain Badiou is one of the few influential philosophers today who proclaims himself to be a Platonist. Already in the first "Manifesto for Philosophy"—published in 1989 in France—he branded this peculiar kind of Platonism "a *Platonism of the multiple*" (*BMPHI*, 103). This proclamation does not only sound very countercurrent today, it also rings very profoundly anti-Heideggerian. And indeed, it is both: it is a counter-

CHAPTER 2

affirmation of Plato against the whole twentieth century which was—
with very few exceptions[5]—unanimously anti-Platonist (from Nietzsche
and Bergson to Deleuze, from the Marxist tradition, the analytic thinkers of the Vienna Circle, and empiricist neo-positivism to existentialists
like Kierkegaard or Sartre, "democrats" like Popper and Arendt, and of
course Heidegger); and it is anti-Heideggerian, since for Badiou Plato is
not the one philosopher in whose thought one can first (and foremost)
situate the beginning of a catastrophic and powerful history of metaphysical forgetfulness.[6] It is rather precisely with Plato that philosophy as
a historically specific and peculiar form of practice has for the first time
seen the light of day.[7] So against Heidegger (and the majority of contemporary philosophers), Badiou affirms that there is something—not
in the pre-Socratic poetic thought but—in Plato that is still contemporary to and relevant for any philosophical thought,[8] and with Heidegger
Badiou somehow insists that this very "something in Plato" is worth being
remembered. So, Badiou's gesture of reaffirming a Platonist position can
also be read as a gesture of anamnesis. An idealism without idealism
cannot simply do away with Plato. Yet, the question emerges of what philosophy needs to remind us (and itself?). Is there also a diagnosis of forgetfulness at work in Badiou?

## Metaphysical Maneuvers of
## Contemporary Materialism

"Democratic materialism"—the contemporary form of ideology well
suited to go along with what he calls "parliamentary-capitalism"—can
be said to endorse a peculiar kind of forgetting. If—as developed in
the first chapter—what determined philosophy as well as the whole
political field nearly throughout their entire history was the old struggle
between materialism and idealism, after the disappearance of idealism
and the complete taking-over of materialism—everyone being a spontaneous materialist—this struggle enters into a new phase of its existence. Although the predominant version of materialism—democratic
materialism—denies that there even might be any struggle anymore, the
ideology-critical approach of Badiou consists in demonstrating that this
denial, this repression cannot be upheld.[9] There is always a return of the
repressed (in this case: of the struggle). The ideological structure—and
the denial on which it is based—of democratic materialism functions in a
way that by attacking the kernel of the former idealism it also attacks the
dialectical moments it was based upon. Democratic materialism thus was

only able to overcome idealism by getting rid of the materialist kernel of idealism itself. With the return of the repressed struggle within materialism, materialism is now—ideologically—split into a materialism denying that there is anything materialistically relevant to idealism and into a materialism which seeks to stick to the materialist kernel of idealism itself. But, as one might ask here, in what consists the materialist kernel of previous idealism? Two answers can be given: first, the materialist kernel of idealism is the dialectic. Second, the materialist kernel of idealism is linked to what Badiou calls an "idea."[10] Democratic materialism did become the predominant ideology of today's world by neglecting, repressing dialectics[11] and in doing so it denied the very existence of what the previous idealists called an idea. With the disappearance of idealism appeared a materialism that seeks to be everything that there is and by problematically totalizing itself (there are only bodies and languages) it turns itself into a weird form of idealism (idealizing the "matter" of bodies and languages to be the only matter there is). So, what one ends up with in this very formal account of Badiou's diagnosis of the contemporary present (in terms of ideology) is also that there is a forgetting at work, maybe more adequately put: there is amnesia. Democratic materialism forcefully forgets, denies, represses, and obliviates the very existence of dialectics and thereby consequently enforces an *amnesia of the idea*. Democratic materialism can thus, referring once again to Heidegger, be called a metaphysics or in Badiou's terms: an ideology.

The democratic materialist metaphysics or ideology—that does not want to be either one—does not only forget the distinction between materialism and idealism (and therefore the dialectical kernel of idealism which is also linked to the concept of the idea), but it does also perform the very move which Heidegger criticized as being the move of metaphysics par excellence. If for Heidegger metaphysics relied on the understanding of "being" in terms of a highest being, this implies that metaphysics takes "being" as being constructible[12] (in terms of the highest being). Insisting on constructability—and the oblivious denial of an antecedent split, which deprives this constructability—is for Heidegger the crucial move of metaphysics. Democratic materialism also insists on constructability, because for it everything is constructable in terms of bodies and languages or of individuals and communities. But as much as Western metaphysics for Heidegger, democratic materialism relies on a very special maneuver that gives its specific constructability its peculiar shape (and makes it intelligible why it is perfectly well suited for the contemporary form of capitalism).

The metaphysical maneuver of democratic materialism as the ideology of contemporary capitalism can most easily be accounted for in relating it—other than Heidegger would ever have done—to a simple scientific, that is, mathematical, insight:[13] consider the order of whole natural numbers (1, 2, 3, 4. etc.). Each of these numbers is in itself finite (each number names the finite point or position where it stands) and so each number and the whole series of numbers preceding each one of them is also finite. But at the same time each of these numbers has a potential infinity of successors. One can easily find a higher number to any number imaginable by simply applying one of the most basic mathematical formulas $(n + 1)$.[14] There is a dialectic of finitude and (potential) infinity with regard to the series of natural numbers. A number is thus an element of an infinite set (a set containing a potential progression ad infinitum) by standing precisely in between the finite (of the preceding series of numbers) and the infinite (of potential successors).[15] This is the precise definition of what one can call *numerical finitude* as each number is the point between the finite series before and the potentially infinite series after it. It should be clear that numerical finitude is nothing but a peculiar relation between the finite and the infinite. But if one considers the numerical finite as simply being finite, this already relies on a specific kind of forgetting (since what is forgotten is the potential—but constitutive—infinity of successors). *What is forgotten is the possibility of (the potential) infinity.* Already when one simply considers the realm of the (infinite set of) natural numbers and seeks to derive from the constitution of this very set a claim about the essential finitude of the number (i.e., of its elements), this implies that one already hypostatizes one side of the defining criteria of what a number as element of the set of natural numbers is.

To put this simply: to claim the number is finite implies a "decision for finitude" ("BIV"), which forcefully forgets the possibility of infinity that is as much constitutive of the number as the finite series of predecessors. One can here translate this forgetful decision involved in such a depiction of the essential finitude of the number into direct political terms: the numericity of commodities, of money, of electoral votes, opinion polls, the very idea of majority votes, and so on—all that constitutes our "era of number's despotism," "the empire of the number" whose main imperative is "count!"[16]—all this relies on forgetting the latent, that is, potential infinity that is constitutive of the number. And this forgetting is what the contemporary "politics of administration" ("BLO," 311)[17] (as one might call the very link of democratic materialist ideology and parliamentary capitalism) employs as one of its most crucial tools (if not as *the* one). Such an account of the number relies on an orientation that constructs everything that it proclaims to exist as being (something) countable. Thereby the very claim of countability relies on the axiom of constructability and the very constructability relies on a decision to finitize the very concept of number. And as anyone today has become counted—as voter, as cell phone owner, as existing body living on the territory of a state, and so on[18]—the type of subjectivity that is implied within this alleged political system is a "voided Subject" (*BRP*, 469); a subject that is precisely voided by being finitized (purified from anything infinite to be ultimately nothing but an individual body with communal language capacities) by the "seduction of commodities and money" (*BRP*, 460). The contemporary oblivion is thus not only a decisive and decided forgetting implied in democratic materialism, which thus is an ideology (or a metaphysics), but at the same time engenders a production of forgetfulness (with regard to his or her own potential infinity) in each and every one. But this very forgetful production of forgetfulness (another more traditional name for this has been: naturalization) is thus perfectly well endorsing and reproducing, producing and enforcing the contemporary capitalist order. But nonetheless and against Heidegger, this is materialism, since one cannot interpret this maneuver in the framework of a simple onto-theological operation (implying the claim that there is something like a highest of all beings).

Yet, the forgetting of the possibility of infinity (of the number) might not even be considered to be the most radical dimension of this ideological forgetting, although the proper dimension of the implicit decision for constructability can only be grasped from taking this into account. There is a twofold forgetting taking place and to delineate this, once again a turn to mathematics is instructive: within mathematics one can demonstrate that there is an infinity higher, or to be more technically precise: more powerful than the (potential) infinity of the natural numbers (progressing infinitely). Therefore there are the whole natural numbers (a series of predecessors and successors) and then there is "something" which cannot be considered to be a successor of the series of natural numbers (otherwise it simply would be another natural number); let us call it $\omega$.[19] One way of rendering this very position of $\omega$ is that this is what the mathematicians refer to as actual infinity.[20] This infinite point that $\omega$ is can be said to surpass the potential infinity of successors precisely by not being a successor; it is rather the place or space where the succession can take place.[21] By being excluded from the potentially infinite succession it is at the same time precisely the horizon of this very succession (that which is the totalizing limit point of the potentially infinite series).[22] $\omega$ is thereby an infinite point that is also an infinite place (by retroactively totalizing the potentially infinite series and at the same time not being a successor) and takes the function of a limit-point (infinite horizon). In this threefold determination $\omega$ can be said to interrupt the repetition of the succession (the repetition of the repeated engendering of new successors) that was defining the realm of the whole natural numbers. Yet, one can now easily generate a successor to ω (which is itself not a successor of and in the same series) by again applying the simple mathematical formula (ω + 1) and one can, of course, continue this infinitely. This amounts to a reopening of succession,[23] to the reinscription of a new repetition. But ω—and this is important—being at the juncture of two successions is itself not a successor of the first series of successions. This is why Badiou calls it an "intervallic infinity" ("BIV") which can itself be considered to be the support of a new series of (potentially infinite) succession.

The best example for such an intermediate infinity is in political terms a revolution (precisely in the function of infinite point, place, and horizon). A revolution breaks with the previous succession model and with the order of succession and creates a new one. ω is an infinite that breaks with repetition but makes it also possible to recommence. Why is all this instructive? It is because it demonstrates that the endorsement of finitude, which is one of the most crucial momentums of contemporary ideology (a result of their constructivist orientation), entails a forgetting of the very existence of the different functions of infinity (point, place, horizon, interruption, and recommencement) in its crucial medium, the number. The philosophical and political (but also artistic and amorous) consequences of this forced and forceful forgetting are far reaching. Hence, an exploration of them is necessary.

## Consequences of Democratic Materialism

One first consequence is that this oblivion implies a denial of the significance of the infinite point *tout court* (it denies that there can be something that is not a successor and thereby it denies the very idea of an interruption of succession, i.e., it denies eventality as such). This leads to the idea that what there is and can be is an endless extension of the quantitative dimension of finitude forgetting and repressing that there can be something like a qualitative leap, like an exception. This is one way of rendering what it comes down to that democratic materialism forgets dialectic, since any dialectic worthy of this name is a dialectic of exception. The extension of the quantitative implies that there is no exception, that is, no dialectic and nothing of politics (recall that revolution was the paradigm for the movement of this dialectics of infinity). All of this amounts to the assumption that everything has a price (i.e., that there is no politics that could not be reduced to the mere number game of economy).[24] This very operation (based on the presupposition of constructability) might be considered to be one of the most crucial capitalist operations *tout court* (i.e., the assimilation of a point of exception into the normality of repetition), since it implies the translation and transfixation of something qualitatively different into something quantitatively equivalent, hence comprehensible and measurable (this is turning an exception into a new commodity that has got a price like all the others). This also implies that everything which does not have a price (i.e., is not quantitatively accessible) does not count, that is, it is insignificant, imperceptible from the perspective of the quantitative regime. This is what also makes intelligible why in capitalist democratic materialism true love does not count much (and is constantly attempted to be quantitatively apprehended),[25] art is only what can be sold on the art market (and the best art is that which is sold for the most), and science is only truly worth any subsidization when it leads to new marketable technology. Everything that seems to be not apprehendable in terms of quantity is insignificant, thus negligible and therefore can be (and needs to be) forgotten. *Quantity governs everything, quality is obliviated.*

A second consequence lies in the fact that ω in its precise determination as place of the potentially infinite repetition (that is constitutive for the number) is forgotten. This consequence is implemented by an act of hypostatizing relation, that is, all the relations that there are between the finite (numbers), and by assigning to them the primacy over the place where their relation is situated. This is to say that the number is treated as a mere relation that can be comprehended in terms of equality and inequality. Finally this means: (necessarily oblivious) holism[26] versus ontology. Thereby what is established is that the only way by which a thing is worth more than another is by the very position it takes within the series (7 is more than 4 but less than 13). With this operation it is not that the exception as something qualitatively different is forgotten. Rather, what is forcefully obliviated is that there can be (and that there is) something absolute. This is why within the political field such a position basically leads to a weak version of cosmopolitism or cultural relativism (no political organization or party within the parliamentary system can claim that its agenda is fundamentally different than any others, it can only claim that its program promises to be—on a numerical level—better than the other). Better or worse, this is what counts; absolute difference is forgotten.

A third consequence is that the very definition of ω as infinite horizon, as limit point to the potentially infinite series of numbers is denied and forgotten. This can be translated into the claim that although it might seem that there is something beyond the mere repetition of finitude, in fact there is not. This operation can also be rendered as follows: the repetition that is recommenced after ω, after the interruption of the first series of repetition, is worse than the first (it is criminal, destructive, dangerous, horrific, etc.). All these consequences are consequences of a forgetting of the infinite. This forgetting takes the precise form of forgetting the very status of ω as non-successor (with its different characteristics). So, in some sense Badiou also (like Heidegger did) diagnoses the forgetting of a difference, of a qualitative difference (or more precisely: the qualitative difference between quantity and quality), of the difference between finitude and infinity (more precisely: between the constitutive infinity of finitude) and therefore of the difference between the denial and the existence of something absolute.[27] If for Heidegger philosophy was able to counter the metaphysical forgetting (and its social, political, and cultural consequences) by revealingly recalling the truth of being (in insisting on the ontological distinction between being and beings)[28] through returning to the language of the poets, Badiou's opposition to the ideological oblivion functions differently. So, why and how is philosophy anamnestic for Badiou?

## Total Recall: Remember (the Idea)

One might start to answer this question by taking two things into account: Badiou not only defends a philosophical position that from the perspective of the contemporary (ideological) doxa could not be more countercurrent, namely Platonism, but he is also one of the few thinkers that started to openly endorse again a political name that also could hardly sound more out of date with respect to today's mainstream political (democratic materialist) positions, namely communism. My claim is that to properly understand Badiou's take on how to counter the delineated oblivion of democratic materialism these two commitments have to be read together. Badiou is not only defending a renewal of Platonism, he is—and very much so—defending a renewal of what he calls the "communist hypothesis" (*BCH*). This double counter-affirmation (of Platonism and communism), as I see it, has to be read together. This is not an arbitrary or merely contingent take on Badiou's position, brought to it from the outset. The necessary (and maybe at the same time impossible) link in his double commitment already becomes perceivable when, in a somewhat empirical manner, two things are taken into account.

Firstly, Badiou reconstructs this history of the communist hypothesis in its different sequences (two of which yet have been "completed") in terms of different historical types of organization of what Badiou calls the "communist idea." The communist idea—which systematically has to be distinguished from the hypothesis[29]—is that which is always marked by a historically specific exception to the given realm of the (politically) possible; a conversion of something previously regarded as impossible into a new "impossible possibility" (*BPP*, 101). The idea whose political name is articulated by Badiou under the title "communism" marks an exception, an interruption of the repetition of the previous successions of possible actions, types of organization, political agendas, and so on. The idea, obviously the Platonic category par excellence, is that which names the very mobilizing force and the real existence in the organization of these exceptions.[30] So, one of the most crucial metapolitical[31] concepts of Badiou's thought can already be considered a bastard, namely a Platonist-communist one. Secondly, it can be stated that Badiou worked for a long time on a now published "hyper-translation" ("BQM"), as he once called it, of Plato's *politeia* to which he gave for a long time the provisional title "On Communism" ("BPAP"). It thus can be an instructive starting point to take this very book (now published under the title *Plato's Republic* [*BRP*]) as offering clues to the understanding of how precisely the anamnesic practice of philosophy within Badiou's system works as well as why Plato and communism have to be read together. For Badiou's *Plato is* countering political oblivion and hence it is a *crucial element of any contemporary materialism* (as paradoxical as this may sound).[32]

In the preface to his re-actualization of Plato's republic, Badiou claims that one of the questions occupying him while working on the project was: "what does 'treating' the text mean?" (*BRP*, xxxii). One might against the background of the thus far elaborated rephrase this question as follows: "What does it mean to render a Platonist text under the heading of communism and at the same time under the condition of hegemony of democratic materialism?" So, what does this mean to translate one of Plato's most famous texts—crucially dealing with the question of politics and justice and how what Plato refers to as "idea" functions in it—in a time when there is only democracy (as the best of all the worst options) and its materialism (as the only ideological option)? How to understand a gesture like this—retranslating Plato under a new title in a specific historical context?

Some brief digressions can be instructive here: in the 1960s Pier Paolo Pasolini embarked on a rather unusual project that he never realized (at least not in the form of a film). He was working on a screenplay about the life of Saint Paul. This film was supposed to "transfer the life story of Saint Paul to our own time" (*PPP*, 16).[33] And it is this precise project which can shed some light on the questions phrased above. This is the case, as Badiou comments on that very project in his book on Saint Paul.[34] What Pasolini, according to Badiou, sought to do was to "turn Paul into a contemporary without any modification of his statements" (*BSPU*, 137)—this is to say that what Pasolini tried to demonstrate is that Paul (as for Hegel the absolute) is with us.[35] Pasolini's aim of transplanting Paul into the contemporary world was conceptually motivated by three different insights, which Badiou articulates as follows: (1) "today the figure of the saint is necessary, even if the contents of the initiating encounter may vary"; (2) "by transplanting Paul, along with all his statements. . . . one sees them encountering a real society . . . infinitely more supple and resistant than that of the Roman Empire"; (3) "Paul's statements are endowed with a timeless legitimacy" (*BSPU*, 37).[36] If one takes these three claims together in an endeavor that seeks to demonstrate that "Paul emerges strangely victorious" (*BSPU*, 39) when faced with the contemporary world, it might become clear why actualizing a seemingly outdated position (of a religious militant) can indicate an obliviated, forgotten, even concealed impossible possibility of a subjective position and of subjective action. But for Pasolini to fulfill this task it was necessary to effectuate a "series of transfers" to "resurrect" (*PPP*, 16) Paul's position in and for the mid-1960s. So why can this reference be helpful for understanding the general direction of impact of Badiou's hyper-translation of Plato? Is Paul for Pasolini what Plato is for Badiou?

To start to answer this question one can assert that what is at stake in both endeavors is the task of transmitting "something" (of a position), which is linked to the peculiar problem of how to transmit it (across contexts and circumstances that differ fundamentally),[37] since what is supposed to be transmitted is not knowledge, but "something" else. Therefore what both Pasolini and Badiou aim at is to provide adequate tools of another kind of "message," for "something" to get through. Yet, while Pasolini's project aimed at placing Paul without any modification of his statements in a more contemporary context in order to demonstrate and remind us of his eternal legitimacy, Badiou's project goes even one step further. Of course—and the above-mentioned mathematical references were meant to rearticulate this point—Plato was the first to delineate the very conditioning of philosophy by non-philosophical forms of practice (namely by art, politics, love, and science, i.e., mathematics), and this very Platonic claim (philosophy is under conditions) is what for philosophy—from a Badiousian perspective—has an eternal legitimacy.[38] Yet, to make Plato's text itself legible and to counter the oblivion induced by democratic materialism, a different kind of renewal is needed. The very name "Plato" stands for a dimension that has been forgotten within the reign of democratic materialism. However, in order to recall what this name stands for, even the means for remembering have to be reshaped since Plato is charged not only with being an utter idealist defending an unsustainable philosophical position but also with being a totalitarian (in his conception of the philosopher-king).[39] So, what is surprisingly attacked in the name "Plato" is also in some sense (although, of course, from a different perspective) that which is attacked under the name "communism": a totalitarian model that is not suited for the real-life world, proven wrong by history, criminal not only by accident but in its essence.

So by seeking to revamp the very text in which Plato deals with the question of justice and political organization (and the critique of the different types of organization from oligarchy to tyranny), Badiou links the question of how to render Plato's "message" transmittable to the question of *how to transmit the very conception of an idea*. One can argue that his hyper-translation is an attempt to realize not the transmission of a concrete idea that could be put into practice proper, but of the very form of an idea. For what today is forgotten is not this or that concrete idea, but rather the very (possibility of the) existence of an idea (that is, of something infinite in its different dimensions). However, to actualize something that seems to be invalidated and forgotten what is needed is not only to transplant artistically the very position one is seeking to defend into the new context, but rather a renewal of the means of actualizing the forgotten position. Simply put: one cannot simply translate Plato's theses without any modification into a contemporary context, as this would precisely not demonstrate their validity; this might rather make them sound unsound. The ideology of democratic materialism works precisely in a way to make certain things unintelligible, unreadable (by rendering them as utterly absurd, nonsensical, and so on),[40] and a simple gesture of transplantation would only further endorse the alleged nullity and meaninglessness of a Platonic position. But if communism might be said to have been an idea[41] and if *the* philosopher of the idea is of course Plato, the question emerges: *how can one actualize the idea of an idea?* This is the question that one can see to stand behind Badiou's act of hyper-translating a text by Plato.

To rephrase the thus far developed argument: Heidegger's as much as Badiou's diagnosis of the present implies that for them philosophy is an anamnestic practice and both argue that what needs to be recalled is not "something" but rather a forgotten distinction. For Heidegger the forgetting of the ontic-ontological difference leads to a hierarchized structure of the ontic sphere (and in the last instance thereby to an empowerment of the subject via technology); whereas for Badiou the forgetting of the distinction between finitude and infinity leads to a demise of the very notion of the subject and its practice. Heidegger counters the effects of oblivion by referring to a forgotten truth by pointing to the poets, who thereby become the bearers of the knowledge of the very existence of this truth (which is the truth of being). For Badiou, things are here a bit more complicated: the forgetting of the distinction instructs his return to Plato and his use of the allegedly idealist category of the "idea." Yet the very concept of a practice that returns to the idea—in its Platonic forming—does not simply return to the forgotten infinity. What philosophy—among other things by means of mathematics—recalls is that there is also and necessarily a dialectics of finitude and infinity at work that constitutes the very form of the idea. Thereby what is forgotten is not only a distinction but rather that there is a dialectics constitutive of the idea.[42] Returning to Plato to resurrect the idea of the idea thus also implies resurrecting dialectics. To counter democratic materialism when materialism is the only option, this cannot but imply to contend that materialism needs dialectics as much as dialectics needs materialism. To oppose democratic materialism, *materialism has to become dialectical.* This is what it means to recall the idea of the idea. However, what does it mean to remind the human animal of that which has been forgotten under democratic materialism? Badiou answers as follows: that for which philosophy has to struggle is that one can think an alternative to the form of life (and practice of living) that democratic materialism defends (one with oblivion at its basis; a life without any exception whatsoever and thus without any dialectics, hence without any idea). This is to say: there can be a life under an idea.[43] The political name for it is communism. Yet how can philosophy under changed circumstances remind the human animal of this?

## Meta-Critical Anamnesis I: Remember How to Remember

What philosophy needs to recall and hence resurrect from Plato is precisely the *concept of the idea* (which Heidegger deemed to stand at the origin of metaphysical oblivion). But things start to get more difficult here: what does it mean to recall the conception of the idea in Plato since Badiou does not simply mimic a (traditional) Platonist position? In fact he insists that the only proper way in which philosophy can be anamnestic is by re-actualizing not only what has been forgotten but also by re-actualizing the very means with which this anamnesis operates. Philosophy hence does not simply recall the idea by emphasizing its dialectical constitution; it can only do this by applying dialectics and this means by dialectically working through the very concept of anamnesis itself. This is how materialism becomes dialectical and this maneuver implies (1) that philosophy is anamnestic for the sake of introducing a distinction[44]—this is the philosophical act referred to in the previous chapter—a distinction between two ways of living, for example, a distinction that forces one to take sides;[45] (2) that therefore the anamnestic practice that is philosophy is militant: it is a *militant anamnesis*; (3) that philosophy is critical in the very literal sense of the Greek verb *krinein*, of distinguishing and deciding; and yet (4) that philosophy can only be what it is by recalling that the very means of reminding the human animal of this forgotten distinction need to be reworked, too, taking into account the historically specific situation and the hegemonic ideology within it. Thus philosophy cannot simply be anamnesic for the sake of being critical. It has to be *meta-critical* (critically re-actualizing the very means of anamnesis) to fulfill its anamnesic task.

So what does all this mean when one looks at Badiou's revamping of Plato's text? This question can be quite easily rephrased into another one: is Badiou's hyper-translation of Plato a book by Badiou or a book by Plato? The most obvious answer might be: both. And indeed, it is a book in which Badiou re-actualizes Plato against the background of his own philosophical enterprise. Yet this is to say that one has to take into account some sort of recursive loop when dealing with the text. The book itself is neither simply Badiousian (although obviously Badiou is a Platonist) nor simply Platonic (as it is Plato re-actualized, retranslated, revamped). Therefore it presents one way in which philosophy can be anamnestic by reshaping the very concepts (and their presentation) by which it brings back to life what has been forgotten.[46] Its essential operation is to remind the human animal in ever-changing historical conditions of the fact that something impossible can happen although it always and ever again will seem (or will have seemed) impossible. One is thus dealing here with a meta-critical and anamnestic book. Hyper-translation thus names a crucial operation of meta-critical anamnesis. *Meta-critical anamnesis is another name for philosophy* (in Badiou's sense).

One of the most crucial claims that can be derived from the book—that is intimately linked with the question of how to recall the very idea of an idea—is presented (close to the very end) in the discussion of what justice and even more of what "happiness" (*BRP*, 291–315) is. It could be argued that this passage presents Badiou's-Plato's answer of how to comprehend the being of an idea. The background of this presentation might be best summed up in Badiou's own words:

> In the Republic, the generic form of being is the Idea. When it is a
> question of designating the principle of intelligibility of the being of the

Idea . . . we must have recourse to the transcendence of the Good. Now, what does Plato tell us immediately afterwards? That the Good is not an Idea, and thus that with regard to the ontological disposition, what is the root of being and the thinkable stands in exception to being, in the form proper to non-being that is the non-Idea. ("BLO," 314)

What this is to say is that one cannot simply recall what an idea is by presenting the concept, the conceptual implications of an idea.[47] Rather the very being of the idea—which Plato calls the Good that is itself not an Idea—necessitates recalling the very status of an exception. But how can one transmit an exception? This question is a question any materialist philosophy has to answer. And this is also what the delineated chapter of Badiou-Plato deals with. So, what is happiness? Happiness is misconceived when it is rendered as something that could describe the objective state of a subject (since then it would be quantifiable and thus we would be in the thick of democratic materialism). Instead it has to be conceived of as that which can only be grasped when there is an exception to the seemingly unchangeable laws of the world and of one's existence. This means that one can only comprehend what happiness is when one is actively partaking in the unfolding of the consequences of an exception. This is also to say that happiness names the very affective state that is the link between a subject and an idea. An idea enters the world via an exception—as *the very nature of the idea is exceptional*—and the idea only becomes what it is if it in some sense materializes in the very world in which it introduces an exception. Happiness—the subjective and affective name for the Good in Badiou's Plato—can thus only be grasped from the subjective interiority of the very process that constitutes the material effects of an exception to the world. Thus if philosophy seeks to bring into existence the very improbable and allegedly impossible possibility of an idea, what it needs to do to fulfill this task is to also affirm in ever new ways the impossible possibility of an exception.

Linking together Plato and communism once again—the double commitment that is constitutive of Badiou's endeavor—what one might say is that philosophy as meta-critical anamnesis has to remind the human animal of what cannot be known. Since what is recalled has the character of a peculiar non-being (the being of the idea, i.e., the Good that is non-being, i.e., an exception even to being), it cannot be known because it can never be anticipated, deduced, derived, inferred. It is necessary, yet impossible. Meta-critical anamnesis operates by recalling the necessarily impossible, the impossibly necessary. This is what philosophy can achieve by defending Plato. And as in its principles communism is and always will have been an exception to the given state of things (as the real movement abolishing the present state of things), to defend Plato is also to struggle for the very impossible necessity of communism. This is why true philosophy—which will always have been exceptionally materialist, materialistically emphasizing the exception—for Badiou (will) remain(s) Platonic. And affirming Plato is thus the first necessary, yet impossible communist gesture; a Platonic gesture of anamnesis, an anamnesis of Plato in times when communism seems as much impossible as Plato. Resurrecting the idea of the idea is why philosophy cannot abandon Plato. But what does this mean in more concrete terms? Or to put this in Lenin's terms: What is to be done?

# 3

# Repeat

## Remembering, Repeating, Working through Materialism

> Quite generally, the familiar, just because it is familiar is not cognitively understood.
> —G. W. F. Hegel, *Phenomenology of Spirt*

> ... *démocratie*. C'est pour moi le nom phallique de notre présent et ce que j'aimerais faire ici c'est en quelque sorte d'écrire la comédie de la démocratie.
> —"BITP I"

> The only way to grasp the true novelty of the New is to analyze the world through the lenses of what is an "eternal" in the old.
> —*ZTF*

### Remembering, Actualizing

Without knowledge of the situation any action is difficult, true action even seems to be impossible. But to render this in more precise terms: real action only becomes possible when pseudo-actions (actions that only reproduce the given situation and its vectors) and true actions (actions that have an influence on and hence transform the fundamental coordinates of the situation) become distinguishable. To act at all one first needs to draw such a line of demarcation. To act an act is needed. However, lines of demarcation always result from concrete analyses of concrete situations—even if in the last instance this leads to the fact that any action has to make the wager if it will have been a true action or not. Hence, the question how to truly act today is related to the question of where does one stand today and what today can be called a real action at all. This is to say that without a line of demarcation between real and pseudo-action ultimately there is no room for action. Only demarcations create the minimum of orientation that is needed to act. This is why the question of what a true action is (today) or how to properly act at all (today) therefore always relates to the historical present of the action and is hence also a question of how an action can be adequate to its own time. The question of how to act therefore is conceptually preceded by another one: by the question of how one can conceive of the historical present of an action and of its essential coordinates. One way of giving an account of the contemporary present of any action seems to be easy at hand—it depends on whether the end of history as most rather unconsciously than consciously believe has now come or not. Everyone lives as an individual in democratic-communal orders and if one does not, one should sincerely hope that one is allowed to do so in the very near future. Those who do not share this kind of hope do not really live in the present of the present. But things start to get complicated here, since one might ask what does it mean to live in democratic communities or also what does it actually mean to hope to do so in the near future?

If in search for an answer one solely refers to the Marxist tradition one can find among many answers two particularly trenchant ones. First, there is the answer of the young Marx who openly identifies democracy with communism when he claims "that all states have democracy as their truth."[1] Democratic in his sense is any type of organization that enables the truth of collective and free self-determination of equals; a truth which will always already be obstructed in or by any state. Second, one finds a strictly opposed position in Lenin's thought who repeats the old diagnosis of Plato by claiming: democracy is a preferable form of the state but in the last instance it is still a form of the state and as any "state [it] is an organ of the rule of a definite class which *cannot* be reconciled with its antipode (the class opposite to it)."[2] Therefore and to finally enable collective free self-determination of equals it has to sink in what Eduard Gans called the "ocean of history."[3] Democracy as such, if only situated within the Marxist tradition, namely between Marx and Lenin, implies a peculiar double determination that locates it somewhere between being a not-statist, free-associated and free-associating organization on one hand and a statist nationalized instrument of dominance on the other. The contemporary democratic present of any action thus oscillates within this tension of non-statist and statist organization.

Alain Badiou starts his reflection on what a true political action today could look like by reflecting on and criticizing democracy. This same maneuver is also performed by another contemporary thinker who could in many respects not be closer to Badiou's project of renewing materialism, namely Slavoj Žižek. Žižek has extensively elaborated in all of his work how to conceive of materialism today, how to criticize the predominant ideological formations and also how to conceive of the coordinates of a true political act today. This is why I think it is instructive to read Badiou's and Žižek's approach to the question of a materialist theory of action in parallel. Initially both seem to recognize the tension that is inherent in the notion of democracy, its conceptual oscillation between non-statist organization and state-form. This oscillation, as one might argue with reference to both of these authors, is repeated historically as tension between content and form. Today the form of democracy is conditioned by the capitalist content and the form of capitalism is conditioned by the democratic content.

Capitalist content in democratic form presents itself in the dominance of interests, desires, and finally in the animal and beastly constitution of man within all contemporary "political" debates. Democratic content in capitalist form presents itself in the practical interpretation of democratic principles, say of freedom as freedom of the worker to sell his own labor.[4] Following Badiou and Žižek one can claim that this mutual and historically specific determination (of the content as well as of the form) of democracy and capitalism has to be thought through to outline what real actions can be in the present times. Only in this way one is able to escape the temptation to act while not knowing the coordinates of the situation and hence the danger of ending up perpetuating them.[5] Reflection on real action today thus demands both: a reflection on democracy *and* a critique of democracy. The latter today takes the form of a concrete analysis of the intimate link between democracy and capitalism, which implies an analysis of the entanglement of the twofold interdependent determination of content and form. A true action can only be an action that is free from the political premises, coordinates, and ideological parameters brought forth by the economic dynamics of capitalism and the form that is determined by it as much as it determines it. From these remarks one can formulate a common ground of the approaches of Badiou and Žižek that can be delineated by stating: only a critique of capitalism that takes the form of a reflection on *and* of a critique of the contemporary form of democracy produces demarcations of real and pseudo-actions and might thus generate orientation. Avoiding such a form of analysis of the concrete historical situation is simply further endorsing the "time of disorientation" ("BCP"), in which any "subjective cognitive mapping is lacking" (*ZID*, 240).

*Reflection on democracy* consequently means to side with young Marx and to question what it can signify today to maintain the hypothesis that one can organize oneself democratically, that is, in a communist way, and this means under the primacy of equality so that a collective practice of equals is installed which *hic et nunc* can be called just. Democracy in this sense would formally and with regard to its content have to be separated from the determinations of capitalism—that is, of the given form of circulation of objects—and indicates a name of a sociopolitical organization that needs to be reinvented. One might state that for Badiou and Žižek this is one way of rendering what they call the "communist hypothesis."[6] *Critique of democracy* consequently means that the existing form of democratic organization under present globalized capitalist conditions, the historical situation that Badiou refers to as "capitalo-parliamentarism" (*BCH*, 38) and Žižek by addressing "democracy as master signifier"[7] has to be drastically put into question to be able to remain anti-capitalist. As Žižek rightly diagnosed: "an anticapitalism without problematization of the political form of capitalism (of liberal parliamentary democracy) is not sufficient, no matter how radical it is" (*ZR*, 101). Badiou sharpens this: "Today the enemy is no longer empire or capital. It is democracy."[8] The formerly historically effective signifier "anti-capitalism" today has lost its subversive core because, to vary the infamous words of Lenin, "all the social-chauvinists now"[9] are anti-capitalists. Boltanski and Chiapello have rightly diagnosed that this brings about very peculiar discursive effects. One of them is that from the 1980s onwards "virtually no one, with the exception of a few allegedly archaic Marxists (an 'endangered species'), referred to capitalism any longer. The term was simply struck from the vocabulary of politicians, trade unionists, writers and journalists."[10] But that about which one seemingly cannot talk (anymore) is precisely that about which one should *not* remain silent.

## Actualizations of Ideology-Critique

Capitalism, although omnipresent and predominant, has become invisible in everyday life. This is due to the fact that it has taken over all the forms—for example the liberal-democratic-parliamentary form— that make it disappear. Capitalism appears as "invisible since it sustains the very zero-level standard against which we perceive something" (*ZV*, 2). However, it is precisely the form of capitalism—democracy—and the *capitalist ex-adaption*[11] of democratic principles that is responsible for and produces capitalism's very invisibility. If against this background one starts addressing the question of what the contemporary present of a real action is, this also implies to investigate the very structures that determine what appears to any agent as being a possible or impossible action.[12] Today the regime of the possible is one that plainly confirms the "reality" of the given and thereby ultimately leads to the fact that anything that is possible has become necessary. The possible is therefore a regime that despite its seemingly endless expansibility[13] approves the necessity of the given. Today one can diagnose a fundamental reversibility of the possible and the necessary. If one inquires about the coordinates of the regime of the possible and the field of impossibility it implicitly and explicitly delineates, one has to investigate that which one can see as possible action and that which one cannot; that which one cannot see within the established parameters—the content and the form—of the contemporary present. This also implies that any action that appears to be possible is an action which is already determined as possible by the coordinates of the situation itself. One hence can infer that possible actions are pseudo-actions, real action has to appear to be impossible. *Voilà*, the first line of demarcation.

Today one cannot but locate real actions in the historical context of capitalism. Or more precisely within the distinction if one acts for or against capitalism, hence within the distinction capitalism/anti-capitalism. If real actions describe actions that transform the coordinates of the historical situation, the question arises what the invisible background is that makes it possible to qualify certain actions as possible and others as impossible. One therefore does not only investigate the (normative and concrete) contents of an action but also its (historically specific) form and thereby also the apparently invisible and historically specific transcendental[14] conditions of this form itself. If in one step actions can be understood as implying a subjective determination of a content that stands in a dialectical relationship to the reality in which it can be realized, since on one side it might simply be determined by this reality or on the other, it might transform the reality (such that there is a subjective coining of a merely apparently objective reality by which the content truly becomes what it is). This means that the analysis (of the form) of action is spanned between two poles: (1) the question of what the present objective possible and impossible forms and contents of the subjective determination of actions are; and (2) the question of how to overcome the dominant forms and contents of actions (since this defines true actions) by also inquiring into what seems objectively impossible and unthinkable. This means the materialist position one is dealing with in Badiou necessarily refers to something that appears to be unthinkable and impossible. It is a *materialism of the impossible*. Hence, how can one raise the impotence to truly act in the face of what today seems possible to a point of impossibility?[15]

Today an essential dimension of the reflection on real action is hence a link between the *historical-objective possible/impossible content and the historical-subjective possible/impossible form of action.* In view of the authors discussed in this chapter, one can contend: Badiou and Žižek remember in this precise sense a lesson of Marx. Already the early Marx asks what a real action can be under given conditions of (capitalistically organized) alienation. "To remember Marx" means to remember and resume his critique of allegedly possible modes of action. This is to remember to avoid a misunderstanding of what materialism is; a materialism of the possible (like in Feuerbach) is precisely not a materialism of the exception and only a materialism of the exception—an idealism without idealism—is a true materialism. Critique then does less imply the upholding of a Kantian form of critique (that constitutively expounds what the conditions of possibility of actions are), but rather to affirm other modes of action, precisely those that seem impossible (this amounts to the claim that an action retroactively constitutes its own conditions of possibility and hence reconstitutes a new transcendental horizon). But "to remember Marx" also means for Badiou and Žižek to remember that real actions are impossible *inside of capitalism* since the form of action it inscribes always already determines all actions via the paradigm of extending and expanding the possible.[16] "Remembering Marx" in Badiou and Žižek therefore means to actualize the critique of ideology as *modus operandi* of any concrete analysis of concrete situations under present conditions. And this also implies that one needs to find a seemingly impossible starting point for any action that truly wants to change the situation and its fundamental coordinates. Such an action has to be absolutely heterogeneous to any form of exchange, any form of circulation of objects. This means that one has to find a starting point for actions that is not exchangeable, or to be more precise: one has to bet on the idea that there can be a present of actions that is not oriented by the primacy of objects; one has to bet on the idea that there can be a non-objective, that is, subjective (and this is not to say solipsistic or relativist) present against the dominant present of (exchangeable and circulating) objects.

Badiou's and Žižek's reflections on the contemporary link of democracy and capitalism can be understood as a form of *ideology critique* and this is to say as actualization, renewal, and revision of Marx, that is, a rigidly anti-capitalist position. Actualization, renewal, and revision have to be understood at the same time as implying a dissociation and critique of that which seems evident and irrefutable and thus possible or necessary. This means, this type of contemporary ideology critique has to tackle any type of naturalization of certain contents and forms of action, since naturalization has always been the first operation of reactionary ideology. If today "democracy" seems to name the sole politically thinkable form then any form of anti-capitalism remains in the last instance capitalist when it proves to be unable to criticize the form of its own critique (by criticizing capitalism but not democracy and hence being negligent of their link). It thereby becomes itself an effect of effects of naturalization of the historically specific form of capitalist circumstances, or to put this in different terms: anti-capitalism becomes a perfidious—and ultimately fetishist—procedure of naturalizing of given conditions. The formula of this impotent anti-capitalism is: "Je sais bien (que je ne suis pas anti-capitaliste parce que je ne suis pas antidémocrate), mais quand même (je crois que je suis anticapitaliste)."—"I know very well (that I am not an anti-capitalist because I am not an anti-democrat) but nevertheless (I believe that I am a true anti-capitalist)."[17] But this is also why one can legitimately ask: in which relationship does the formal critique of democracy exist towards an anti-capitalist position? On the one side one can remark that a merely abstract opposition to capitalism—and who is today not, from Hollywood to the most reactionary parliamentarians, somehow an anti-capitalist[18]—without a critique of its specific political form, that is, democracy, remains powerless against the capitalist dynamic. Even worse, it is doomed to reproduce it. On the other side one also has to remark that a merely abstract opposition to democracy also remains within a position of a systemic substanceless substance of contemporary historical developments, that is to say precisely within the realm of capital that unites both, the anti-democrats—who present themselves subjectively as terrorists (with a small "t") or fundamentalists—and the liberal democrats.

Abstract anti-capitalists and abstract critics of democracy remain immediate prisoners of the form or of the (contentless) content that they attempt to criticize. Neither the abstract negation of capitalism nor the abstract negation of democracy is enough to outline a model of true and free political action and its consequences. Freely paraphrasing Kant, one can hence state: *anti-capitalism without critique of democracy is impotent* (and turns into parliamentary opposition or into something like the anti-globalization movement, which in the last instance makes no difference and either remains simply ineffective[19] or even reproduces the system); *a critique of democracy without anti-capitalism is blind* (and leads to nihilist terror or obscurantism).[20,21] One might thus infer that Badiou's and Žižek's project remembers Marx because both of them undertake an actualization of ideology critique, which entails an investigation of the form and the content (of apparently possible and seemingly impossible) actions. Both of them "remember Marx." If this is the case it is decisive to ask which Marx is remembered by whom. I will argue that Alain Badiou remembers the early; Slavoj Žižek remembers the late Marx.

Badiou attempts, following the early Marx, to comprehend the present ideology as a regime that emphasizes and relies solely on that which is humanly possible; as a type of materialism whose founding axiom is that there are only individuals and communities or that there are only bodies and languages. To affirm a materialist position today, Badiou recognizes the (peculiar) legitimacy of democratic *materialism*; there is no simple return to idealism. But he also remembers the early Marxian insight that there exist only individuals and communities as long as there is no exception to this realm of existence. Already early Marx understands the critique of ideology as affirmation of an exception to that which is. The early Marx insists that there are only exploited and exploiting or more generally alienated individuals and communities as long as there does not exist something that he names "man as species being."[22] The species-being against the traditional readings names a dimension that consists in the fact that any historically specific form of seemingly evident determinations of man can be revised and new determinations can be brought up in a process of "universal production."[23] The early Marx does not blame the Hegelian deduction of the necessity of the existence of the state "for depicting the essence of the modern state as it is but rather for presenting what *is* as the *essence* of the state."[24] One can actualize this phrase in the following form: "The democratic materialist is not to blame for depicting the essence of the present situation as it is but rather for presenting that which *is* as the essence (and this means as the truth) of the situation." *Democratic materialism is the contemporary myth of the given.* One can thus say that already the early Marx insists: "There are only alienated individuals or communities *except* that there is man as species being." Badiou's actualized critique of ideology, in its two infamous versions ("There are only bodies and languages except that there are truths" and "There are only individuals and communities except that there are subjects" [*BLoW*, 1–41]) is a critique of ideology as affirmation of exceptions to this very ideology. This is what it means to remember the very foundational moment of early Marx.

Žižek remembers late Marx. For if late Marx writes to Lassalle that his *Capital* is "at once an exposé and, by the same token, a critique of the system,"[25] then Žižek remembers the same gesture. "Remembering Marx" means for Žižek to find a form of (re-)presentation (*Darstellung* in German) that is able to challenge, provoke, and criticize the link of the level of content and form between democracy and capitalism. To criticize an ideological formation that replaces any antagonism with agonism because it relies on the idea that there is possibly a "plurality on principle"[26] one needs "sideway glances" (*ZV*, 3). These sideways perspectives are needed to avoid any form of spontaneous ideological identification with that which already determines in an invisible manner the coordinates of any action. One needs for example a presentation of the emancipatory potentials of the Terror of the French Revolution or a presentation of the impossible ground of all that appears to be given (for example, one needs to depict that and why in the heart of democracy lies the permanent state of exception).[27] Badiou and Žižek offer two ways of actualizing

Marxian ideology critique: on one side as affirmation of the seemingly impossible exception, on the other as a seemingly impossible (re-)presentation of the impossible. "To remember Marx" means to criticize ideology and today it also means to affirm a materialism of the impossible, as early Marx did. Or it implies a critique of ideology via a (re-)presentation of the impossible ground of all possibility, as it can be found in the late Marx. Actualization of ideology critique is the common enterprise of Badiou and Žižek that leads into the unity of differences of early and late Marx. Ideology critique is hence a crucial element of any contemporary materialism; of any idealism without idealism.

## Repeating: How Can One Be (a) Truly Post-Hegelian (Hegelian)?

> This is where Hegel vacillates, namely, in the vicinity of the rock
> that we Marxists call "primacy of practice," and Lacan the real.
> —*BTS*, 19

Today it is thus crucial to remember Marx. However, is it enough to remember him? Should one not repeat more than his gesture today? Does remembering Marx and thereby actualizing him mean: Marx once again? All these questions already indicate that to demonstrate the actuality of Marx also in some sense means to "repeat Marx." This means that the projection onto the future and the repetition of the past can coincide in one moment. To think together projection and repetition implies to repeat Marx's gesture under new conditions. One can say that this is precisely a procedure of what I call *meta-critical anamnesis*. It is such a repetition that one can identify in Badiou and in Žižek. But "repeating Marx" in this way also means that it is necessary to again work on or digest Hegel, the most important cornerstone of the formation of Marx's thought. This means first to show on one side *against the present democratic-materialist critics of Hegel* who consider his notion of the absolute and of absolute knowing to be ridiculous and to show on the other side *against Hegel himself* why (a certain) Hegel is not enough to think how to act in the contemporary situation. The Marxian gesture that is to be repeated is thus to show that Hegel was in some aspects not Hegelian—and this means not dialectical—enough and that he contradicted certain insights of his own dialectical thought. This implies that there shall not be any alliance with the democratic-materialist ideology that attacks Hegel for being a megalomaniac idealist. But there shall solely be an alliance with the materialist elements of his dialectic and this means to insist upon the "rational kernel of Hegelian dialectic"[28] even against Hegel himself. This is an essential component of the operation of repeating Marx. "Repeating Marx" implies therefore also to repeat Marx's struggle with Hegel, his struggling with Hegelian dialectics. One can now infer that there are two possibilities of how to perform this repetition and there are many reasons to claim that one is paradigmatic for the project of Alain Badiou, the other paradigmatic for the project of Slavoj Žižek. One thus passes from the unity of Badiou and Žižek to an articulation of their differences.

On the one hand "to repeat Marx" means to again perform the transition from Hegel to Marx. Then one has to get again from late Hegel to early Marx—and one might then also ask if Feuerbach, the river of fire (*Feuer-Bach*) that all emancipatory thinkers have to cross, would somehow be a necessary element of this transition or not.[29] If this is the case, one has to support Badiou's thesis that the contemporary present resembles the 1840s, that is to say the time of early Marx.[30] Taking this position one would then have to repeat all the steps Marx undertook in his period of formation: from a rewriting of the Marxian thesis on Feuerbach, to a rewriting of his *Economic-Philosophical Manuscripts*, from re-actualizing the *Holy Family*[31] and the *German Ideology* to ultimately a redoing of the *Communist Manifesto*.[32] Repeating Marx thus would mean: one needs to work at generating a new early Marx. The communist hypothesis would then also be a hypothesis about the possibility to repeat the theoretical-practical gesture of early Marx in the here and now. "Repeating Marx" means in this first Badiousian version also to again raise the old question (of Lenin), namely what could be considered to be contemporary sources and components of a contemporary Marxism, a contemporary materialism. The answer to this re-actualized question is therefore for Badiou, the idealist without idealism, today linked to the names of Plato, Descartes, and Hegel.

On the other hand, "repeating Marx" can also mean to repeat and actualize Marx above all as a critic of political economy, as the theoretician of capital. The contemporary situation in which any political action will take place is still first and foremost the times of capitalism that can still be grasped in the most adequate way from the viewpoint of Marx's theory.[33] But accentuating this position "means that the most urgent task of economic analysis today is again to repeat Marx' 'critique of political economy'" (*ZR*, 121). This is to say, if this critique is to be repeated it needs a re-actualized form; one that can be up-to-date with the contemporary situation and does not deteriorate to being an abstract critique of the link between capitalism and democracy that is then said to be embodied in merely abstract forms of universality—say in the system of right—or to a reduced analysis of the specificity of class relations that are determined by capitalist society. For even a critique of abstraction needs to be supplemented with "the properly Hegelian procedure which uncovers the universality of what presents itself as a particular position" (*ZV*, 131). Žižek's repetition of Marx is one that assumes that one can give consistency to the following formula (which obviously comes close to an idealism without idealism): "Marx + Hegel (−Marx) = Hegel."[34] Hegel first seems to be the vanishing mediator to repeat Marx (twice in this formula), yet he is the only remainder after one starts from and then subtracts Marx. This is the very background against which Žižek proclaims a "return to Hegel" (*ZLN*, 260). He starts from late Marx to return to (the late/early, or rather: a timeless) Hegel without abandoning the insights and lessons of the critique of political economy. "Repeating Marx" then means to show how and in what sense one necessarily has to think "Marx + Hegel (−Marx) = Hegel," since first one needs to assert the validity of the critique of political economy, then one needs to relate it back to Hegel, subtract the traditional form this critique has taken, and one ends up with Hegel. This is a double repetition (of Marx and Hegel), subtracting from both, from the classical Marxian critique of political economy and from the classical interpretation of the Hegelian system, the very elements which make them inapt to account for the contemporary situation—both lack a good dose of dialectics.[35]

This claim is paradigmatically apparent in Žižek's diagnosis that in contemporary capitalism anyone occupies the position of the Hegelian monarch but as a "king in a constitutional democracy . . . a king that decides only formally, whose function is merely to sign off on measures proposed by an exclusive administration" (*ZTF*, 134)—something not even Hegel had foreseen (while he of course delineated the stupidity inscribed into the very function of the monarch, he did not anticipate the universalization of this function). "Marx + Hegel (−Marx) = Hegel" as form of a repetition of Marx (and Hegel) implies that one does not only need to constantly add to a renewed Marxian position the Hegelian insight that any true (and this means universal) action can only be performed from a particular, that is, singular position; one also needs to supplement the Marxian critique of political economy with Hegelian content and Hegelian form and thus assimilate Marx within a reformulated Hegelian position (so, Marx becomes something like an obviously necessary vanishing mediator).[36] Repeating Marx for Žižek hence is returning to Hegel; however, this can only be done by staring from a post-Hegelian standpoint, namely the one of Marx.[37]

Both Badiou and Žižek thus share that today true actions can be described starting from two essential assumptions: (1) it is imperative to repeat (early or late) Marx, and (2) it is imperative to affirm that this repetition (if it attempts to again overcome Hegel but also if it is supposed to lead back to him) has to take place under radically post-Hegelian conditions; that is to say it has to take place after the death of idealism and traditional Hegelianism. And this can either mean that Hegel is generally to be left behind or that one has to return to Hegel while acknowledging and criticizing where he has not been dialectical enough. One can note here that after Hegel the historical conditions of philosophy have been transformed in a way that it is impossible to repeat Hegel in a simple manner—this is again to say it is absolutely clear that there cannot be a simple return to idealism. Therefore a repetition of Marx is needed to truly accept that contemporary philosophy stands under post-Hegelian conditions. One can only be (or remain) a Hegelian when being a Marxist first.

"To repeat Marx" can then only mean to include the historically specific conditions of post-Hegelian philosophy into philosophy or better: to take them as the very starting point. As Žižek claims: "What even the most fanatical partisan of Hegel cannot deny is that something changed after Hegel, that a new era of thought began which can no longer be accounted for in Hegelian terms of absolute conceptual mediation."[38] But what precisely happened after Hegel? One can present the post-Hegelian condition in the following manner: after Hegel there have been theoretical and practical inventions and events that necessarily jolt his systematic framework and come with the exigency to fundamentally transform philosophical practice. What were those events? One can for example, and all this can be found in either Badiou or in Žižek, think of the invention of psychoanalysis and with it of the invention of a new perspective on love and sexuality; one can think of the development of set theory with Cantor who demonstrated that infinity can be measured and that therefore there cannot be a set of all sets and ultimately also generated a new type of formalization;[39] one can think of the invention of new political forms of organization with the Paris Commune, the Russian or Cultural Revolution that have materially proven that forms of collective non-statist organizations (even leading to the abolishment of private property) are in fact thinkable and realizable. Now, what does it mean to repeat Marx under these conditions?

First, as I argue throughout the present book, it means that it becomes necessary to develop a new form of materialist thought, a new form of materialist-dialectical—that is, idealist without idealism—thinking. "Repeating Marx" in the contemporary present, and this also means under post-Hegelian conditions, implies to articulate again the question of what it can mean to develop a dialectics that makes real action thinkable and is at the same time contemporary to its own time. The question of real action thus becomes a materialist question, a question of materialism or to be more precise: it becomes a question of materialist dialectics. Only such a question can ultimately receive a truly materialist answer. If this means, as for Badiou, to pose the question how it is possible to be fully post-Hegelian—and therefore to again perform the transition from Hegel to Marx—or if it means, as for Žižek, that one needs a radical return to Hegel—to perform the transition from Marx to Hegel and thereby propose another Hegel—all this does not change the fact that "repeating Marx" is a formula which is implied in any renewal of materialist thought and this means in any renewal of materialist dialectic. Without Marx, no materialism. Yet, this implies that "repeating Marx" comes with the exigency to work on dialectics.

## Working Through: What Is Your Dialectics?

> Dialectics, this old Platonic name of philosophy, has received a
> new impulse with Marx.
> —A. Badiou[40]

To repeat Marx today thus means to work through dialectics. And repeating Marx by working through dialectics is—as the motto quoted above indicates—in some sense to work through Plato (and hence to work through the very status of philosophy itself). But how can one do this? If "repeating Marx" implies that there has to be a working through of dialectics so that there can be a materialist theory and practice of true action under given historical circumstances, one can also identify another implication of this repetition of Marx. Any working through of dialectics has to be a working through of the notion of negativity. After Hegel, and this is a way to read the post-Hegelian condition, the notion of negativity is not the same as it was before. And at the same time the notion of negativity is the central concept of any dialectics. What to make of this? It helps to relate this diagnosis to one of the most interesting claims concerning contemporary forms of politics that was articulated by a French militant organization formerly known as "organisation politique,"[41] now called "contre le mauvais gouvernement, les volontaires d'une politique à la distance de l'état,"[42] and it takes the following form: the twenty-first century has not yet begun.[43] This claim addresses that when it comes to political action we are still thinking in the terms of the twentieth century. We are still embracing the old model of negation. What were those terms?

It is possible to render the claim mentioned above intelligible if one considers the victorious forms of political action or more adequate of revolution that took place in it. One can, for example, consider the Leninist model: it was a party-based model of organizing collective political action and the central aim of the party was taking state power. So the political framework Lenin was thinking and acting within was one in which the central issue was victory and this very issue was defined in terms of taking power—taking power only to transform the state from within, into a non-state, into the famous dictatorship of the proletariat that would eventually lead to the withering away of the state as such. In consequence this victory was only possible if the mode of organization itself was a military one able to confront the dominant forces, the dominant powers of imperialism—that is to say: also military and police forces—on its own terrain, that is, on the terrain of the state. The central question that Lenin attempted to answer was therefore: how can we be victorious, how can we win the war?[44] This is why the organization had to be a military one, employing if necessary violent means to counter the system. This question is clearly a question that he inherited from the Paris Commune.[45] The underlying logic of the theme of revolution that means the victorious insurrection that takes power was therefore what, in somewhat Althusserian or more precisely Badiousian terms, one can call an expressive dialectics.[46]

This model of an expressive dialectics designates, following the famous scheme Lenin formulated, that masses are divided into classes, classes are organized by parties, and parties are led by leaders.[47] So the avant-garde of the party, that is to say, the professional revolutionary leaders, had to express the contradiction immanent to the masses due to their organization into classes. What this whole conception is based upon is a very powerful interpretation of what abstract and determinate negation is. There is an abstract negation inherent to the social organization of masses into classes,[48] that is, class struggle; this negation that articulates itself in the form of domination of one class over the other can be overcome if it and what it fundamentally relies upon, that is, the use of violent force of the military and ideological power of the state apparatuses, is itself determinately negated. Political action was only able to be victorious if it was conceived of in terms of determinately negating the present abstract negation of the domination of one class over another. Now, this model of thinking resistance and resisting political action—in terms of state revolution organized by a centralized party—encountered fundamental obstacles that it was unable to overcome. To conceive of emancipatory political action, resistance or revolution within the constellation power-state-party was indeed victorious when it came to taking power but it was not when it came to the exercise of it. This can be seen in the fundamental failures of the final outcomes of the October Revolution but also in many respects different but formally comparable in the Cultural Revolution.[49] The centralized party that had taken power came with a tendency to (immanently capitalist) bureaucratization, a tendency that the Trotskyites, quite adequately, called state terrorism[50] and the Maoists themselves called reformism.[51] This is why today the word revolution is completely obscure.[52] No one knows what it could mean. The revolutionary idea, as can be seen for example in the adaptation it received under Stalin—although in certain sense one might argue that Stalin already took a reactive and defensive position against the universalist core of Leninist politics[53]—the revolutionary idea was swallowed by what Hegel once called a logic of suspicion[54] that described the general state of things.

One can see in Stalin a literally perverse universalism: if the October Revolution was supposed to address anyone, under Stalin it is precisely anyone that was suspected of being a counterrevolutionary. Now, all these are moments that indicate that the model of the party with all its implications (victorious resisting insurrection, taking state power, etc.) is saturated today.[55] The central point for addressing the question of political resistance today is thus to give an answer to the question of how to conceive of and how to invent a non-military discipline and new forms of organization that are detached, or better: subtracted from power, the party, and (first and foremost) from the state. This is both a political and a philosophical task. Why should this in any plausible way also be rendered as a task of contemporary philosophical thinking? Because the twentieth-century model of revolution as present in Lenin relied upon a specific expressive dialectics which included an interpretation of how determinate negation has to be thought and put into practice when it comes to concrete political action. With the saturation of the (power-) party-state model necessarily also emerges what Badiou called a "crisis of negation."[56] If negation is the central category of any Hegelian, but also post-Hegelian—say Marxian—dialectics and today the task is to find new means of political organization and a new popular discipline, one can claim that the essential task lies in rethinking negation, in rethinking dialectics. Rethinking negation and dialectics is needed not to remain in the schemes of the twentieth century when it comes to conceiving of political resistance or more broadly: of any concrete political action. Rethinking dialectics is needed to think politics concretely and concretely means to be able to take into account the experiences of the twentieth century and the knowledge that the means employed in it are saturated, and also start thinking what emancipatory politics can be here and now, that is to say: what forms of organization and discipline can be invented without falling into the deadlocks and while avoiding the impasses of the last century. Or to put it in Freudian terms: one should repeat, remember, and work through dialectics.[57] And this means: to repeat, remember, and work through its central category, the category of negation. Only in this way one might be able to exit the twentieth century and let the twenty-first century finally begin.

Thus, repeating Marx means working through negativity. "Working through Marx" then also means to reflect on what today may be adequate forms for a renewed materialist understanding, for a renewed materialist theory and practice: for a new manner of conceiving of negativity. One can substantiate this claim by pointing out that for Badiou and also for Žižek the name "Marx" stands like no other for a working through of dialectics—to be more precise a working through of Hegelian dialectics. The early Marx depicts a *dialectic of the exception* with his definition of "real communist action" and the conceptual link between the proletarian impoverishment[58]—the proletariat as that which loses all substantial determinations—and what Marx calls the human species being; the late Marx depicts a *dialectic of critical representation (one is tempted to say: a dialectic of critical reason)* with his outline of the (revolution of) productive forces and their relation to proletarian class-consciousness. "Working through Marx" therefore means for Badiou and Žižek each in his own way to "work though dialectics," and this ultimately means to respectively "work through negativity."

Žižek makes this explicit when he claims that "at the very center of what I am doing generally" is a thinking through of a central category of psychoanalysis—of the death drive—and of "the central feature of subjectivity in German idealism"—namely of Hegel's "self-relating negativity."[59] Žižek remembers, repeats, and works through Marx to get to a new dialectics and to a new conception of the notion of negativity. Badiou, whose whole oeuvre can be read as a working through of dialectics,[60] also starts his attempt to establish a new materialist dialectics by dealing with Hegel.[61] Badiou likewise remembers, repeats, and works through Marx. How to distinguish these two ways of working through Marx, working through negativity? An important article of Badiou, in which he introduces a distinction between three types of negativity, offers a useful tool to answer this question.[62] What is at stake in the subsequent discussion is the answer to the following question: Mr. Badiou, Mr. Žižek, what is your dialectics?

Badiou offers an account of different types of negation. The first form of negation that he introduces is the classical one that can be found in Aristotelian *Metaphysics*.[63] Aristotle develops a framework for conceiving of negation in a general manner as he shows that thinking in general is determined by three principles: (1) the principle of identity that signifies that any proposition is equivalent to itself, that is, to its truth content; (2) the principle of contradiction that signifies that it is impossible that in the same context the proposition P and the proposition non-P can be true at the same time; and (3) the principle of the excluded middle that signifies that for a proposition P holds that it is either true or false—either P is true or non-P is true. The power of negation in this Aristotelian model is structured in a twofold manner. First, there is a power of exclusion inherent to negation: the proposition P excludes the validity of the proposition non-P. Second, there is a power of a forced decision inherent to it: either P or non-P is valid, there is no third option. For classical negation never holds that "yes" and "no" are valid at the same time and in turn it always holds that either "yes" or "no" is valid. Classical negation is what Badiou calls the "kernel of classical logic" ("BTN," 1878). But as one can easily see there are not only classical forms of negation. Already when remaining within the framework of these three principles one can easily infer other logical combinations that lead to other forms of negation.

Negation is only classical when it follows the principle of contradiction and the principle of the excluded middle. One can also think of a form of negation that only follows the principle of contradiction but not the principle of the excluded middle; one can think of a negation that only follows the principle of the excluded middle but not the principle of contradiction and finally one can think of a negation that follows neither of the two principles. This last form of negation loses all power of negation because it neither prescribes a decision nor does it exclude anything—the fourth form of negation knows negation only as itself negated.[64] The second form of negation, only following the principle of contradiction but not of the excluded middle, is what Badiou calls the "intuitionist logic of negation" ("BTN," 1879), the third, only following the principle of the excluded middle but not of contradiction he calls paraconsistent. As he put it: "In fact the potency of negation is weaker and weaker when you go from one to three. . . . In intuitionist logic, the negation of P excludes P itself, but not some other possibilities which are in fact somewhere between P and non-P. In paraconsistent logic, the negation of P excludes that sort of space between P and non-P, but not P itself. So, P is not suppressed by its negation" ("BTN," 1879).

It is important to note that for Badiou the classical logic of negation corresponds to the discourse of ontology. For his definition of being qua being—that is to say from a set theoretical perspective being is discursively presented as a multiplicity of multiplicities whose consistency is only guaranteed by the void, the empty set[65]—the principle of extensionality is fundamental: this means that an element of a set belongs to the set or does not belong to it. Either P (the element belongs to the set) is true or false, there is no third option. The difference between two multiplicities—or two sets—thus can be followed from the fact—and only from it—that one element of a set is not an element of another.[66] If one accepts the Badiousian framework this means that any form of negation that complies with the principle of contradiction and of the excluded middle is not only classical but also ontological. But if classical negation is ontological, what is the status of the intuitionist logic of negation? Badiou's answer is: it covers the logic of appearance. The ontological determination of what is a multiple, of what is a multiplicity can and has to be distinguished from how a multiple appears, with which intensity, in which guise; if it appears in the shadows or in the brightest light. Although one can show the intuitionist logic of negation is grounded in the classical one—because something cannot appear absolutely and with maximal intensity in a world and at the same time not appear in it—it is not true that in the realm of appearances one has to decide between P and non-P. A multiplicity cannot appear and not appear at the same time, cannot exist and not exist at the same time, but it can appear in multiple ways and forms or intensities. There is itself a multiplicity of third possibilities. P can appear more or less intense than non-P or vice versa. Therefore the principle of contradiction is valid but not the principle of the excluded middle—P can appear as Q between the absolute appearance P and the absolute non-appearance non-P. P can appear somewhere in between the maximum and the minimum of appearances. This form of negation is therefore not only intuitionist but also linked to the discourse of appearance, that is to say to phenomenology.[67]

To delineate the third, the paraconsistent form of negation, following the principle of the excluded middle but not of contradiction, one has to introduce besides ontology and phenomenology that which Badiou calls an event. An event is logically related to being as well as to appearance. One can therefore ask: (1) What sort of multiplicity does an event name (ontologically)? (2) How does an event appear (phenomenally)? (1) An event is a contradictory multiplicity whose definition is to belong to itself—it has the property that axiomatically is prohibited (following the axiomatization of Zermelo-Fraenkel) for any other multiple (or set).[68] This means that on the level of ontology an event is neither classical—because it does not comply with the principle of contradiction—nor intuitionist. From this perspective it can be called paraconsistent. But one has to be more precise here. For an event might be in itself nothing but paraconsistent, but the way Badiou defines it indicates another crucial aspect: an event is nothing but the ensemble of the consequences it will have produced. An event is measured only by the consequences it is able to generate and can therefore only be thought in the linkage of being and appearances.[69] Because if the event, not to be a miraculous intervention, is itself nothing substantial, one has to claim that the only thing that appears are its consequences. (2) How does an event appear? Initially, the event is phenomenally the identity of appearance and disappearance. It is the paraconsistent "vanishing mediator";[70] but this does not change the fact that one can only decide what it will have been after considering if it had concrete consequences or not. Therefore its (ontologically) paraconsistent form necessitates a decision. When it is not clear if something has happened or not, a decision is needed; a decision that has to take the form of a "yes or no" and can never take the form of a "yes and no at the same time." An event thereby conjures the classical form of negation; it demands the power of exclusion and the power of decision. If an event is nothing but the ensemble of the consequences that it yields one can claim that these consequences are only measured by the fact that one either said "yes" or "no" to the forced choice that it necessitates; and the consequences are what follows from this yes or no, from the acceptance of the choice or the indifference towards it. An event is hence in a certain sense diagonal towards the classical, intuitionist, and paraconsistent form of negation.[71] But what does that mean?

One can start by stating that an event is a sudden change of the laws that regulate the realm of appearance. Something that seemed impossible appears in the form of a previously unthinkable possibility. Therefore it is not directly the creation of "something" new, but rather the creation of a new possibility, of a formerly nonexisting possibility.[72] If it were the creation of something new, an event would mainly be destructive.[73] But it is precisely by generating a new possibility that it also enables the integration of something of the old in the construction of something new—something new that emerges by unfolding the consequences of this new possibility. But the whole question whether an event is an event—at least on this level—is linked to another one, namely to the question of how far-reaching the change is that this new possibility produces. The greatest change that an event can inaugurate is the transformation of something that does not appear in a world—for example non-P does not appear in it—into something that appears in a world—into P. Or to put it differently: an event is what is capable of transforming the appearance of the workers that "are nothing" as the *Internationale* has it—that is to say: that do not appear at all in the world—in a way that they become "all"—that is, appear maximally—and it is that which thereby changes the historically specific logic of appearance. This transformation is evental; it is followed by true actions of resistance and follows the classical logic.

This is because the workers that did not appear in the world now appear maximally. This means that the consequences of an event also have to be further conceptualized from the perspective of the two other logics, the intuitionist and the paraconsistent one. This leads to the following logical setting: either the consequences of an event are classical—non-P appears instead of P—or intuitionist—non-P appears as Q which does not replace the appearance of P by the appearance of non-P (the workers appear but this appearance does not generate a new formation of the laws of appearance but rather enacts a reform or modification of these laws); or finally the consequences of the event are paraconsistent. In this case the fundamental framework of appearance is respected and maintained; the distinction of P and non-P is not touched at all. The paraconsistent form of transformation leads to the fact that it remains unclear if a transformation of the frame and of the laws of appearance happened or not. From the perspective of the world everything remains the same, the event and the non-event remain identical and the consequences are null.[74] And as one is clearly able to follow: if this is the case, one abolishes the very eventality (i.e., consequences) of an event. Evental consequences, as one can resume, can either be classical (maximal and evental), intuitionist (moderate and factual), or paraconsistent (minimal and non-evental).

If any world of appearance is organized intuitionistically then any real political action must follow the classical logic of negation; pseudo-actions clearly follow the paraconsistent logic. But again one needs to be more precise: if true political action has to be organized classically and mobilizes the double power of negation—of exclusion and forced decision—then the development of consequences of the exclusive decision takes place within an intuitionist regulated world (since any world is governed by the intuitionist form of negation as shown above) in which multiple ways and alternatives of their materialization are possible. To take this into account it is also necessary not to assume that one single "yes" or one single "no" with regard to an event may be sufficient as foundation for all subsequent consequences.[75] In fact, they have to be unfolded in many nuances within the realm of appearances.[76] And it also has to be clearly remarked that an event—due to the fact that it appears within the phenomenal world in the form of a classical negation—is not shared by everyone. Not everyone affirms that something happened, not everyone answers the forced choice with a "yes"—some remained untouched by the event of the October Revolution, for example. One needs to conceive of a relation between the three logics because the ontologically paraconsistent event appears as classical negation (something has happened or has not happened and there is no third option) within an intuitionist framework in which a multiplicity of consequences are possible and at the same time there is a paraconsistent opposition to them, since not everyone gives an affirmative answer to the forced choice of the event. This also implies that even within the procedure of unfolding the consequences—which Badiou calls fidelity[77]—there is always a temptation to transform the form of the choice, that is, the "yes or no," into an avoidance of the choice, that is, into a "yes and no." "Yes" something has happened but "no" I do not have to draw consequences from it. This is the paradigmatic form of paraconsistent temptation. Or as one may say: this is the logic of seduction. Against it one has to constantly perpetuate the power of exclusion and forced decision to not abate the unfolding of consequences. There has to be a continually perpetuated "yes"—which is also why the only imperative of an ethics of truth is "Continue!"—which constantly while taking place inside a world subtracts from all differences—national, local, gender specific ones, and so on—that appear and are declared to be essential in and for the world. True political action is the concrete articulation of a *constantly perpetuated classicism* within a world, in which it takes multiple different shapes; political action is the concrete articulation of the permanence of exclusion and forced decision against paraconsistent temptations.

It is precisely the relation between the three negations, the three logics of negation, that presents the matrix of a new dialectical conception. It is dialectical as it is a relation of different types of negations that stand in its center and at the same time it is materialist because it considers the concrete consequences produced by the relations of the negations. It is materialist because it begins with an exception and it is dialectical because without substantializing the exception one cannot but think it dialectically. But this matrix depicts thus far only the objective side of a renewed materialist dialectics. It is also imperative to consider its subjective side.

## Addendum: From Objective to Subjective Materialist Dialectics

To resume:[78] *The ontologically paraconsistent event appears in the form of classical negation within the realm of the phenomenal world that is organized according to the intuitionist logic, and the consequences of an eventual emergence, taking multiple different concrete forms, are essentially either paraconsistent or classical.* Now, the central question is how does the procedure of unfolding the consequences of an event start and how is it perpetuated? I already indicated that it can only start with a "yes." Everything begins with an affirmation of the forced decision that an event introduces. An event subtracts all differences that play a role within ordinary appearances by condensing them into one point, that is to say into a choice between a "yes" (something happened and I have to draw consequences from it) or a "no" (nothing happened).[79] Subtraction here gives rise to the primacy of the principle of contradiction over the principle of the excluded middle, the latter not being valid in intuitionism. An event is no event without its subjective affirmation, an affirmation which initially inaugurates the procedure of fidelity. An event is a vanishing mediator, the clinamen[80] that appears as an irruption of something,[81] which can only gain consistency through a primary "yes," which then has to be perpetuated and repeated constantly—this repetitive process does not know any immanent limitation of its own. The event is itself nothing objective but can only be what it will have been through a subjective intervention whose starting point is what I call a *determinate affirmation:*[82] a "yes" to a concretely determined choice. But at the same time one "yes," one determinate affirmation, is never enough.

Although one determinate affirmation already changes the situation—since it makes something appear which did not appear before[83]—one is never enough. The "yes" has to be repeated in a situation that is already changed due to the first "yes"—say in love it is not enough to affirm the possibility of something new; profane questions of organization are also crucial and in them the first "yes" is repeated in ever-changing situations; situations, in which one determines say where to go for a holiday, how to spend time together, if to move in together or not, and so on. The subjective determinate affirmation has to be apt to sustain the "yes," to sustain classicism facing a world that changes because of the unfolding consequences of previous determinate affirmations—and how this is to be done cannot be foreseen or deduced in advance. The "yes" has to be sustained although it is unforeseeable how. Only in this way the contingent emergence of a new possibility can retroactively gain consistency—or to put it in other words: only through the consequences that are unfolded step by step, or more precisely "point by point,"[84] only through the continuity of "yeses" can an event retroactively be considered as what it will have been and gain some objectivity. The objective side of the renewed materialist dialectics thus fully depends on the subjective determinate affirmation and its continual reiteration and vice versa.[85]

*Objective is only what will have been objective by the retroactive effect of the consequences that are at the same time nothing but the sustained classicism of subjective determinate affirmations in a changing world, which changes precisely due to the effects of these affirmations. The totality of the self-determination relies on the (newly emerged) possibility of a choice, whose proper potency is hence unfolded in this very process.* One can also say that the constant upholding of the subjective determinate affirmation of the emergence of the retroactively objective classical negation inside the intuitionist framework and against any paraconsistent temptation is a dialectical development that always—this is precisely an insight from the logic of retroactivity—relies upon something that is not itself dialectically deducible. If the consequences that change the world are engendered by something, namely an event, which itself is nothing but what it will have been, not to fall back into a pure intuitionist framework, one has to insist: materialist dialectics to remain materialist has to introduce something that cannot be deduced dialectically[86]—for the event in any other way would substantialized. Yet, it also should be absolutely clear that this non-dialectical momentum is not something which simply lies logically prior to the dialectical unfolding of consequences. It is not "something" substantially undialectizable. The non-dialectical moment is something which itself has to be comprehended as being produced by the dialectical movement itself; or in other words: the event—as that which is not deducible from any dialectic whatsoever—is what it will have been only through the dialectical unfolding. Hence, the non-dialectical element is "something" which constantly is reproduced, is reinitiated in each step of the dialectical path. Materialist dialectics not to fall back into the historically specific political shortcomings of (previous modes of dogmatic) expressive dialectics has to be understood as a procedure of unfolding consequences, of the attempt to cope with something that due to the logic of retroactivity logically lies prior to it as it is produced as that which lies prior to it. Materialist dialectics not to totalize dialectics—and therefore hypostasize only one form of negation,[87] for example the intuitionist one—has to be a dialectics of dialectics (drawing of consequences) and non-dialectics (the contingent emergence of a new possibility). Materialist dialectics should entail what I will call a *dialectics of dialectics and non-dialectics.*[88]

*True action upholds the permanence of classicism,* the permanence of the power of exclusion and of forced choice that generates consequences, which appear in multiple ways and are constantly directed against any paraconsistent temptation.[89] The structure of temptation or seduction lies in saying "yes and no" at the same time. However, if one accepts the delineated coordinates of working through materialist dialectics, and if this already depicts what Badiou's version of a renewed dialectic is, what is the matrix of Žižek's dialectics? If one takes his project of combining Hegel's notion of self-relating negativity and Freud's notion of death drive (read through Lacan) seriously, how to conceive of their dialectical relationship? One may start with some preliminary remarks: Hegel's notion of negativity seems to be intuitionist, since it follows the principle of contradiction but not the principle of the excluded middle: the negation of negation is in Hegel not identical to an immediate affirmation.[90] Negation of negation in a very profane sense might rather be read as a concept of affirmation, an affirmation, as already Nietzsche famously argued, made out of two negations. Negating something does not simply negate something, but it rather also leads to something that can only appear through the act of negation. However, if Žižek tries to bring together Hegel and Freud, can one conceptualize the Freudian death drive in terms of negation? Which of the three modes of negation would apply to it? With some vulgarization and far too many abbreviations, could one not claim that the death drive is a drive that in some sense longs for its own non-satisfaction—a "pure drive to repeat without any movement of sublation or idealization" (*ZLN*, 500)?[91] Is not the structure of the death drive, as reconstructed by Žižek, precisely that of a peculiar insistence on something, an "'undead' persistence attached to a contingent particularity" (*ZLN*, 490)? And could one therefore not say that it does follow the principle of the excluded middle but it does not obey the principle of contradiction and hence can be conceptualized by recourse to the paraconsistent form of negation?

But things are more complicated here because Žižek's materialist dialectics entails a redoubling of the paraconsistent form of negation—which at the same time leads him down a path different from Badiou's. Žižek seeks to redouble paraconsistent negation and to link it to the principle of contradiction that governs intuitionist logic. To elucidate the series of steps involved in this approach, one may reconstruct them in the following manner: one is always already moving within ideological coordinates and one is always already familiar with ideological operations. The (contemporarily) most elementary way of relating to them can be said to take the form of the fetishist disavowal, whose infamous slogan is: "Je sais bien mais quand meme"; "I know very well but nevertheless . . ." This is how Žižek, with reference to Mannoni,[92] re-actualizes Marx's infamous definition of commodity fetishism as the nodal point of any ideology critique, as the crucial starting point of any critique proper.[93] The formula for fetishist disavowal, for this crucial building block of contemporary ideology, can also be read as expressing (a reactionary) paraconsistent logic of negation. This paraconsistent type of negation works like any ideology proper works, namely it fills the gaps and holes produced by certain apparent inconsistencies in the world. To put this in other terms: paraconsistent logic is the new opium of the people. This is comparable to what Marx claimed with regard to religion. First one needs to suspend its effect to then start the real business of critique. This is because comprehending the nature of religion leads to the insight of why its opiate impact exists in the first place. To cut a long story short: there are contradictions structuring the (social) reality of human beings living under capitalism. Religion is a (contradictory) product of these contradictions.[94] On one side, it functions like opium generating a delusion with regard to the real state of things. Even if the real world is contradictory, high on religion we still feel good about it. On the other side, religion nevertheless bears the mark of this real world. Since without it there simply would be no religion. Religion exists as Marx diagnosed because there is no true "realization" of equality, freedom, and justice. Human beings create a fictional realization, lacking a real one. But religion functions like an opiate because it forecloses the very insight from which it originated. It exists due to contradictions, yet its existence obfuscates its own origin. Human beings create religion to deal with real contradictions, but it is only the fiction of resolving them without actually resolving them. This fictitious nature is why Marx called religion an "inverted conscience" which nonetheless entails a "general theory of the world."[95] It contains a theory of the world in which there is religion *because* there is religion. A world without religion would imply a different manner of treating contradictions. Religion comprises a general theory of a contradictory world in which these very contradictions necessitate a need to obfuscate them. Thus for Marx *the believer* knows that there are contradictions in the world (otherwise there would be no fictitious realm of religion) but he nonetheless *does not know what he knows* (religion is inverted conscience or: unconscious). *The believer believes* in a fiction *that he does not know* to be a fiction and *this is why he believes* in it. It is this fiction (that resolving contradictions *of the world* without resolving them *in the world* is still a way of resolving them) which enables him not to believe in what he knows but to repress it. Religion is a way of *believing* (in a fiction) *without* truly *believing* (what one knows)—it is a manifestation of a drive not to know. This is why for Marx we first need to believe what we know.

Žižek follows Marx on this methodological path. Fetishist disavowal, that is, reactionary paraconsistent logic, is a means to prevent change from happening, since it obstructs the very access to contradiction—one knows, but one does not believe what one knows. Hence paraconsistent logic obfuscates the access to very contradiction—one might say: to class struggle—which governs any (intuitionistic organized) world. This is why, for Žižek one first has to get from paraconsistent reactionary negation to the principle of contradiction. Hence the first step is a step in which one assumes one's own knowledge. But this is done only to then reemploy, repeat, and redouble the paraconsistent logic of negation. What is this supposed to mean? It means first and foremost that the paraconsistent type of negation can, as in Badiou, serve different functions. In Badiou the event seemed to have a paraconsistent status with regard to ontology, but paraconsistency also appeared precisely as a seductive threat to the continuation of the unfolding of evental consequences. Something similar is at work in Žižek's dialectics—yet, he starts in an inverse manner. First one has to counter reactionary paraconsistency, then after moving to contradiction one is able to return to paraconsistency and see a new, a different quality in it. So, paraconsistent negation, contradiction, and paraconsistent negation again—this is the beginning of Žižek's dialectical sequence. Yet, any dialectic does not only consist of three but four terms—a point that for example Hegel refers to in terms of a repetition of the immediate as result, or, more technically, in terms of "quadruplicity" (*HSL*, 836).[96] The proper question is here, how to generate the fourth term. Žižek's proposal is that this can be done by repeating this very movement twice, by repeating the immediate move from paraconsistency to contradiction again as immediate result, since this very repetition generates a minimal difference between the first and the second.

First one needs something that demonstrates, as Žižek puts it "that the real universality does not lie in the neutral domain of translating one culture into another," that is in translating one of particular appearance of a non-excluded middle(s) into another one; what one needs to see is that universality lies "rather [in] the violent experience that beyond our cultural lines of demarcations we are united by the same antagonism."[97] The first move generates the insight that although we think we are all individualized, we are nonetheless still depending on the same anonymous divide, on the same contradiction. What we share is what divides us. Therefore one can see why Žižek's position constitutively relies on a "shift of perspectives" (*ZLN*, 242). He demonstrates that any paraconsistent logic of ideology obfuscates and invisibilizes the contradiction at the ground of any phenomenal world.

But this perspective shift enables the insight into the real underlying principle of organization of any world, which is contradiction or more precisely antagonism. One can note that this means to introduce "a totally different Universal, that of antagonistic struggle which, rather than taking place between particular communities, splits each community from within" (*ZLE*, 53) The shift of perspective is in its very mode of operation depicting a splitting, a split that governs everything. The shift by moving from one to the other side embodies the split it depicts. It is important that one is truly dealing with a shift of perspectives. This is why for example the predominant difference between democracy and totalitarianism is for Žižek not a proper shift of perspectives, since both of them are nothing but the same side of a coin whose true other side lies elsewhere. Hence the distinction between democracy and totalitarianism impedes the insight into what the real political choice may be; it is only one ideologically naturalized side of the true distinction between democracy and totalitarianism on one side and communism or real emancipation on the other. To again depict this in a rather formal manner: the transition from the ideological paraconsistent "yes and no" to the intuitionist "yes or no" is a necessary prerequisite. One shifts from a constant "and" that functions as principle (of a pretended choice) to the real act of choosing sides ("or") in an antagonism. This is why Žižek can claim that with this shift comes the insight that one is not dealing with "a conflict between particular agents within social reality . . . but [with] an antagonism . . . which constitutes these agents" (ZLE, 201). So this is the first shift of perspectives.

However, this movement is not yet enough to account for Žižek's dialectics. One needs another, a second shift. The second shift of perspectives makes it manifest that these perspectives are perspectives, that is to say one asserts a radical relativism. Why is that? Because one can deduce that with this change from paraconsistency ("and") to the principle which governs intuitionism ("or") one only gains the principle of contradiction (represented by a "yes or no" choice) but one does not get the true principle of the excluded middle—one thus only got rid of the false "yes and no" of ideology. But the "or" of a choice that is itself without force is insufficient. Therefore one also needs the principle of the excluded middle to arrive at a classical logic of negation (or to arrive at what Badiou calls an eventual rupture of the truth of a situation in the phenomenal world), which is what Žižek calls an act.[98] For this very reason it is necessary to again move from the intuitionist logic to the paraconsistent one; one only arrives at the act via repetition.[99] The act embodies repetition in its most radical manner. Rendered in different terms, this implies: repetition precedes the act. Only this repeated movement, this double shift allows one to get from the wrong "yes and no" of ideology that obstructs the principle of contradiction to the true "yes and no" (that is the death drive) and hence this repetition is needed to also and again obtain the principle of the excluded middle. Or to put it differently: one needs to get to the point where *one can only say "yes or no" to the true "yes and no" (of repetition by means of repetition itself)*. One thus arrives somewhere where there is truly the choice of a "yes or no" with regard to that which longs for its own non-satisfaction (and hence follows the structure of a "yes and no" but a proper one). To make this overly clear: one needs to arrive at a decision ("yes or no") with regard to the death drive (that is itself structured by a peculiar "yes and no"). Hence one needs a proper "yes or no" with regard to the constitutive "yes and no."[100] One may put it in the following manner: one first needs to get from "yes and no" to "yes or no" to then get to a true "yes or no" with regard to a true "yes and no." This is to say the principle of excluded middle and of contradiction are necessary to generate a classical logic (or as one might say with Badiou, to generate an ontology).[101] Therefore one needs to again move back from the obtained antagonistic contradiction appearing behind the multiplicities of non-excluded middles to the paraconsistency of the "yes and no." This is a precondition for distinguishing between a fake "yes and no" of ideology and a true "yes and no" of the death drive. What does this imply?

It implies that one needs to move again (a third time now!) from the paraconsistent logic to the intuitionist organized world because only in this way the attained classical logic can be given a phenomenal appearance; it needs to be inscribed into the world. Only by again moving from paraconsistency to intuitionism again can there be an inscription of the true "yes and no" into the world that produces a change of coordinates, an act.[102] In the last and fourth step the immediate, that is classical, logic, repeats itself in the form of a result because it then becomes retroactively clear that it will always already have been present in the paraconsistency of ideology (principle of excluded middle) and intuitionism, that is the phenomenal world (principle of contradiction).[103] One needs these four steps to attain the classical logic in Žižek's materialist dialectics. But ultimately, from a Badiousian point this leads to one crucial question which can easily be transposed into a series of questions.

If Žižek situates classical logic precisely in this double shift between the paraconsistent and intuitionist logic of negation, what precisely is the position that theory takes in it? Or in different terms, what is the position of philosophy if, as one can still insist, in this very movement it is not possible for ontology to be a condition of philosophy (as it is for Badiou)? Ontology cannot be a condition for philosophy because one only attains the classical logic of ontology through the process of this double shifting movement of philosophy, philosophy as analytical discourse, as movement of the act of thought itself. At least if my rendering of Žižek's powerful dialectics can be defended—and I suggest that it can—it seems that this movement of shifting perspectives does describe the movement of philosophy itself; a movement of philosophy that constantly borders on non-philosophical conditions, yet a movement which can never fully assume their existence.[104] Žižek depicts a movement that constantly breaks the unity of philosophical practice by pointing to its (historical, economic, political, etc.) conditions (one might even at first glance articulate this in a rather traditional Marxist sense), that is, he opens philosophy (again) to non-philosophical practices. And he does so to reaffirm philosophy. This is strictly in line with Badiou. So, is there any—a minimal—difference in their proposed dialectics? There is.

Yet, there is only a difference—as always—under (certain) conditions. If there is a difference, a minimal difference between the two, it depends on how one articulates the very *relation* between philosophy and its conditions.[105] One option of articulating this can be resumed by pointing out a possible danger in rendering this very relation. To put it in the most traditional form: if there is one way, one concept of how to relate philosophy and its condition, does one not encounter the old problem that this is the ultimate solution presented by and within philosophy itself in a timeless manner? One may rephrase this by asking if the ultimate sublation of all contradictions would not be to attain the notion of contradiction as such?[106] Would not philosophy then be a discourse which gains its consistency via reference to the antagonism, that is, the inconsistency in all other discourses? It would be the only discourse which would be able to have a proper concept of inconsistency. Or to put it differently: why is philosophy as movement from the false "yes and no" of ideology to the "yes or no" of contradiction or antagonism and ultimately to an affirmation of the true "yes and no" of the death drive not precisely a very classical interpretation of Hegel's absolute knowledge? How to avoid a stance which ultimately withdraws from affirming the proper historicity of extra-philosophical conditions? How to avoid philosophical transcendentalism (or in different terms: Kantianism)? This is to my mind the true question that one can raise from Badiou's working through of dialectics.

## Coda: How to Posit Presuppositions?

On the other side one might argue that absolute knowledge in Žižek's account would amount to uttering the most de-substantialized Socratic statement, namely: "I know that I do not know." The knowledge of my own not-knowledge then would be—this is Žižek's ultimate twist—the knowledge of that which I do not know that I know, such that I know that I do not know what I know. Yet, if this way is precisely one way of rendering what for the assumption of the unconscious means psychoanalysis (it can be reduced to the statement that "I do not know what/that I know"), Žižek's version of (absolute) knowledge could be said to be a knowledge of or about the unconscious. This knowledge is obviously opposed to any fake "yes and no" ("I know very well that I do not know what I know but nonetheless I act as if I only do not know what I do not know and hence I still know something").[107] So, why not simply praise this as an account of Hegel that finally liberates the latter from all clichés and ultimately is able to offer what decades of analytic philosophy dreamt of but were unable to "deliver"? Because I think one may ask the old question that was always raised with regard to Hegel: does this rendering not come close to presenting an ultimate sublation of all forms of practices, of all non-philosophical conditions into philosophy?[108] Badiou's system is able to avoid this consequence, but is Žižek's dialectical schema apt to avoid suturing philosophy to a (retroactive) ontology of the drive, an ontology which emerges from or in a more precise rendering: *is* the very movement of philosophy?[109] To put this in in renewed terms: for Badiou philosophy depends on extra-philosophical practices; might not for any Badiousian the danger of Žižek's position lie in the fact that the very conditions philosophy depends upon are posited by philosophy itself? And if this were to be the case would this not imply the loss of the non-dialectical element of any contemporary materialist dialectics? Does pointing Badiou against Žižek, as fashionable as this may have become, not here boil down to an affirmation of non-dialecticity against a very subtle, unacknowledged-even-subverted-and-hence-still-obtained-continuity of dialectics? Imagine Badiou and Žižek in a café. Would not the former need to ask the latter: my dear Slavoj, are you really post-Hegelian?[110]

To reformulate the quarrel in a Hegelian language: Could one not state that Žižek initially claims that any "in itself" is nothing but what it is "for others"? He hence, siding with Hegel, breaks with the idea that subjectivity could be simply correlated with interiority such that its determination would be internal determinations. Rather, everything a subject (or any thing) is, is what it is externally. There is a clear primacy of exteriority and if you ask: "what is the subject in itself?" the initial answer that can be given is that it is simply what it is for others. Any thing, any subject, is what it is only when it entered into the sphere of relations with others and thereby gained its proper determinations. I am what I am, say, as a father only because of the relations I have to those others who address me precisely as someone being in the position of the father (my son or daughter), and so on. In this sense what a subject in itself is, is nothing but its being-for-others. This also implies that chances are quite high that the best chess player in the world, who constantly loses to everyone in chess, may not be the best chess player in the world. This initial point can be schematized in the following manner:

In itself → Being for others

In this schema the arrow symbolizes the process in which the in-itself gains its determinations by entering into relations with others. The in-itself is hence the outcome of the process of its becoming determined by and through others.

That is to say as soon as the in-itself enters into the sphere of holistically describable determinations, it will have become what it actually is; this is the defining character of any symbolic setting. If one now poses again the question of what the "thing in itself" is, the repetition of the question introduces an additional twist. Why? Because the thing in itself will have been different after it became a thing for others. Hence, of course, the first answer to the question is still that the thing in itself is nothing but the determinations it has for others, yet one can also ask by shifting the perspective a bit: one can ask if it is clear that the in-itself is nothing but what it is for others, how do we conceive of this "nothing," of the in-itself-in-itself? This is then obviously more than just a tautology, because one can derive that the in-itself after entering into the determinations is nothing but the determinations it is. The in-itself-in-itself is nothing (the in-itself of the in-itself is only graspable via the becoming for others of the in-itself) or more precisely it is even less than nothing: simply because it was "nothing" but what it is for others and right now, it is even less than this—there is not even pure nothingness. Hence one is dealing with a nothing which even lacks proper nothingness, since it is that which lies prior to all determinations, even negative ones. This dimension, because it only emerges as a by-product of the process of determination (the in itself gaining determinations), does itself not even have a negative determination and hence lies prior to any determination. The insight into the in-itself-in-itself, the insight that the in-itself is split between what it is for other and itself, emerges from the process in which the in-itself gains its determinations. This is why the split of the in-itself (into in-itself-in-itself and in-itself for others) is a retroactive effect of the process of determination itself.

One deals here with "the pure form of dislocation ontologically preceding any dislocated content" (*ZLN*, 38)—because the in-itself appears as a retroactive effect of the process of determination, but thereby it seems to be the ground of this very process. One can also state that the in-itself-in-itself is not located in its being for others, although the in-itself is nothing but what it is for others. The in-itself of the in-itself can only be thought after the in-itself became for others, thereby it seems to be determined by it, yet it is not. One may schematize this in the following manner:

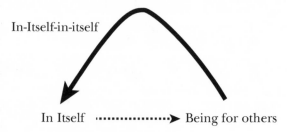

With this shift of perspectives one proceeded a further step and is now also able to see not only that the in-itself-in-itself does emerge from the process of gaining determination and that it thereby retroactively splits the in-itself. One can also ask the question of how to conceive of the relation between in-itself and its in-itself, which again is nothing but a repetition of the initial question ("what is the in-itself?")—but from a different perspective. By rephrasing it in this way one is able to indicate the possibility of the in-itself-in-itself also having a retroactive effect on what seemed to be the initial definition of the in-itself (it is nothing but what it is for others). The in-itself becomes (in) itself by entering into symbolic determinations, this retroactively generates the insight into the split, divided form of the in-itself (into in-itself for others and in-itself-in-itself). This is to say that this split, the empty in-itself-in-itself rede-termines, again retroactively, the first in-itself. The split of the in-itself determines the in-itself. But the catch still lies somewhere else, namely in the fact that after the insight into the constitutive split of the in-itself (into in-itself-in-itself and in-itself-for-others), the in-itself-in-itself is the instance that will have had a determining influence on its other half (the in-itself-becoming-for-others) or in short: this peculiar nothing without nothingness, this less than nothing will have been the determining factor of the entire first process of determination from which it emerged. It is something like a retroactively posited presupposition of the whole pro-cess that nonetheless is only accessible from this parallax, from this dialec-tical sequence (first process of determination, first retroaction, splitting of the in-itself, second retroaction). This may be schematized as follows:

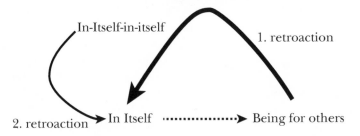

This schema shall make clear that it is only the second retroaction—the retroaction of that which lies prior to all symbolic determinations of the process of its own genesis[111]—which deserves the name "drive" in Žižek.[112] What hence emerges in the first retroaction is not "something" but a split, even an invisible split within the in-itself; what then happens with the second retroaction, with the drive, is that something which lies prior to symbolic determination although it is only constituted by it, determines the former. This is the fundamental parallax constitutive of any Žižekian dialectics and it is constituted through repetition, not of something but of, say a question, that step after step unfolds a new and slightly different perspective. Žižek himself resumes this in the following words: "This shift is deeply Hegelian, forming a kind of "negation of the negation": "we begin with the consistent 'big Other,' the self-enclosed symbolic order; then, in a first negation, this consistency is disturbed by the remainder of the Real, a traumatic leftover which resists being integrated into the symbolic and thus disturbs its balance, rendering it 'barred,' introducing into it a gap, flaw, or antagonism; in short, inconsistency; the second negation, however, requires a shift of perspective in which we grasp this intrusive leftover of the Real as itself the only element that guarantees the minimal consistency of the inconsistent big Other" (*ZLN*, 661).

And it shall be clear that the last schematization implies a different perspective on all previous schemas; it implies a proper shift of perspective, whereby the in-itself-in-itself will always have been the determining factor of the others and hence the whole sequence of the schemas needs to be included into the last one—this is the invisible fourth schema, in which the third schema entails a depiction of its own becoming. The last step implies that the totality of the whole dialectical sequence (the immediate in-itself repeated as unfolded result) now took a different guise, which is to say that one is not only dealing with three but with four dialectical steps, in which it is clear that the "radicalized diffraction is revealed as another name for parallax, the shift of perspective needed to produce the effect of the depth of the Real, as if an object acquires the impenetrable density of the Real only when its reality reveals itself to be inconsistent: the observed X is real only insofar as it is the impossible point at which two incompatible realities overlap" (*ZLN*, 949). But does this rendering not clearly bring Badiou and Žižek closer together? Does his insistence on the idea of pure multiplicity grounded in the void not also imply the contention that one has to think the in-itself as *being-split* (separating itself from itself)? One might even suggest that Badiou speaks of being qua being, whereas Žižek speaks of nothing qua nothing. Yet from a Badiousian perspective this ultimately amounts to being the same.

To my mind it depends on how one reads the claim that the in-itself-in-itself (this split entity emerging via the very process of determining the in-itself) retroactively determines the whole procedure of determining the in-itself. Why? Because if this implies that there is something, which from the proper logic of retroaction can be said to have been "driving" the in-itself to become for others, hence if there is some necessary driving force of the process of determination itself (the in-itself-in-itself determines the in-itself-becoming-for-others although the latter precedes the former), one cannot but assume that there is not only a retroactive product of the process of becoming for others (namely the in-itself-in-itself) and not only does this product seem to invert the logic of retroactivity (by being that which drives the initial in-itself to become for others), but one also has to deal with the implication that there is a retroaction on the logic of retroaction, something like a retroactive retroactivity itself. Does not this very maneuver (in the process of determination emerges something which retroactively will appear as having been the driving force of this very process) come very close to affirming—in a retroactive and de-substantialized manner, but nonetheless—the following: at the end, in the beginning there is movement? Could this not be, and this is obviously the worst-case scenario, be read as if there were a driving force, which itself is nothing but a retroactive product, a retroactively retroactive motor behind all concrete determinations? The true question is hence if that which lies retroactively prior to all symbolic determinations—the real real, the posited presupposition—can be depicted in terms of symbolic determinations or not. The act of positing presuppositions implies movement, the presuppositions do not. The presuppositions do imply movement if they are rendered as if they are acting upon the positing itself, and hence the danger that one can see with regard to such a depiction is that one identifies a type of movement somewhere where it does not make any sense to speak of movement any longer. Žižek seems to suggest that there is movement, which is indistinguishable from pure repetition and hence from absolute non-movement—this is what he calls drive, the second retroaction. The problem that may arise here is simply that however unsubstantial this movement might be, however indistinguishable it is from non-movement, as soon as one calls it movement, or more precisely drive, one seems to assert more than can be asserted.[113] To put this in different terms: if Žižek asserts that the second retroaction implies an indistinguishability of stasis and movement—because one is essentially dealing with the "nature" of the split of the in itself, that is, with the inconsistency of being—the danger that emerges is that what "indistinguishability" means for him can only be accounted for in terms of movement—in terms of a shift of perspective, in terms of an operation performed, in short: the danger lies in becoming a negative, de-substantialited, retroactively retroactive Aristotelean. Against this Badiou seems to suggest that indistinguishability implies that nothing can be said about this very point. Žižek and Badiou affirm a split in the beginning, a primacy of the two. It is imperative to investigate how this primacy can be conceptualized. The real question concerning the difference between their respective positions, between two modes of conceptualizing the renewal of materialist dialectics comes down to the following: is that which is prior to any determinations and hence prior to what can be thought (as any thinking relies on determinations) itself "moving" thought or is it that which can only be indexed by thought? What does it mean to refer to "being," to the "in-itself"—is it an operation (a movement between the poles) or a name, is the in-itself-in-itself identical to the subject or not? The danger lurking behind certain answers to this question is Aristotle; the royal path to materialism bears the name Plato. But to clarify this struggle more adequately, let's turn to Descartes.

# 4

# Repeat Again

## Exiting the Woods of Materialism

Nevertheless I will work my way up. . . .
—*DMFP*

What I did not notice is that I owe a lot of things to Descartes. I
have always said this about Plato, but not about Descartes.
—"BSP III"

I am not where one thinks that I am, being there where I think
that one thinks that the Other is.
—A. Badiou

## For a Cartesian Manifesto

Briefly before the calendric beginning of the new century, in 1999, Slavoj
Žižek diagnosed that "a specter is haunting western academia . . . the
specter of the Cartesian subject. All academic powers have entered into
a holy alliance to exorcize this specter."[1] He claimed that it was high time
for all Cartesians to "meet the nursery tale of the Specter of Cartesian subjectivity with the philosophical manifesto of Cartesian subjectivity itself."[2]
What is Badiou's position in this? Is he a thinker of Cartesian subjectivity?

To begin with one may say that there is without a doubt a clear Cartesian element in Badiou's thought. But the difficulties begin as soon as
one wants to pinpoint in what precisely it consists. Things become more
intricate if one takes into account some simple indications: Badiou claimed
that "there are only three philosophers: Plato, Descartes and Hegel"
(*BLoW*, 527). This claim obviously entails the stipulation that Badiou's philosophy takes its shape also as a working through and re-actualization of
Descartes's oeuvre. This can be supplemented by the fact that Badiou struc-

tured his second major work, *Being and Event*, into a series of thirty-seven meditations—an obvious and explicit reference to Descartes's *Meditations*. And moreover, this same book ends with a meditation on Descartes.[3]

It is astonishing that in most of the literature on Badiou only two of the three philosophical references have been present thus far: Plato and Hegel. This is because in Badiou's work Hegel, on one hand, is present because his first major work, *Theory of the Subject*, begins with a long discussion of the structure of Hegelian dialectics (*BTS*, 1–21); one of the meditations of *Being and Event* (*BE*, 161–71) and one chapter of *Logics of Worlds* (*BLoW*, 141–52) is devoted to Hegel; Badiou himself referred to *Being and Event* as his *Science of Logic* and *Logics of Worlds* as his *Phenomenology of Spirit* (*BLoW*, 8) and he openly asserted that today it is necessary to work through (Hegelian) dialectics with the objective of giving it a renewed materialist guise. Plato, on the other hand, is clearly and overly present because Badiou himself called his take to be that of a "*Platonism of the multiple*" (*BMPHI*, 103); he proclaimed his plans to shoot a movie on the life of Plato; he has taught a seminar under the title "For Today: Plato"[4]; and also published what he himself once referred to as a hyper-translation of Plato's *Republic*.[5] I am here tempted to nonetheless offer a twist on one of Badiou's famous formulas to clarify his position, namely that for him: "There are only Plato and Hegel, except that there is Descartes."[6]

With this I do neither wish to suggest that Descartes is more important for understanding Badiou than Hegel or Plato nor that he is the true hidden kernel of his entire project. But I want to suggest that it is important to reconstruct the Cartesian element in Badiou's thought, since it allows us to grasp the systematic link between a renewal of (Hegelian) dialectical thought (that is to say: a renewal of the category of negation that leads to a *dialectics of dialectics and non-dialectics*) and a re-actualization of the (Platonic) eternity of ideas (that is linked with an *idealism without idealism*). Descartes is the vanishing mediator between the Platonic and the Hegelian dimension of Badiou's philosophy. Obviously, the entirety of his work can only be grasped by taking into account all three thinkers. However, the aim of this chapter is to trace and clarify systematically where Cartesian elements within Badiou's philosophy are at work and how he reworks them—this is crucial work to be done, for if there is any thinker of the two, of the famous dualism (of body and soul) it is without any doubt Descartes. In the course of my investigation I will show that Badiou's philosophy presents what I will call a *Cartesianism for the twenty-first century (to come)*. However, first two additional remarks.

First, the Cartesian element in Badiou's thought cannot be limited to one specific domain, as it touches upon vital insights of his whole system. Descartes's thought cannot only be related to Badiou's ontology, but also to his conception of the relationship of philosophy and mathematics, his theory of truths, and his (specifically modern) theory of the subject. This implies that there is not only one Descartes in Badiou. "Descartes" is rather the name of a philosopher whose theory resonates with Badiou's, someone who presents a complex (and from time to time contradictory) set of claims. One may say that Badiou's system takes something which in Descartes is (generically) more than himself radically serious. This inner-Cartesian excess connects with several issues at hand in Badiou's system: (1) the speculative meta-ontological claim that the Two is what needs to be thought to think pure multiplicity; (2) the claim that there is a relation between infinity and (the creation of) eternal truths; (3) the assertion of a specific role of philosophy in "disoriented times" ("BCP"); and (4) the depiction of a theory of the subject.[7]

Secondly, Badiou begins his *Being and Event* with the following periodizing remark:

> We are contemporaries of a *third epoch* of science, after the Greek and Galilean . . . We are equally contemporaries of a *second epoch* of the doctrine of the Subject. It is no longer the founding subject, centered and reflexive, whose theme runs from Descartes to Hegel and which remains legible in Marx and Freud . . . Finally, we are contemporaries of a *new departure* in the doctrine of truth, following the dissolution of its relation of organic connection to knowledge. (*BBE*, 3)

The coordinates of the contemporary situation Badiou announces are all post-Cartesian. What hence needs to be stated up front is that his philosophy in its entirety considers itself to be post-Cartesian. However, one can claim that the whole question is what the "post-" in "post-Cartesian" means. What is at stake is what it means that Badiou is as much a *post*-Cartesian, *post*-Hegelian, *post*-Platonic thinker, as he is a post-*Cartesian*, post-*Hegelian*, post-*Platonic* thinker. He remains a Platonist (with his reference to eternal ideas) and is at the same time a post-Platonic philosopher (insisting that the eternity of the ideas has to be created by finite subjects); he remains a Hegelian (because disciplined thought as such has to be dialectical)[8] and is at the same time a post-Hegelian (as infinity has to be grasped in a proper post-Cantorian way which overcomes the distinction between bad and good infinity).

A fundamental Badiousian insight is that to remain faithful under changed historical conditions to what has been presented under these names in philosophy implies both remaining a Platonist, a Hegelian, and a Cartesian, *and* to find new means to articulate what in all of these thinkers is worth being faithful to, what in all of them is more than just themselves. Badiou's philosophy is Cartesian, Platonic, and Hegelian precisely in relating to something that exceeds any concrete historical articulation. Hegel's system is among other things conditioned by the French Revolution, Plato's philosophy is conditioned by Greek mathematics, and Descartes's thought is conditioned by new inventions of Galilean science. The *lesson of Badiou* is to be faithful to that which in these philosophies is more (i.e., generic) than themselves *because* it is what conditions them. This is why a true philosophical position is only faithful when it is *constitutively heretical*. What he once claimed with reference to Lacan therefore also applies to reading Badiou as a post-Cartesian thinker, namely that "one is not obliged to read into this a complete rupture with Descartes" (*BBE*, 432). But how to remain faithful to Descartes and be contemporary to innovations (within science, politics, etc.), this is the question to be answered subsequently. Why this question is also a heretical one becomes intelligible when one considers the fact that today it more or less seems impossible—at least within academia—to be a Cartesian.[9] Žižek's analysis mentioned in the beginning thus proves to be correct. So, what is Badiou's contribution—in search of "another philosophical style . . . a decided style, a style in the school of Descartes" (*BIT*, 28)—to the manifesto Žižek envisaged?

## Two to Remember: The Cartesian Adventure of Subtraction

> Not one Origin, Two.
> —R. Schürmann[10]

What has been frequently misread in the reception of Badiou is the claim that being qua being can be conceived of as pure multiplicity. This idea has often been rendered in a way that states that being as such *is composed* of (nothing but) pure multiplicity.[11] Being thereby as many readers over-hastily claim is multiple. As if he himself was aware of the danger of this misunderstanding, Badiou once wrote: "I said that being is presented as pure multiplicity (sometimes I shorten this perilously by saying being is multiple)" (*BBE*, 58). Already in 1982, in his *Theory of the Subject* he stated that

> dialectics states that there is the Two, and intends to infer the One from it as a moving division. Metaphysics posits the One, and forever gets tangled up in deriving the Two. There are others, like Deleuze, who posit

the Multiple, which is never more than a semblance since positing the multiple amounts to presupposing the One as substance and excluding the Two from it. (*BTS*, 22)

Taking this remark seriously—and Badiou remained faithful to it throughout his oeuvre—necessitates that any ontology of the multiple has to start from thinking the Two. Why this is can be grasped when this (axiomatic) thesis is linked to arguments which can be found in Descartes: (1) a demonstration that any discourse needs to be sutured to a void; (2) the idea that one can have a clear and distinct idea of the unimaginable; and (3) that the idea of infinity is much easier to grasp than the idea of the finite.[12] It is important here to show how Badiou takes up and repeats these Cartesian elements. I will start the reconstruction by recourse to the two most famous and influential Cartesian arguments: (1) the proof of the existence of the Cogito, and (2) the proof of God's existence, or to be more precise: of God's being.

1. Descartes starts his investigation from a proper philosophical axiom, namely that we are all equal because we can all think ("Good sense is the best distributed thing in the world, for everyone thinks himself to be so well endowed with it" [*DM*, 46]). That no one wishes to be endowed with more implies that the nature of all man is equal—as "there are differences of degree only between *accidents*, but not at all between *forms* or natures of individuals of the same *species*" (ibid., 47). Following Descartes we all share the same "form," the same "nature," the same, as one may put it (formal and as it will become apparent: empty) substance. But what is this (formal, empty) substance?[13] How can one comprehend this pure form suspending any degree of accidental differences (this is again the question of how to conceive of the in-itself-in-itself)?[14] Descartes sets off to a powerful *adventure of subtraction*. Famously he begins by claiming that the only thing we already and veritably know is that we can err. We thus have to subtract all the sources of erring, failure, and false judgment to come to an adequate understanding of what this pure form is in which our equality is grounded. As he puts it in his *Meditations*:

> I will meditate once more on what I once believed myself to be, prior to embarking upon these thoughts. For this reason, then, I will set aside whatever can be weakened even to the slightest degree by the arguments brought forward, so that eventually all that remains is precisely nothing but what is certain and unshaken. (*DMFP*, 108)

One should emphasize a certain ambiguity at the end of the last sentence: what remains is precisely *nothing* and this nothing cannot be shaken and is therefore absolutely certain. So how do we arrive at this point? How does the *adventure of subtraction* take its course?

At first Descartes subtracts all devices of rhetoric and all means of language—as he claims "those who possess the strongest reasoning and who best order their thoughts in order to make them clear and intelligible can always best persuade others of what they are proposing" (*DM*, 49); he subtracts theological justifications to come up with a real uncontestable proof, comparable to proofs in mathematics. Because otherwise it "would be necessary to have some extraordinary assistance from heaven and to be more than a man" (ibid.); he goes on and subtracts any reference to already established philosophical doctrines—"there still is nothing in it about which there is not some dispute" (ibid.); he subtracts all other scientific explanations—"as for the other sciences, I judged that, insofar as they borrow their principles from philosophy, one could not have built anything solid upon such unstable foundations" (ibid.). But all this is still not enough to conduct what Descartes wants to put forward: an "attack" on "those principles which supported everything I once believed" (*DMFP*, 105). The *subtractive method*—putting a minus in front of anything—has to be continued in an even more radical manner.

He thus continues to subtract all seemingly evident opinions—which is not at all an easy enterprise "for long-standing opinions keep returning, and, almost against my will . . . take advantage of my credulity, as if I were bound over to them by long use and the claims of intimacy" (*DMFP*, 107)—all habits,[15] all concrete sensuous experience, then sensuality *tout court*, even logical reasoning—"because there are men who make mistakes in reasoning, even in the simplest matters in geometry" (*DM*, 60), and ultimately ends up subtracting any (concrete) thought—"I resolved to pretend that all the things that had ever entered my mind were no more true than the illusions of my dreams" (ibid.). In the end "it is as if I had suddenly fallen into a deep whirlpool; I am so tossed about that I can neither touch bottom with my foot, nor swim up to the top. Nevertheless I will work my way up" (*DMFP*, 107).[16] But why should it be possible to work one's way up from the abysses of subtraction? Because, as Descartes famously claims, when in the attempt to acquire an absolute certainty (that also accounts for our formal equality) I subtract anything, I cannot subtract that it is precisely me who subtracts. Thereby Descartes comes to demonstrate the existence of the cogito.[17] It is the absolutely empty point of which one can only claim *that* it exists[18] after having subtracted—minused—all other qualities. It is that which has no extension and yet it is the absolute point to which any discourse—any accidental and differential symbolic setting, or any situation, as Badiou would have it—is sutured. As Badiou reformulates Descartes: "There is

an existent whose being *cannot* inexist: the subject of the *Cogito*."[19] This is
to say that any concrete thought, any sensation or imagination, and this
also means thinking in general (because thought is necessarily mediated
by a discourse), relies upon "something" which in itself has no extension,
no content except that it exists.

This is the Cartesian subject, the subject of the cogito. It is, as Badiou put it, "the inactive residue, this is to say, the non-operative residue
of thought which is the 'I think' as such. Note that the 'I think' is constitutively in Descartes the 'I think nothing'; for if it were the thought of
something it would be attacked by doubt, because any something is hit
by doubt."[20] Badiou is fully right in asserting that to think the cogito is
to think the "I think" as thinking nothing: *thinking the 'I think' is thinking
nothing but thought itself.* One might even go as far as to claim that thinking
the "I think" is precisely to think nothing.[21] *Thinking the "I think" thinking
nothing is to think Nothing.* This is why one can speak of a Cartesian *adventure of subtraction* which ultimately leads to Nothing.[22]

For, the "I think" subsists, better: persists even when I subtract everything. Even if I subtract my "body" and pretend "that there was no world
nor any place where I was, I could not pretend, on that account, that I did
not exist at all" (*DM*, 61). This is, as he claims, why doubt is necessary. It
is necessary to find a point which is radically subtracted from any positive
form of knowledge. The cogito is hence not previously given to knowledge. It is what has to be found by means of subtraction of any unstable
source of knowledge. It is as if Descartes three hundred years ago already
read Badiou's remark that "a subject is nowhere given (to knowledge). It
must be found" (*BTS*, 278).[23] And Descartes, after looking for it, thought
he found it and located it (once and forever) as the empty and void (pre-
and unworldly) place of any discursive (or structured symbolic) setting.[24]
This is the first central Cartesian claim: any discourse whatsoever has to
be sutured to something void, subtracted from all accidental and thereby
differential differentiations. This pure point rather grounds any consistent discursive domain, any worldly sphere. It is

> a pure point, that is a void, it implies a certain assertion of existence but
> is void of content . . . For him [Descartes] as for Plato, it is a void point
> which authorizes the discourse on being; it is the void which convoked
> to the point where the discourse assures itself of the real.[25]

Yet at the same time for Badiou the problem with Descartes's argument lies in identifying this empty and void point with the subject. For
Descartes the real of any discourse is the void subject; the real of any discourse for Badiou is still void, but this void is precisely not a or the subject.

Badiou will uphold the Cartesian claim that any discourse (on being)—
any situation[26] whatsoever (and also the situation that is ontology)[27]—is
sutured to a void but he will give this idea a specific post-Cartesian twist.
For Badiou, this void precisely needs to be extracted from its identification with the subject, it needs to be anonymized. I will return to this
point, as it is one of the distinctive traits of Badiou vis à vis Descartes (and
Lacan).[28] But to fully grasp Badiou's take on Descartes one also needs to
reconstruct Descartes's proof of God.

2. After having concluded his subtractive adventure by finding and
placing the void cogito in the heart of any discourse, Descartes derives
implications that concern the existence, the being of God. Descartes,
at least in the *Discourse on Method*, starts from a simple idea: I can doubt
because I know that I can err and my judgments can be mistaken. If this
is the case then I can infer that I am able to doubt because I made the
experience of committing errors. I can doubt because I (know I) am not
perfect (I know that I know nothing).[29] This is to say ex negatively I can
infer that having the concept of imperfection or the concept of lack (that
I gain through my experience of imperfection and lack), the proper understanding of this very concept contains its own negation. Experiencing
imperfection thus entails the possibility of the absence of this very experience. The experience of "something" negative (negatively) implies its
own negation. This is to say, the concept of imperfection and lack which
I gained from an experience of negativity implies its own negation and
this means that from it one can infer perfection. Perfection hence is the
absence of imperfection and as the experience of imperfection is the
experience of an absence (of negativity, lack), one can infer the being
of the absence of this absence. This is to say that Descartes's argument
functions according to a self-reflective application of the concept of lack
onto itself, which generates a further concept, namely the concept of the
*lack of lack*. Absence, lack, is thereby in itself reflexive and logically leads
to the idea of its own abolition. Hence, what I ex negatively[30] find in myself is the idea of perfection (that is: lack of lack).

Moreover, as Descartes argues, as my own imperfection results from
my constitution—it results from me being composed of two different substances (an extended one, i.e., my body, and a not extended one, i.e., my
soul, i.e., the void cogito)[31]—what is perfect necessarily has to suspend
the very source of imperfection (because perfection is what negates the
negativity implied in my own lack [of perfection]), that is, this twofold[32]
constitution. Descartes can in this way deduce, as he "saw clearly that it
is a greater perfection to know than to doubt" (*DM*, 61), that something
perfect—which he in a classical terminology refers to as "God"—must
exist, because without any doubt it can be inferred and hence it must be.

For, that which is perfect would not be perfect if it were not. Perfection (lack of lack = God) must be as it is what can be drawn from the experience of negativity, of lack, which is as origin of doubt itself beyond any doubt. The first certainty in Descartes is therefore neither the cogito, nor doubt, but rather the lack of certainty that enables the cogito and also to derive God's being.

Descartes here deploys what Badiou calls an

> "ontological argument" which names "a proposition of existence which develops from a concept [*sens*], for example . . . from the fact that the sense of the infinite itself infers the existence of God. From the concept [*sens*] of infinity in us one can necessarily deduce an existence."[33]

Descartes starts from a concept—the concept of imperfection (lack)—and then derives the notion of perfection from it; that which is perfect also has to be infinite not only because what is finite and hence limited cannot be perfect, but also because I am finite due to my bodily constitution and I gain the concept of perfection ex negatively. And this whole demonstration starts ex negatively from the I, from an imperfect entity and seems to unfold nothing but the concept of what I find already latently entailed within myself. Yet this raises the question of how to conceive of a perfect existence, of something infinite, unlimited. Descartes's argument is far more radical than it is usually rendered. He claims that

> what brings it about that there are many people who are persuaded that it is difficult to know this and also even to know what their soul is, is that they never lift their minds above sensible things and that they are so accustomed to consider nothing except by imagining it (which is a way of thinking appropriate for material things), that everything unimaginable seems to them unintelligible. (*DM*, 62–63)

Such a limitation of thought is what Descartes strictly opposes. That which is perfect has to exist and as imperfection is grounded in the impure composition of substances; Descartes deduces that it is necessary that what is perfect is not composited. This implies that God is "something" non-material, "something" which does not appear. He has no body and one thus needs a radically different manner to conceive of him. Anything that appears (in a world[34] or in a discourse) is imperfect due to its bodily constitution and this is why God has to be that which is (pre- or) non-discursive. God has to be that which is even more subtracted from any bodily materialization or existential quality than the cogito is. He has to be that which will always and ever have been logically "before" the discourse or the world—as he is its creator, this is to say logically "prior" to it.[35]

God is that which we cannot comprehend (discursively). He is that of which we cannot have an image, a representation. But we can think that which we cannot comprehend (= God). As Badiou rightly claims: "For Descartes, it is the exterior of the place (God) that is infinite, since the place of my thought, guaranteed in its being by the Cogito, is finite, and is therefore not capable of supporting alone the idea of the infinite" (*BNN*, 42). This is to say that due to the fact that the cogito is a purely empty and void point—and any point is by definition finite—the cogito cannot be the grounding principle of that which is by definition not finite—as finitude is at the same time an index of imperfection.[36] "He [Descartes] makes sure not to infer the infinite from reflection or from the Cogito as such . . . Descartes' problem is elsewhere. . : [it is that] the idea of the infinite is without common measure with its place, which is my soul" (*BNN*, 41). Badiou can claim this because the soul is "that part distinct from the body of which it has been said previously that its nature is only to think" (*DM*, 67) and thus is identical with the cogito. But the cogito as empty point is finite and if the idea of the infinite and perfect is derived from the imperfection of my cogito, one can infer that the place of the idea of the infinite is finite and has thus not common measure with what can be derived from it. Yet even though our cogito is a pure finite point, this does not at all hinder us from thinking that which is perfect and also infinite, that which is not limited (in any internal or external way). Or to put this radical idea in a formula: *Although we are finite, we can think that which we cannot think.*[37]

We can think that which will always have been logical 'prior' to the world and the discourse and is thereby necessarily unthinkable—at the same time it is only accessible when one starts from the existence of the discourse or the world on. But what does this mean? It means that we can have a clear and distinct idea of the perfect, the infinite—as "there cannot be any[thing] that [is] so remote that [it is] not eventually reached nor so hidden that [it is] not discovered" (*DM*, 54–55)[38]—and no kind of mysticism is involved. One can have a fully rational, clear, and distinct thought of that which cannot be thought—although it still holds "[a] being is thinkable only insofar as it belongs to a world" (*BLoW*, 113–118). There is a "clarity of the incomprehensible . . . There is a clear and distinct incomprehensibility of God which does not lead up to be a confused notion" (*BN*). In different terms one might say that God has a being which can be thought but that he does not have any attributes of (worldly) existence—as any existence implies to belong to a discursive setting even as its void point. Descartes thus proves that we can conceive of *that which is but does not exist.* He proves that one can think "being qua being" (*BBE,* 3)—being in its beingness, so to speak—but in thinking it *one thinks being as being unthinkable*—it is even less than the existing Nothing that is the cogito. Nothing exists, God as *being qua being* is and does not exist.[39]

*We can think the unthinkable.*[40] We can do so because we can even subtract—in the still ongoing *adventure of subtraction*—the existence of the cogito because if there is "something" which created the cogito and if it is the empty limit point of any discourse, we can think that which retroactively precedes it. Descartes should not be misread here: his point is not simply that we can infer the being of God from the existence of the cogito. It is rather that when the cogito exists and it is the zero-point of any discourse that we can (and must) retroactively deduce, that there will have been something before the discourse (which is what created it). Another way of putting this is to claim only via the limit point of the discourse, and this means only after and because of the discourse, one can think *that which will retroactively have been "prior"* to it.[41] But one does only think if one thinks it.

Although we know that the existence of cogito is indubitable for Descartes and we cannot think ourselves as not-thinking, this empty point not only allows for but also forces a thought upon us that immanently "transcends" thought itself. What lies "at the centre of the Cogito, is not immanent, but rather transcendent" (*BBE,* 432). Because: if to exist in a fundamental but also quite empirical sense implies to appear in a world, the cogito argument has proven that there is something—a thing that thinks—which although it grounds every discourse does not at all need to appear in it—the cogito is *not* the body. The radical gesture of Descartes now lies in the claim that the thing which has no other attribute but to exist—the empty point of the cogito—allows for and forces us to think (a) being that has no attribute at all; not even that of existence (this is God):[42] *God is but does not exist,* while the cogito exists without any criterion of existence. It is only from the cogito that we can think that which we cannot think because it just is (and will hence always have been prior to thought).[43]

## Two to Repeat: Descartes Turned from His Head onto His Feet

> I would say that the debate bears upon the localization of the void.
> —*BBE,* 432

How to read Badiou's system against this Cartesian background and defend it against the misreading I referred to at the beginning of the chapter? To now properly enter the Badiousian cosmos: as is well known, his *Being and Event* offers the most systematic presentation of his so called meta-ontology.[44] He starts off by laying a complex set of propositions which I will briefly reconstruct in a *tour de force* as they need to be taken into account to adequately unravel the Cartesian heritage in his thought. The most fundamental of these propositions for the present context are: (1) being is not composed of numbers and this also implies that "it should be taken quite seriously that the 'one' is a number" (*BBE*, 24). This means (2) that being is not one.[45] (3) But at the same time: being as being is also not multiple.[46] "Being is neither one (because any presentation itself is pertinent to the count-as-one), nor multiple (because the multiple is solely the *regime* of presentation)" (*BBE*, 24). This remark is important as it represents a fundamental statement with regards to how ontology functions when addressed from a meta-ontological perspective—that is to say: from within philosophy. These three claims about being need to be read together, but to do so one needs to understand Badiou's most central claims about ontology.

Ontology is the "discourse on being" (*BBE*, 25). It can be identified with mathematics, or more historically specifically with set-theoretically based mathematics.[47] Why? Because set theory is able to do two things at the same time: (1) by presenting pure multiplicities, it presents the form of any presentation–it presents presentation. This is to say, set theory is not the one and only presentation of being—this is clearly impossible as there cannot be only one presentation of being (see point 2 above),[48] otherwise being would somehow be immanently linked to the One. But by presenting multiplicities of multiplicities (inter alia embodied by the variables it uses) it also presents the multiplicity of presentations as such. (2) Set theory can show that the consistency of any presentation derives from its structure and that any structure is structured by the specificity of a count, of a count-as-one; what is counted as one are multiplicities. So, if set theory is able to present pure multiplicities without counting them as one—this is what Badiou necessarily needs to claim—set theory presents presentation, any thinkable structured and consistent presentation operating according to a count-as-one. But this also implies that set theory, that is, ontology, is itself a (structured) presentation or what Badiou calls a situation. For it consistently presents multiplicities (of presentation) and this is only possible via counting-as-one. Therefore it holds that set theory also operates under the regime of a count-as-one and it counts "something" which logically has to precede its count; otherwise it could not have been counted in the first place, for the count is an operation on something logically "prior" to the count even though it is only accessible afterwards.[49] This "something" is the "matter" on which the count-as-one operates.

Given this framework, Badiou initially demonstrates that what set theory counts as one is itself internally *less than one*—set theory counts multiplicities as multiplicities. But why can it do so? Because it does not start from any definition of what the multiplicity is. It counts something as one without defining, without giving a determinate operator, of how the operation of the count proceeds. *It counts something as one without knowing what it is that it counts.* For set theory has the "structure of an implicit count" (*BBE*, 57). This is why it can consistently count and present multiplicity-as-multiplicity. Rendered in a simpler manner: one can start from any concrete situation or object (may it be a tree in the yard) which appears as one (one tree) and dissect it into its components (for example the trunk, the branches, the leaves, the stem, and other parts of the leaves) and then continue with this dissemination ad infinitum. Any element itself consists of elements and they again are composed of others unto infinity. In this way one ends up with an infinite process of dissemination of all the components into what they are made of. If one now reflects on this very process of decomposition, one is led to the claim that anything consistently presented as one in any given situation (any "whole or single body" [Hegel 2004, 47] as one might put it with Hegel) is composed of multiplicities of elements which themselves consist of multiplicities of elements and so forth. This is precisely what set theory can present by presenting presentation. One could also claim it presents the most indeterminate instance of what a count-as-one is.[50] Therefore the question arises of whether there is ultimately "one" (form of) multiplicity (atoms, for example) that constitute that which initially was presented as "one" (one tree) or if there is nothing but an infinite dissemination of multiplicities.[51] Badiou opts for the latter answer. Set theory subtracts all qualitative attributes of that which it counts—very akin to Descartes. It presents multiplicities of multiplicities and thereby the multiplicity of any presentation. It *presents presentability.* This is why ontology—that is, set theory—is the most abstract discourse on being because (1) ontology is still a situation and thus counts something, some multiplicity as one and because it (2) can present under its count-as-one that which is constitutively not-one, it counts-as-one-minus-(counting-as-)one. *Ontology counts as one without counting as one.*[52] Set theoretical ontology from a meta-ontological, that is, philosophical perspective is a *subtractive discourse* (on being).

Broadly speaking, what is subtracted within set theory is primarily the definition of what a set is. Set theory is a theory about something which it does itself not define. A set is an operative category.[53] Any set has elements but they are themselves sets, so what is counted as one are sets and sets only. But, and this is crucial, the elements of a set have nothing else in common than to be elements of the same set. Two sets differ solely with respect to their elements—either two sets have the same elements and are thus the same set or they are distinct "globally" due to a distinction grounded in one (or more) of their elements. What is counted as one (set) is itself inherently multiple (i.e., a set of sets). But of what is this multiple (a set) a multiple? First answer: a multiple of multiples, a set of sets. But what then is the multiple of multiples composed of? Second answer: of nothing; only of that which Badiou calls the void. The void is nothing but the pure and empty name of being. But, and this is essential, if set theoretical ontology counts-as-one that which is not one (by subtractively counting-as-one-minus-one), this means that what will have been before the count is *neither one*—as the one already has been subtracted from the indeterminate count—*nor multiple*—because what set theory presents are multiples of multiples and it thus has to be claimed that it still counts "something" as multiple. That which is counted as pure multiplicity is composed of the void which thereby can neither be one nor multiple. The void therefore "*is unique*" (*BBE*, 69). This is why Badiou can claim that *being* as such—subtractively indexed in set theory via the name of the void—*cannot be presented*. Its most fundamental mode of presentation is pure multiplicity. This mode of presentation makes being "sayable for humanity" (*BBE*, 27). In ontology being presents itself as *being unpresentable*. It can only be indexed by a pure name, the name of the void that is subtracted from any presentation and hence presents nothing. Being is that to which the realm in which multiples of multiples are presented is subtractively sutured.

Badiou's version of this insight reads like this: The "*void* of a situation" is "this suture to its being . . . every structured presentation unpresents 'its' void, in the mode of this non-one which is merely the subtractive face of the count" (*BBE*, 55).[54] This means that everything set theory presents is composed of a "*sole term . . . without concept*" (*BBE*, 57). All multiplicities of multiplicities are composed of nothing; this is why the void is not localizable as it is everywhere, universally included. It is globally included in any term (multiplicity) and locally everywhere (any singular element is composed of it). *Ontology* "can *only* be theory of the void" (ibid.) because "being *qua being* . . . is neither one nor multiple" (*BBE*, 58). Ontology has to be a theory of the void by being *a theory of the suture* (of any discourse to being). Here the ontological primacy of the Two over the multiple becomes fully apparent. The void "is subtracted from the one/multiple dialectic" (ibid.). Ontology is a situation, thus it counts-as-one, but what becomes thinkable via its form of presenting presentation is that, what will have been counted will always have been logically "prior" to the count, although only accessible and thinkable afterwards. *What gives consistency to ontology's presentation is unpresentable.* The *Two pre-*

*vails* as pure multiplicity can only gain its consistency when referred back to the void of which it is composed. Thus the dialectic of one-multiple retroactively produces what will have preceded this very dialectic, namely the void. Recall again Žižek's reconstruction of the distinction between three forms of judgment in Kant (*ZID*, 286): The positive judgment assigns an attribute to a subject ("X is dead"); the negative judgment negates this attribution ("X is not dead"), and this is what makes it possible to translate this judgment into a positive one ("X is not dead, that is to say, X lives"). Finally, the infinite judgment assigns a non-attribute to a subject ("X is undead, that is to say, neither X lives nor X is dead"). With reference to Badiou one can claim that the distinction of the one and the multiple is linked to the realm of positive and negative judgments (say: X is multiple, X is not One) but the void as the other side of this distinction (one-multiple/void)[55] is something comparable to the infinite judgment: *The void is Un-One / Un-Multiple.*

The question here is: how to conceive of the relation between on the one side the one-multiple-distinction (dialectics) and the void on the other?[56] The way I read Badiou it is neither a positive relationship which could be described by positive judgments, nor is it a negative relationship. It is an *un-relation*[57] linking the positive and negative judgments (one-multiple) and the infinite judgment (void), that is to say the relationship between the two sides can only be rendered intelligible via the form of the infinite judgment.[58] This is why one can claim that the void will always have been prior to the discourse of the one and the multiple although it is only graspable as retroactive effect of the discourse itself. *There is an un-relation of the dialectics of the one and the multiple (= discourse) and the un-one, un-multiple which is the void.*[59]

This is what the primacy of the two within Badiou's system comes down to. And it represents the most fundamental meta-ontological claim of Badiou's philosophy. On one hand there is the distinction of the one and the multiple and its complex dialectic within set theoretical ontology and on the other side, although this side is only retroactively produced by this very dialectic, lies "something" which is diagonal towards this distinction.[60] It should be clear by now that Badiou's meta-ontological primacy of the Two over the multiple can be read as a repetition of one of the two Cartesian claims reconstructed above. Badiou also claims: *one can think that which one cannot think* (because thinking requires presentation and the void is per se unpresentable). But here things get more difficult. For Badiou repeats Descartes's claim in a very specific sense—any discourse is sutured to the void: and ontology as the most fundamental and the most abstract discourse can demonstrate that this is the case by presenting any form of thinkable presentation. But at the same time Badiou differs from

Descartes because the void is the subject. This distinction needs some elaboration. Thus far I have demonstrated that the void is the sole term of which the multiples of multiplicities are composed. Thereby it is—and this is essential to take into account—not localizable. It is rather the unlocalizable void point in which manifests both that the situation is sutured to being and to "*that-which-presents-itself*, wanders in the presentation in the form of a subtraction from the count" (*BBE*, 55).[61]

Thus it bears some characteristics of the Cartesian cogito and some of the Cartesian God. It is a point, void of any determination, to which any discourse, any situation is sutured—this is what makes it comparable to the cogito. It is as such unpresentable, it can only be thought within the realm of a structured presentation as that which is unthinkable, for any thought presupposes structured presentation—this is what makes it comparable to the Cartesian God. It can be thought as that which cannot be thought and it is precisely that which cannot be thought to which any discourse is sutured. So the void takes its position in between the Cartesian subject and the Cartesian God. What is this supposed to mean? Here one passage from an early conversation between Badiou and Natacha Michel is quite instructive. Badiou therein claims:

> To say that the subject is a process and even, as the book [*Theory of the Subject*] does, a braid of a process is at the same time to de-punctualize it—it is not the cause, it is not the primordial source, fundament, certainty of itself—and to de-totalize it—it is not the absolute of spirit, the reason of history, it is not the integral recollection of experience. (Badiou 1982, 3)

Here it becomes clear what distinguishes Badiou from Descartes and what makes him into a veritable post-Cartesian thinker. The subject is not "the solution to a problem of possibility or unity (possibility of intuitive certainty for Descartes, of synthetic judgments a priori for Kant)" (*BLoW*, 101). The subject is a process, it is not a point. So the void as the point—locally and globally, that is, universally included—cannot be identified with the subject. The void is an unlocalizable point; the subject is a process which always—as Badiou insists from his early works onwards—takes place in a singular and historically specific situation. *The void is not the subject, the subject is not the void.*[62]

What does this mean for Badiou's Cartesianism if there is one? It means that there is no transcendental domain involved in his meta-ontology. That to which any discourse is sutured is not the localized void point of the cogito although any discourse or situation is sutured to a void point. But this void is not localizable and thus cannot be the subject—

since otherwise it could be the founding cause of the discourse, even if this cause were to be constitutively lacking. So Badiou disentangles the two Cartesian claims. First he demonstrates the necessary suturing of any discourse to the void—comparable to the Cartesian cogito argument. Then he develops the necessary primacy of the two over the multiple for any materialist ontology by showing that one can think the unthinkable— comparable to the Cartesian proof of God's being. Finally he insists—by de-punctualizing and de-totalizing the subject—that the void is not the subject. The subject is not pre-given, it has to be found. How to find the subject if it has to be dis-identified from the void? The answer to this is why the whole debate between Badiou and Descartes (and also Lacan) "bears upon the localization of the void" (*BBE*, 432). Because

> for the void to become localizable at the level of presentation, and thus for a certain type of intra-situational assumption of being qua being to occur, a dysfunction of the count is required, which results from an excess-of-one. The event will be this ultra-one of a hazard, on the basis of which the void of a situation is retroactively discernible. (*BBE*, 56)

This claim entails that the subject does not ground anything—it is "the local or finite status of a truth" (Badiou 1993, 93), the subject is a process—but this very process is grounded in the localization of the void. And the (supernumerary) name for this localization is "event." The event as localization of the previously unlocalizable and unpresented void is that which enables the subject to come to being, it allows for subjectivization. Here is the precise passage from which one can grasp the meta-ontological claim that in any materialist ontological the two needs to prevail over the multiple and from which one can infer the necessity of not only thinking the two but the three. And the three is nothing but a *torsion of the two*.[63] The subject is not the void, but for the subject to emerge and to be sustained (as a process) the two is not enough. One needs think, so to speak, two-plus-one, the three. Recall Badiou again:

> Dialectics states that there is the Two, and intends to infer the One from it as a moving division. Metaphysics posits the One, and forever gets tangled up in deriving the Two. There are others, like Deleuze, who posit the Multiple, which is never more than a semblance since positing the multiple amounts to presupposing the One as substance and excluding the Two from it. (*BTS*, 22)

But materialist dialectics also needs to state and defend the Three. The question is: why is this necessary?

CHAPTER 4

Two to Work Through: Against the
Reactionary Two, or Creating Eternity
(without God)

> What knots man and God together is nothing other than truth
> as such.
>     —Badiou 2007, 167

Today we live under the predominance of a very specific, reactionary, and obscurantist interpretation of the two. This ideological interpretation claims that everything that is can be reduced to two fundamental components: bodies and languages, or individuals and communities. This ideology as Badiou stated is a materialist one: democratic materialism.[64] Against this Badiou put up the axiom of what he calls materialist dialectic ("*There are only bodies and languages, except that there are truths*" [*BLoW*, 4]) according to which "the materialist dialectic advocates the correlation of truths and subjects" (*BLoW*, 34). But how to understand this axiom in the context thus far developed? Where does the exception to what there is come from? The answer, given in the unfolding of the argument in Badiou's *Logics of Worlds*, originates from a reading of Descartes. He first points out that both democratic materialism and any materialist dialectical thought share the presupposition that what there is are bodies and languages or individuals and communities—although the first substantializes, even naturalizes this presupposition. Then Badiou turns to Descartes, who traditionally is considered to be the proponent of the classical philosophical form of the two called dualism. Against this reading Badiou claims:

> Descartes' doctrine is commonly identified with dualism: the substan-
> tial "there is" is divided into thought and extension, which in man
> means: soul and body. Nevertheless, in paragraph 48 of the *Principles
> of Philosophy*, we see that substance dualism is subordinated to a more
> fundamental distinction. This distinction is the one between things
> (what there is, that is to say substance, either thinking or extended)
> and truths . . . What a remarkable text! It recognizes the wholly excep-
> tional, ontological and logical status of truths. Truths are without exis-
> tence. Is that to say they do not exist at all? Far from it. Truths have no
> *substantial* existence. That is how we must understand the declaration
> that they "are nothing outside of our thought" . . . Descartes speci-
> fies that this criterion designates the formal universality of truths . . .
> Note that the crux of the Cogito (the induction of existence through
> the act of thought) is a truth in this sense. This means that a truth is
> what thought goes on presenting even when the regime of the thing is

suspended (by doubt). A truth is thus what insists in exception to the forms of the "there is." Descartes is not a dualist merely in the sense conferred to this term by the opposition it draws between "intellectual" things . . . and "corporeal" things . . . Descartes is a dualist at a far more essential level, which alone sustains the demonstrative machinery of his philosophy: the level at which things (intellectual and/or corporeal) and truths (whose mode of being is to (in)exist) are distinguished . . . Consider the . . . passage which also links truths to the infinite of their (in)existence . . . And it is true that a truth is an exception to what there is, if we consider that, when given the "occasion" to encounter it, we immediately recognize it as such. We can see in what sense Descartes thinks the Three (and not only the Two). His own axiom can in fact be stated as follows: "There are only (contingent) corporeal and intellectual things, except that there are (eternal) truths." (*BLoW*, 5–6)

What a remarkable reading! Badiou is able to demonstrate that the Cartesian dualism relies on a fundamental distinction: between the realm of the "there is" which comprises intellectual and physical entities and the realm of truths on the other. In this way Descartes becomes a central proponent of dualism, of a dualism which can oppose the ideological hegemony of the "there is" (which is nothing but individuals and communities or bodies and languages) by insisting on the very possibility of an exception.

But what does this more fundamental dualism come down to? It comes down to claiming that, of course, no materialist can argue against the material domain of existence, against the "there is" of bodies and languages or of individuals and communities without falling into some sort of mysticism, religion, or bad idealism. But it also comes with the insight that *this type of materialism is not materialist enough*. It is not materialist enough as it suppresses the central materialist ontological insight: it suppresses the primacy of the two by substantializing or naturalizing it. One direct consequence of misreading the ontological primacy of the two over the multiple consists in the naturalized substantialization of what "there is," bodies, languages, individuals, communities. This is due to a perfidious rendering of the primacy of the two which in the very moment of its alleged affirmation immanently negates this very primacy. Democratic materialism claims to say "yes" to the primacy of the two ("yes, there are only bodies and languages"), but at the same time it utters a silent "no" to dualism proper. Democratic materialism is a materialism of a simultaneous "yes" and "no" to the two. Against this one needs a (dialectical) materialism of the "yes" or "no," an affirmative materialist dialectics, an idealism without idealism.

The democratic materialist claims: yes, there are only bodies and languages, and continues to draw the consequence that one can present everything within the realm of bodies and languages because there are no exceptions to this realm. But the ontological primacy of the two—as Badiou's Cartesian meta-ontology shows—can only be properly understood if any presentation, even the most fundamental one, relies upon "something" which cannot be presented in it. Thereby one encounters *the problem of how to localize that which cannot be presented.* This is a problem the democratic materialist does not know anything about as he is without any effort able to localize all the bodies, languages, individuals, and communities—if worse comes to worst, they are localized by being excluded.[65] So, against the alleged affirmation of the primacy of the two—and one should also note here that this is why democratic materialism presumes to be always able to construct a consistent totality[66] of all bodies and languages, a totality of the "there is"—Badiou turns to a more fundamental two which he locates in Descartes's philosophy. Democratic materialism attempts to count-the-Two-as-One[67] making a whole out of it—and thereby naturalizing what "there is." Against democratic materialism's body-language-dualism one can oppose a Cartesian body-language-truth dualism, against the individual-community-dualism a Cartesian individual-community-subject-dualism. For: "We are not obliged to obey the Two, i.e., the state of things" ("BSP II"). The true primacy of the two contains the *impossibility of totalization,*[68] the primacy of the Two necessarily leads to thinking an exception to the "there is" (of any presentation). Materialist dialectics is thus a dialectics of the exception which introduces a split into the materialist "there is." Yes, *there are* only individuals and communities, except that *there are* subjects. Only this split "there is" is truly materialist. There need to be two "there is's."[69] Materialist dialectics thus performs a "materialist reversal of materialism."[70] The proper two is only graspable from the position of a three.[71]

It is thus necessary for any materialist thought to insist on the three (one-multiple/void) to uphold the ontological primacy of the true two over the multiple. The three then presents the split, or better: *the scene of the split* within the "there is"; it represents the insistence on the exception to the two-counted-as-one. The three is the two-counted-as-two; the two of the "there is"; the insistence on the exception. But what this exception indicates is that there is something unpresentable, something inexistent within any given world or presentation. Within any "there is" there is more than there is: "there is" a split "there is." So what one can learn from Descartes, if one follows Badiou, is that one has to be a dualist to remain a materialist and a dialectician.[72] But:

> This opposition is also one between two conceptions of freedom. For
> democratic materialism, freedom is plainly definable as the (negative)
> rule of what there is. There is freedom if no language forbids individual
> bodies which are marked by it from deploying their own capacities. Or
> again, languages let bodies actualize their vital resources. Incidentally,
> this is why under democratic materialism sexual freedom is the para-
> digm of every freedom. (*BLoW*, 34)

Democratic materialists love sex in which one is allowed to freely con-
sume the other, to express one's desires in the most direct manner, and
they feel threatened by love,[73] as love is always a risky exception to that
which there is. One might also frame this in slightly different terms: the
law of the body is a specific desire that Kant would have called pathological and its linkage with different forms of languages is a means of
articulating this very desire. Thus the freedom the democratic materialist
proposes is a freedom of the body, a freedom of its expression—this is
why it ultimately is the freedom of human (bodily) rights. In opposition
to this, freedom from a materialist dialectical stance "presupposes that
a new body appears in the world" (*BLoW*, 34).[74] This is to say: only via an
exception to that what "there is" can "something" which formerly has
been inexistent come to exist, that is, appear in a world.

This is what localizing the void means. It means localizing an exception. An exception that has material consequences is nothing but an
event and as its effects produce something that previously did not appear
in a world: a new (subjective) body. This is to say: only via the localization of the void within a specific situation—the void which is not the
subject—can a subject—in the material form of a new body—emerge.
Without such an exception we remain within the fake democratic materialist realm of the two of individuals and communities. There is only a
true two if there is a three; there is only a true two if there is an exceptional event which localizes the non-subjective void and as a consequence
makes a subject appear in a world. An event generates a previously un-
foreseen possibility, an "impossible possibility" (*BPP*, 101) which produces
as its consequences—and an event is nothing but the ensemble of the
consequences it produces—something which will have been unprecedented in the given situation or world. Yet, how to grasp this as a common
Cartesian and Badiousian line of thought? One first answer can be given
if one considers that what also appears with the emerging subject—and
we should not forget: the subject is a process (of the unfolding of the consequences of an event)—because it is produced by it is a truth. So, if the
exception within the "there is" is an exception which is linked to truth

(in Descartes) or to the subject and to truth (in Badiou), how to understand this claim? One can answer this by rephrasing it and by splitting it in two: (1) what is the status of truths in Descartes and Badiou? and (2) how does a truth relate to the subject?

1. What is clear thus far: for Descartes and Badiou a truth is an exception. And both also claim that truths are not relative; they are eternal. As Badiou puts it:

> I believe in eternal truths and in their fragmented creation in the present of worlds. My position on this point is entirely isomorphic with that of Descartes: truths are eternal because they have been created and not because they have been there forever. For Descartes, "eternal truths" . . . cannot transcend divine will. Even the most formal of these, the truths of mathematics or logic, like the principle of non-contradiction, depend on a free act of God . . . Of course, the process of creation of a truth, whose present is constituted by the consequences of a subjectivated body, is very different from the creative act of a God. But, at bottom, the idea is the same . . . Eternal necessity pertains to a truth in itself. (*BLoW*, 512)

This point is fundamental: truths are not eternal because they have been there since before the beginning of time, they have been created.[75] Descartes is similarly explicit with regard to the creation of eternal truths, as one can read in a letter to Mersenne: "The mathematical truths, which you call eternal, have been established by God and they entirely depend on him as much as the whole rest of the creatures."[76] And he explains how radically this creation has to be thought in a further letter:

> And again that God had willed that some truths are necessary this is not to say that he necessarily willed them; for, to will that they are necessary and to necessarily will it or to be necessitated to will it is a completely different thing.[77]

Truths are eternal and they have been created. This is what Descartes and Badiou share. For Descartes, eternal truths have been created by God out of a free act of will; for Badiou, truths will have been by finite subjects.[78] What does this amount to? One further clarification can be derived from a remarkable text that Jean-Paul Sartre published in 1947 on Descartes's notion of freedom[79] from which Badiou takes up certain elements. Sartre systematically explores how to conceive of Descartes's notion of freedom that is linked to the idea that God does not necessarily will anything. Rather, even eternal truths are the product of "the absolute contingency of a free creative will" ("SCF," 195)[80] which he places within his notion of God. This is why "God" is also the name of infinity (of freedom), the infinity of an absolutely free and creative will.[81] In Descartes one thus finds a concatenation of several important points: truths are eternal, but they have to be created; truths are created by an act of absolute free will and this freedom is linked to absolute contingency—no regime of necessity is involved. And as Sartre adds creation of truths then signifies that they appear in a world—as any truth God creates has to appear for otherwise it would not be ("SCF," 192). This is what one can—via Sartre—read in Descartes and this is what—taking up Sartre's reading—is explicit within Badiou's proposal. He also "posits that their creation is nothing but the appearance of their eternity" (*BSP* II). For he also holds that truths are eternal, they are created, and their creation is linked to (a moment of an) absolute contingency, that is to say an event.[82]

If in Descartes God is the unthinkable that we are able *to think as unthinkable* then what we think in thinking the unthinkable God is precisely the absolute contingency as ground for the creation of eternal truths. We think that which is unthinkable as grounding the (impossible) possibility for a creation of truths. We think that which we can impossibly think, namely we think *the impossible as ground of the creation of truths*. This becomes even more apparent when one considers another passage from Descartes's *Meditations*:

> It is only the will or free choice that I experience to be so great in me that I cannot grasp the idea of any greater faculty. This is so much the case . . . that I bear a certain image and likeness of God. For although the faculty of willing is incomparably greater in God than it is in me . . . nevertheless, when viewed in itself formally and precisely, God's faculty of willing does not appear to be any greater. (*DMFP*, 124–25)

I am the most Godlike in the freedom of my will.[83] And the freedom of God's will is the cause for the creation of eternal truths. But if God's freedom is essentially synonymous with absolute contingency[84]—which is one element that we think in thinking the unthinkable—my freedom comes down to being the unthinkable in me. This is why Badiou reading Descartes can claim that "for Descartes God is the subject, the Other in the Subject [*L'Autre* en sujet]."[85] One could from this infer the following: I am so free—and thus Godlike—that I am able to *do the unthinkable*— this is to say: create eternal truths. But Descartes himself did not draw this precise conclusion, as Sartre indicates ("SCF," 196), as he left creation to God. This is the precise point where Badiou will be more Cartesian than Descartes. But how to conceive of the relation between subject and truths in Badiou and Descartes? Or one could again ask differently: how does one uphold the materialist dialectical claim that truths are as much eternal as they are created while getting rid of God?[86]

2. Against the reactionary and fake two of democratic materialism the exception of the three is needed. The three counts the two as proper two and enables us to conceive of the absolute contingency which lays the ground for any creation of eternal truths. This is what Badiou takes up from Descartes. But as things stand with Descartes, one can say that he mulches several points together which Badiou—as a proper *post*-Cartesian thinker—attempts to disentangle. Descartes insists on the necessary suturing of any discourse to the void cogito. But thereby he is also inclined to claim that the subject itself is a truth. As Badiou put it: "The crux of the Cogito (the induction of existence through the act of thought) is a truth" (*BLoW*, 4).[87] But if it is universally true and any truth is created by God, this necessarily implies that this truth—that is, the subject of the cogito— must have been created by God. Thus the cogito is a truth created by God. What is remarkable here is that Descartes's argument is quite ambiguous. Either one reads it in a way that claims that the truth of any discourse is the void subject of the cogito—this would be the traditional rendering— from which one then can infer—if indeed it is a truth—that it must have been created by God. In this way one identifies the subject with an eternal truth; one eternal truth consists in an empty point which is sutured to any discourse. Or one reads Descartes in a way that one insists upon the radical freedom of God, on the absolute contingency of his creation—even of the creation of the subject—and one thus infers that any subject whatsoever originates from absolute contingency. Depending on how to emphasize the different parts of the Cartesian line of argumentation one ends up with two different Descartes. One Descartes who argues for the identification of the subject with a void point and with a constantly present truth (that is the subject) or one Descartes who argues for the contingency as ground of the existence of the subject (much closer to the deceiving evil genius). This is the precise point where one can draw the dividing line between a Cartesian and a Badiousian-post-Cartesian argument.

In Descartes the subject is itself a truth, in Badiou it is a fragmentary agent of the creation of truths—it emerges as a consequence of absolute contingency but is then itself able to create something eternal (it is able to do the impossible or unthinkable). Subjects in Badiou are fragments of truths, in Descartes they are (is there more than one subject in Descartes?)[88] a truth. This marks the distinction because the conception of truth changes in opting for one of the two sides: either one ends up with a conception of truth which is the subject as void point created by God; or one ends up with a conception of truth as creation which relies on an absolute contingency and produces the emergence of a subject as the very agent of the creation of a truth. The subject thus is related in two different ways to localizing the void. One can assert that Badiou and Descartes agree that this localization is related to contingency. The difference is that everything changes if one leaves God aside.[89] For Badiou an event localizes the void[90] and enables the emergence of a subject, that is to say: subjectivation. But if an absolute contingency grounds the subject and the subject is an agent of the unfolding of the consequences of the emergence of this very contingency—this is one possible definition of what Badiou calls a truth—it is clear that the subject cannot be situated in a point anymore. The subject needs to be a process, for it is the active agent of a procedure. And this also implies that truth cannot be situated in a point within a given discourse, however empty and subjective it might be. It also has to be a process itself. Truths can only be properly grasped when they are considered to be *truth procedures*.

This leads to a further consequence: the localization of the void cannot coincide with a localization of the subject in a singular point. If the subject is a process and thus cannot be the (latent although *constantly present*) truth of any discourse, one needs to think the emergence of the subject, the beginning of the creation of a truth. This is why for Badiou subjectivization consists in the emergence of a new possibility.[91] As depicted, this possibility is a possibility of a new (subjective) choice. One can say "yes" or "no" to an event—only a "yes," a *determinate affirmation* generates subjectivization.[92] This is for example why Badiou can claim:

> The "there is" of the subject is the coming-to-being of the event, via the ideal occurrence of a truth, in its finite modalities. By consequence, what must always be grasped is that there is no subject, that there are no longer some subjects. What Lacan still owed to Descartes, a debt whose account must be closed, was the idea that there were always some subjects. (*BBE*, 434)

This means that only from an event, from an absolute contingency a true two emerges. One needs the three—that is, the absolutely contingent event—to generate a true two (a two as two) against the fake two (the two-as-one-totality) of democratic materialism that is easily sustainable without considering any exception. The three is the torsion of the two. Although Badiou will admit that freedom is linked to contingency, to impossibility or even unthinkability, for him freedom is a *result* of something absolutely contingent. There is no free choice without an event which contingently localizes the void of a situation. *Freedom is not* an ever-present *capacity*. An event is that which creates the conditions of possibility for a voluntary and free subjective affirmation. But at the same time the event is nothing but the ensemble of the consequences it will have yielded (and the agent of these consequences is the subject). An event is thus the creation of the conditions of the possibility of the consequences of an event—that is, of the event itself. This is why it had the paradoxical structure of naming a multiplicity which belongs to itself. An event is the emergence of a possibility of evental consequences that are only evental consequences if the event will have been an event.

The free choice of a "yes" and "no" with regard to a contingent event is thus nothing but the materiality of the event itself, which needs to be sustained as long as possible. This is the place of the impossible in Badiou. For Descartes the unthinkable is linked to contingency and it is the very paradigm of freedom. From a Badiousian perspective, one needs to claim in somewhat paradoxical terms that Descartes in his rendering of this conceptual relationship was too Sartrean. Descartes conflated the contingency as ground of the creation of eternal truths with contingency as the essence of freedom. What in Descartes designates the infinity of freedom, namely God as creator of the subject of the cogito, becomes something quite different in Badiou's rendering of this constellation. Nonetheless already Descartes introduces a notion of freedom which is radically different from the predominant democratic materialist one: a freedom of absolute contingency that is present—*extimately* present as one might put it with Lacan (Lacan 1992, 139)—as the internal other within the subject. Badiou takes up the Cartesian idea that something radically contingent can produce a true and this is to say a free choice—between a "yes" and a "no"—which enables this very subject to do something which previously seemed impossible—that is, to be a proper subject and hence create an eternal truth. Badiou takes up Descartes's two axioms (the cogito as void point and God as that which is unthinkable and synonymous with absolute contingency, thus infinite with regards to his free will) and reshuffles them.

He links them in a specific way to the only two existential axioms that can be found in—at least certain versions of—set theoretical ontology: the axiom of the empty set and the axiom of infinity. The first axiom claims: "There is a set such that no set is a member of it." Or in a different formulation: "The unpresentable is presented, as a subtractive term of the presentation of presentation." Or again: "a multiple is, which is not under the Idea of the multiple." One can see here even clearer that this axiom stands in an analogous position to the cogito argument. The second axiom, "the second existential seal" (*BBE*, 156), claims: "There exists an infinite ordinal." Or more precisely: "There exists a limit ordinal."[93] One can here leave aside the complex technical exploration of the theory of ordinality and only concentrate on the consequences of this axiom against the background developed thus far. First one might say that this is not an axiom that in any form can be related to God—that is, to a localization of the infinite in a place outside the world. Rather it comprises the claim that the infinite exists and because to exist means to appear within a discourse, it means that the infinite as infinite exists in the worldly realm. But one needs to bear in mind that there are very specific conditions for it to come to exist in a world. And one of them is first and foremost that there needs to be an event.

One can reconstruct the connection of the two axioms in Badiou as follows: if any situation whatsoever is sutured to being through its own specific void, then the absolutely unpredictable and thus contingent event localizes the void and enables subjectivization. Becoming a subject means to be forced to decide if what happened was an event or not ("yes" or "no"); if what has happened will have had consequences or not. But any event is nothing but the ensemble of the consequences it yields[94]—although it is at the same time the enabling cause of these very consequences. So, how to conceive of the development of these consequences with regards to the two axioms? Badiou's answer is that what produces these very consequences and thus changes the previous situation is a subjective process which he calls fidelity (*BBE*, 201–64). But as any act of fidelity, any step in the unfolding of consequences, changes the given situation—for it produces something which did not exist before—there can be no rule or law which could regulate once and for all how a subject might forever remain faithful. The absolute contingency which provides the ground for this process can never be abolished and returns in any step of the unfolding of consequences. Fidelity thus remains a potentially infinite series of bets, wagers, since a throw of the dice will never abolish chance.

This contingency is also the reason why there are no immanent limitations to the process of unfolding consequences and thus what the event enables is by definition infinite.[95] This is where the axiom of infinity kicks in. It assures that the realm of consequences, the process that is the subject and that is the material unfolding of what the event will have been is constitutively infinite. One can thus claim that the Cartesian freedom here takes a very different shape with regards to infinity. Subjective freedom is no longer the instance which makes us Godlike because our freedom is infinite. Freedom rather first means to become a subject through a forced choice of "yes" or "no" with regards to an event. But what follows onto the first determinate affirmation is a potentially infinite series of determinate affirmations, which unfold the consequences of the absolutely contingent event. Thus freedom is that which is somehow made possible by the event and needs to be sustained and upheld no matter what—without any transcendental guarantee. This is what distinguishes Badiou from Descartes—as God is the transcendental guarantee embodied as the other in the subject. There is freedom only because of absolute contingency, because of the localization of the unthinkable void—which thereby becomes thinkable—but it is itself not infinite. What is infinite is the process in which the subject develops the consequences of the absolute contingency. *Infinite is the repetition of acts that force one to be free;* freedom is the result of a repetition of classicism and no infinite capacity. Since the proceeding of this unfolding operates via always finite choices—of "yes" and "no." *The subject is finite; what it produces is per se infinite.*

What is produced in this process of free subjective determination which is enabled by the emergence of absolute contingency is thus something eternal: an eternal truth. Badiou by thinking the three, the exception to what "there is" insists on thinking the true two. He thereby insists on repeating Descartes; on that fact there are *two notions of freedom* at stake. The democratic materialist one is similar to what Descartes claimed about the lowest degree of freedom:

> However, the indifference that I experience when there is no reason moving me more in one direction than in another is the lowest grade of freedom; it is indicative not of any perfection in freedom, but rather of a defect, that is, a certain negation in knowledge. (*DMFP*, 125)

This is what the freedom of individual and communal opinions about bodily desires articulated in allegedly free language discourses comes down to: *pure and simple indifference.* This is why Badiou, taking up Descartes, can claim that "the reactive subject is the subject who says the 'event is not important' and so on, but that is not unfaithfulness, it is a sort of indifference" (*BIT*, 188).[96] Therefore the suppression of the exception, of the real two—only graspable via thinking the three—leads to an identification of freedom with its lowest grade—indifference. Against the materialist dialectician Descartes insists that "the more I am inclined toward one direction . . . the more freely do I choose that direction. Nor indeed does divine grace or natural knowledge" (*DMFP*, 125). True freedom for Descartes and for Badiou consists in side taking. Only side taking—the absolutely free choice of God or the forced free choice of a worldly subject—is able to produce eternal truths.

One can thus sum up Badiou's disentanglement of the Cartesian theses: in the place of the Cartesian God stands the void—both are thinkable as being unthinkable, as *unthinkable being.* The place of the cogito became the discursive index—the empty set—of any situation of something which will always have been prior to the situation—already from the cogito one can come to thinking the unthinkable God. The notion of infinity and the notion of freedom are newly constellated. What for

Descartes was the *essence of freedom,* that is, absolute contingency, becomes in Badiou the very *condition of freedom.*

The notion of infinity is in both thinkers linked to freedom. But for Descartes infinity is the infinity of the will, while for Badiou infinity delineates the realm of consequences that a finite subject traversing the situation is able to unfold via finite bets. But thereby Badiou turns Descartes from his head onto his feet as only with this move it becomes intelligible how Badiou can still uphold Descartes's two claims: there are truths and truths are eternal; eternal truths are created within a world. The proper post-Cartesian materialist twist within Badiou's reception of Descartes lies in the claim that eternal truths are created, not by God, but by subjects; by subjects that are themselves the product of absolute contingency. By saying "yes" to that which was formerly unthinkable—unlocalized—and thus impossible, subjects come to be and they are able—in a Godlike fashion—to create something eternal by unfolding (potentially) infinite consequences. Subjects are thus not—as in Descartes—themselves truths but rather become the agents of a material, worldly creation of something infinite. A creation of eternity, here and now. Confronted with the impossible it becomes possible that they do the impossible: they create what in the seventeenth century only God was able to create.

This is one way of understanding the 11th thesis Badiou formulates at the end of his *Logics of Worlds*: "I need neither God nor the divine. I believe that it is here and now that we rouse or resurrect ourselves as Immortals" (*BLoW,* 513). This might be called one of the most important ingredients for any Cartesianism for the next century. What it teaches us is that we are more than our individual bodies are (able to). We can, here and now, live as immortals. *We can do and think the unthinkable.*

## Coda: Meta-Critical Anamnesis: Remembering the Impossible, or Cartesianism for the Twenty-First Century (to come)

> I am trying to be heroic in an age of modernity.
> —"Song for Clay," Bloc Party

> [A] new birth beyond all the facts and markers of time.
> —*BLoW,* 508

Rarely will one find a thinker who is more obsessed with understanding the last century than Alain Badiou. And rarely might one find someone whose diagnosis is more devastating. In one sentence for him: the twenty-first century has not yet begun. The reason for it is that we are still thinking—for example within the realm of political actions—in the terms of the twentieth century—we for example still refer to "revolution" in the way Lenin or Mao did although this clearly seems impossible today. This is why he called our times "a time of disorientation" ("BCP"). Now, this disorientation then can also be rendered as one direct effect of the (ideological) predominance of the fake two of democratic materialism over any materialist dialectical stance. We are all lost in the ossified realm of bodies and their pathological constitution (petty fetishisms, etc.), in the woods of the commerce of languages (the expression of arbitrary opinions), the alleged complexity of our individualities and their relationship to the communities we think we belong to even if we are arbitrarily born into them (family, nation, state, etc.). After what has been elaborated thus far, it might come as no surprise that against the contemporary disorientation of democratic materialism and its nihilistic counter-tendencies Badiou once again turns to Descartes. For in times where there is no principle of orientation, no true subjective position to take and any form of fidelity to past events seems to be suspended and the old means of fidelity are saturated, Descartes is the thinker to turn to. Why? Because the adventurer of subtraction also proposed the idea of a provisory morality for the time in which one did not already find an absolute certainty (*DM*, 56–57).[97]

Today contemporary disorientation is embodied in different forms of indifference: phenomena of indecision, fake- or non-engagement, and obsession with an allegedly free freedom of choice. Not to choose one side and insisting on the possibility of having the choice seems to be preferable to choosing anything at all. Today everyone seems to be obliged to choose without choosing—embedded and overly occupied with choices that are none.[98] This is the structure of the fake two of democratic materialism: choosing without taking sides; by opting for something without consequences; one seems to be lost within the endless games of saying "yes" and "no" at the same time. One is thus within the realm of the lowest degree of freedom. Actually, a quite fitting definition of contemporary capitalism.[99]

The organizational framework that democratic materialism establishes for this persistent non-choice are parliamentary elections that are, at least for Badiou, therefore ultimately nothing but an organization of indifference.[100] The contemporary infamous risk-society has at the same time abolished any risk[101]—the only risky business seems to be the financial one. The abolishment of any real choice immanently implies the omnipresence of the most permissive society ever seen and the predominance of an infinite realm of the possible—all that is possible necessarily

becomes necessary. The reliance on the category of the possible ultimately proves to have had three implications. (1) Having opted for the
possible implies that one always already has opted for one very specific
model of change, namely change as an extension of the possible. (2) It
shows that this process of extension implies that, say, equality can only be
thought gradually, again: as expansion of the possible.[102] (3) Siding with
the possible hence inevitably implies taking sides with the primacy of inequality over equality, due to the fact that inequality is always something
that seems impossible to any given realm of the possible. Equality thereby
becomes something one can maximally wait for.[103] Why? Because siding
with the possible implies that a change of what is possible becomes itself
impossible—and thereby one ends up with a historically specific realm
of possibilities that are actualizable. To expand, in a seemingly infinite
manner, what is possible is already to accept one final borderline: the
impossibility of organizing the impossibility of inegalitarian statements.

The possible is a stable, a statist regime that although it constantly
seems to change, never truly changes.[104] In other words, to side with the
regime of the possible is to support and advocate the actual state of things
and to stick to the actual state. The realm of the possible delineates a
specific form of a realm of thinkability.[105] Consequently, the seemingly
infinite extension of the possible is necessarily limited and finitized by
an always historically specific impossibility that it naturalizes as much as
it seeks to naturalize itself. This is why siding with the regime of the possible necessarily leads to a naturalizing propaganda of the given realm
of the possible.

Starting with the possible means naturalizing it and also naturalizing the impossibilities it specifically encounters. This is also why the most
fundamental paradigm of the possible today has become the natural.
Naturalization here means that the only orientation offered by the possible is inscribed in the axiomatic equation of: "existence = individual
= body" (BLoW, 2). What is possible is what is bodily and individually
natural. What is possible is what is there—in the form of bodies that
exist as natural entities determined by their needs and so forth. Therefore from the perspective of the regime of the possible what exists are
solely individual bodies and their "structure"; our appetites, our small
pleasures, our bodily needs is what one should stick to. The materialism
of the possible is in the last instance a materialism of the biological and
animal body that follows the paradigm of the naturally, the naturalized
possible.[106] The materialism implied here is "bio-materialism" (BLoW, 2);
a *bio-materialism of the possible.*

Badiou diagnoses with Descartes that today everyone seems to "be
imitating travelers who find themselves lost in some forest" (DM, 57).

CHAPTER 4

However, Descartes brought up this image of the traveler in the forest to afterwards propose a solution of what to do in moments when there is no principle of subjective orientation. For one

> should not wander about turning this way and that, nor, worse still, stop in one place, but should always walk in as straight a line as they can in one direction and never change it for feeble reasons, even if at the out- set it had perhaps been only chance that made them choose it; for by this means, even if they are not going exactly where they wish, at least they will eventually arrive somewhere where they will probably be better off than in the middle of a forest. (*DM*, 57)

Even the most contingent idea chosen by chance if one does stick to it, this is Descartes's point, can lead to some form of orientation. So what to learn from this for the contemporary situation? To limit the answer to a few Cartesian elements one can here even answer with a simple and con- densed formula: one has to *counter the reigning indifference* produced by democratic materialism *with a different form of indifference.*[107] This becomes clearer when one remembers one fundamental definition Badiou gives of what a truth is: "a making indifferent of the constituted knowledges."[108] This means that any truth—anything that truly has a universal dimen- sion although it is unfolded by finite subjects—disregards the established regimes of differences and particularities (individual, bodily, or commu- nal ones) and consists in the exemption of everything that "there is." So against the *disorienting indifference* of the fake two (of bodies and lan- guages) one needs to put up an orienting *subtractive indifference* of a true two which is constitutive of any "generic orientation of thought" (*BBE*, 510). This subtractive indifference minuses in fidelity to Descartes all the seemingly unavoidable particular differences and naturalizations implied in the "there is." Badiou has outlined what this act of *subtractive indifferen- tiation* has to entail that one is indifferent (1) with regard to numbers, (2) with regard to the established regime of the possible, (3) with regard to particularities, (4) with regard to the alleged antinomy between what is considered to be authoritarian and what is rather tolerant, and (5) with regard to the separation of repetition and projection ("BSP II"). The first point insists that the concept of "majority" is in itself not a criterion of truth—as Descartes already stated: "the majority opinion is worthless as a proof of truths" (*DM*, 53)—and that, say, ten militants are worth more than a zillion passive voters. The second point insists that the possible is a regime of repression and not of liberation. The third point insists that a truth can only begin from something which is immediately valid for anyone and disregards all attachment to particular life worlds and naturalized specificities. The fourth point insists that one cannot know in advance which form of discipline, which form of authority will have been adequate to create something new. Any true creation generates its own norms; it hence cannot be evaluated by a transcendental (external) standard, and this implies that one can never know in advance if someone will get hurt.[109] The fifth point finally insists that an exception is neither a simple repetition—it is not only a continuation of tradition—nor a pure projection; neither simply the old nor simply the new, for the idea of newness is always threatened to become a nicely marketable product.[110] Any dialectic of the exception entails rather a synthesis of repetition—as something unthinkable or impossible within a given historical situation already has taken place a couple of times before—and projection, a synthesis of singularity and universality. Such a synthesis is what Badiou calls an "idea."[111]

All these *strategic indifferences* are central elements of countering the fake two of democratic materialism which lies at the ground of the contemporary disorientation.[112] All these indifferences are needed to insist that there can be a split within the "there is," that is, an exception, to insist that there is a possibility of the impossible, of the contingent occurrence of an absolute contingency which allows for the doability and thinkability of the unthinkable.

Thus philosophy in times of disorientation does not have a critical duty in the classical or traditional meaning of critique. It does not only take a decisive distance towards the world of the "there is" and differentiates between what is and what ought to be. Rather, it has to take a radically post-Cartesian stance that nonetheless repeats Descartes: it has to come up with a renewed notion of the unthinkable, of absolute contingency or the contingent emergence of the absolute and it can only do so by remembering that something absolutely contingent already has taken place several times under different historical conditions. Thus *philosophy has to remain Cartesian in an unprecedented way*: it has to develop a Cartesianism for the present, for the twenty-first century (to come). But if nowadays the contemporary thinking of the two relies on a speculative meta-ontology, what such a Cartesianism must advocate is also *a meta-critical stance*.[113] This meta-critical stance philosophy can only take—propagating the thinkability of the unthinkable—if it remembers that within its own history it already fulfilled this task several times. It thus takes a meta-stance towards the simple idea of distancing oneself from the world as it is. It is rather a renewed way of conceiving of this distance in renewed historical circumstances. And philosophy already has been able to remind the individual that it can become a subject by recalling the contingent emergences of allegedly impossible events within the history of mankind. This is somehow akin to what Lacan said with reference to what happens in a true love when he claimed: "to give one's love is very precisely and essentially to give as such nothing of what one has."[114] Philosophy as love of wisdom does something similar: it recalls as such nothing of what one knows, *it recalls precisely the Nothing of what one knows as this is what is the subject. It insists that one has to remember what one never knew.* This is why philosophy (will) remain(s) Platonic.

One can thus understand Badiou's claim that

> the individual does not escape this fate. If it pleases you to come into being qua subject, you will be forced, as you well know, expressly and against all existing customs to found the party of yourself: harsh, concentrating force and the power of abnegation to an extreme point, and following its condition of existence which is not to love oneself too much. (*BTS*, 41)

This is to say: one does not only have to change the world of bodies, languages, individuals, and communities but also to become multiply indifferent towards it, one also has to change oneself. Because one can, without having the capacity to do it. One can because one already did. Philosophy's task against disorientation and against the reactionary interpretation of the primacy of the two is a means to remember the impossible in a new way, with new means. Philosophy recalls actions of the impossible, thoughts of the unthinkable under changed conditions. This is why for any contemporary actualization of Cartesianism it is imperative that philosophy is anamnestic and meta-critical. This is why philosophy is a *meta-critical anamnesis*. If, maybe in a thousand years, the twenty-first century will begin someday, *meta-critical anamnesis* will have been a preparation for this very beginning.

# 5

# Working Through

## What Is to Be Done with Philosophy?

> The nature of philosophy is that something is eternally being
> bequeathed to it. It has the responsibility of this bequeathal. You
> are always treating the bequeathal itself, always taking one more
> step in the determination of what was thus bequeathed to you.
> —A. Badiou

### The Nonexistence of Philosophical Subjects

One thing seems to be evident within the oeuvre of Alain Badiou: there
are no philosophical subjects. There does not seem to be any question
about this. Philosophy does not include any effective subject position; no
subject is in itself, *an sich*, philosophical. And it also seems to be quite evident why that is. Any subject following the Badiousian definition is a finite
and locally active agent of a process of unfolding the consequences of an
event. Consequently, there are or there can only be subjects where there
can be events and hence there can only be subject within the conditions
of philosophy, within love, politics, art, and science, but there cannot be
any within philosophy. This means that the claim "that there are no philosophical subjects" can be directly inferred from another one, from the
answer to another question, namely: can there be philosophical events?

The straightforward answer Badiou gives, and has been giving,
throughout his work is: no. No, philosophy cannot produce any events
and therefore it cannot comprise any subjects. Why that is also becomes
easily evident. What is produced by a finite and local agent of the post-
evental unfolding of consequences is what he calls a truth. But there is no
doubt about one thing: there are no philosophical truths—as there is, for
example, no single philosophical claim, argument, or thesis about which
within the history of philosophy there has not been some sort of quarrel,

some philosopher contesting the concept of another. It still holds what Descartes wrote in his *Discourse on Method*: "Concerning philosophy I shall say only that . . . there still is nothing in it about which there is not some dispute, and consequently nothing that is not doubtful. . . ." (*DM*, 49). Therefore for all philosophers it is still valid what he inferred from this: "I was not at all so presumptuous as to hope to fare any better there than the others" (*DM*, 49). To formulate this in more technical terms, that philosophy can defend truth but cannot produce truth leads to the insight that one cannot justifiably claim that philosophy has a truth-effect, for example in the sense that it could or would render truths possible, could or would generate the very conditions of possibility of a truth which then would be developed by a subject within an extra-philosophical situation. To put it in Badiou's own words in which Descartes's resonate: "if philosophy has truth procedures as conditions, this signifies that it does not itself produce truths. In fact, this situation is quite well-known: who can cite a single philosophical statement which one can meaningfully say is 'true'?" (*BMPHI*, 35).

So philosophy does not know any subjects, since it also does not imply in its practice the possibility of an event or of a truth. However, philosophy—as meta-critical anamnesis—has a task that can be characterized as much by its radical simplicity as by its renewed historical complexity, something that turns the formally simple task to be concretely a quite difficult one. It is simple because throughout its history philosophy never did anything but sustain and articulate in different historical contexts and thus in different historical styles the claim that there are truths (*BC*, 23),[1] the claim that there is something absolute, non-relative—in its history it did do so even by reference to God. But this task is at the same time quite difficult because philosophy, precisely due to the varying historical setting and circumstances within which it has to repeat its gesture, can never just repeat the previous ways of articulations of this claim. It *cannot* claim *the same it in the same manner*. It has to repeat but cannot repeat the old form of repeating; it has to repeat, yet it has to investigate how to do it. Philosophy always has to come up with and invent new means. It has to come up with a new and different philosophical style for the same claim. Only thereby can it uphold its essential thesis: that there are truths.

This is why taking into account the history of philosophy one can dissect the shape of what Badiou calls a *creative repetition* ("BPCR")— creative because it has to find new means of articulation and because it is conditioned by what happens in the extra-philosophical fields of practice and thought, this is to say it is conditioned by events taking place in love, science, art, and politics—and it is repetitive because it is only creative to newly reestablish its old and never-changing claim. Philosophy has to be repetitive, for if it were not there once could exist something like a last and final articulation of its claim. One could thus imagine an overcoming of its historical conditioning and also something like a final stage of philosophy, a complete revelation after which everything changes and then nothing will ever change again. This radical overcoming of its own historicity one might even call—by recourse to the traditional and stereotyped renderings of Hegel—the *Hegelian threat to philosophy*.

There are no philosophical subjects. But to fulfill the task of philosophy and to be at the height of its own time, the philosopher has to be radically attentive to everything that is happening in the extra-philosophical conditions. This is why for any philosopher, "Custos quid noctis?"[2] is the essential question, because "a philosopher is a poor night watchman," as Badiou once wrote, who stays "awake" and is "not allowed to sleep" as he attends the moment in which he can finally proclaim that we all have to "wake up as the time for thinking and acting is here" ("BPCR"). This is also the reason why he can claim that any philosopher himself has to be in some sense a political militant, a scientist or mathematician, an artist and a part of an amorous subject. Or to be more precise:

> Philosophy is very close to love but without the violent support of desire, very close to political engagement but without the constraint of a centralized organization, very close to artistic creation but without the sensible means of art, very close to scientific cognition but without the formalism of mathematics or the empirical and technical means of physics. ("BPCR")

This passage should be read as a postulate that anyone in philosophy has

> to practice the conditions of philosophy. To know and to study modern poetry, to work through recent mathematics, to endure and to think the two of love, to be militant in political invention—such is the strict minimum to be expected of those who claim to be philosophers.[3]

Without such minimal practice of the conditions the philosophers would and could not know what to look for, would not and could not even dare to take the risk of calling something, say, in politics "eventual." Philosophy would thereby simply become identical with the university discourse, that is, with an administration of knowledge that in its contemporary form, namely analytic philosophy, is just another version of positivism (of existence)[4]—but this ultimately leads to abolishing the category of truth *tout court* or identifying it with more or less complex procedures of rule following.[5] Yet, the abolishment of the category of truth implies the self-abolishment of philosophy.

So, there are no philosophical subjects but the philosopher has to be on the lookout for new political, artistic, scientific, or amorous subjects, unfolding post-evental truths. And this is why Badiou claims that the future of philosophy depends on its "capacity for progressive adaption to the change of its conditions" ("BPCR"). Without being able to detect, to track, and to name subjects—subjects that "exist only in the strict order of one of the four types of genericity" (*BMPHI*, 106)—and without being able to think the truths they deploy, without these tracking skills philosophy could precisely not do its job. It could not create a space sui generis for different, seemingly incompatible truths that emerged in different domains, a space in which they become compossible after all, that is to say where one can think of what they have in common precisely because they are truths. The future of philosophy thus depends on the philosopher's practice of the conditions, on the skill of recognizing the impossible yet emerging events and their effects as something new which then forces philosophy to reshape and redefine itself, its means, its guise. This is what it means that a philosopher has to practice the conditions, for philosophy in its perpetuated creative repetition is first and foremost an act, an action. But what is this action that is philosophy? Badiou answers: "Philosophy is first and foremost this: the invention of new problems."[6] The act of philosophy is hence a *creative problematization*. Philosophy as creative problematization is an invention, the invention of a yet unseen problem—of a problem not so much for and of philosophy but of the political, amorous, artistic, and so on situation. This is why the philosophical act which is a creatively repeated problematization essentially implies, as demonstrated in the first chapter, (1) a decision, a separation, a clear distinction—say between knowledge and opinion, truth and falsity. Philosophy is an active incision of a line of demarcation that necessarily contains (2) a hierarchy.

This is to say that the distinction that philosophy's problematization introduces implies a normative, hierarchical dimension, a hierarchy between the two sides that the philosophical act itself inscribes. Therefore problematization is always problematization of the evident, the naturalized given. Philosophy is never neutral, but always partisanship. It is the creative repetition of a normative separating and problematizing act, a hierachizing action which attacks the dominant current. This is why philosophy is always an action which creatively de-naturalizes the evidences of an artistic, political, and so on situation. But why should that be the case? The answer again is quite clear: because philosophy is precisely *occupied with that which is not*. As Badiou puts it: "So we can say that philosophy, which is the thought, not of what there is, but of what is not what there is (not of contracts, but of contracts broken), is exclusively interested in relations that are not relations."[7] This can easily be made evident. If philosophy's only claim is that there are truths and truths are always the result of a procedure of unfolding the consequences of an unforeseeable, this is to say previously considered to be impossible event by faithful subjects within the conditions, this means that philosophy deals with that which is not there before the event, that which—as any event—stands in a relation of exception to what there is. Philosophy does not think what is there, it does not even think the "*is*" of what is there—because philosophy is *not ontology*—but it thinks what "is" exceptional to the "is" of "what there is." It thinks what *supplements* being, it focuses on truths made possible by events and deployed by decided and determined subjects. Philosophy is thus occupied with exceptions to what there is, exceptions that force people to decide and say "yes" (or "no") to an unpredictable event, which force a determinate affirmation, a decision, and create a distance to the pure and simple there is. Philosophy's repeated creative act of problematization is centered around these categories: *decision, distance, exception.* Exception to what there is, distance to the realm of the naturalized given, decision of a subject within the conditions. This is why philosophy in its very essence is not democratic, because decisions and their consequences, the affirmed distance to what there is and the exception to it are also not democratic by nature and they are the very material basis of philosophical thought. Philosophical action as such is by definition a non-democratic action.[8]

So, there are no philosophical subjects but there is something like a philosophical act. *Philosophy is an action without a subject,* to rephrase this in Althusserian terms.[9] But if there are no and there cannot be any philosophical subjects, one may raise the following question in mind: Who is it that proclaims the very nonexistence of the philosophical subjects? From which position is it articulated? That there are no philosophical subjects is clearly neither a political, artistic, amorous, nor a scientific claim. And the place of its enunciation as it is valid for philosophy *tout court* can also not be political, scientific, and so on. So therefore it can only be the philosopher, philosophy itself which declares and announces the nonexistence of philosophical subjects. *Philosophy to remain philosophy proclaims the nonexistence of its very own subjects.* This again makes perfect sense as philosophy is precisely occupied with that which is not, with that which inexists, thus it has to declare that there is an action of that which is not, of that which seems impossible, of that which inexists. So, the claim "there are no philosophical subjects" is what a proper subtractive (but also essentially, affirmative) claim looks like. This is why philosophy not only claims that there are truths but can only claim that there are truths on the condition that there are extra-philosophical conditions of philosophy in which there are subjects and by excluding philosophical subjects.

So, philosophy declares, even prescribes the nonexistence of philosophical subjects to avoid the historically false and megalomaniac idea that truths might originate in philosophy. It would otherwise no longer be in a position of the owl of Minerva, the philosopher would no longer be a lonely night watchman but he would rather and maybe also harshly cry along with the Gallic rooster, to which Marx once referred.[10] In such a rendering thought would maybe not precede being, but it would precede truths. And one can immediately see why this would be highly inconsistent. Because it would lead into the paradox that thought would precede thought (since truths are nothing but products of thought). That thought precedes thought is precisely what can be deemed to be the idealist formula. Now, to avoid the danger of a simplified idealism and of idealizing itself, philosophy has to repeatedly insist that there cannot be any philosophical subject. Philosophy cannot fulfill its task all by itself. Otherwise it would give in to the temptation of addressing not that which is not but would start with something that is (or ought to be). Philosophy to remain philosophy has to start from inexistence and this inexistence is first and foremost the inexistence of its own subject. Philosophy has to start philosophically with a proclamation of inexistence: it claims that there *is* something that inexists. And the philosophical subject's place is precisely that which *is* but does not exist.[11]

## Philosophy Today: Saturation, Reaction, Obscurity

So there are no philosophical subjects. But to resume: philosophy is an action that creatively is repeated as a way of problematizing the naturalized given order; an action which inscribes a normative, a hierarchized distinction and thus affirms the necessity of a choice (and thereby of change) and insists on the possibility of truths which always stand in exception to that which is just there and hence it affirms that which is not. All of this sounds undemocratic. So what is the status of philosophy today under the obvious reign of what Badiou once called our holy cow, namely democracy? How is the contemporary philosophical situation in objective democracy?

To give an adequate diagnosis, one can again start with some very simple, empirical observations. Philosophy as such finds itself attacked everywhere right now. Philosophy departments are being closed, analytical philosophy reigns within the departments—claiming that the essence of truth is accessible by referring to the linguistic form of our everyday judgments—anti-intellectualists in power-positions are not even bothered anymore with claiming that those doctors unable to cure anybody are worth nothing, they simply abolish the conditions of their very existence. Thus the practice and thought of that which stands in exception to what there is, seems to be confronted with quite exceptional times. Philosophy betting on the exception of evental truths under the reign of democracy becomes threatened in and due to its non-democratic substance. As Badiou put it in his first *Manifesto*: "We shall thus posit that there are four conditions of philosophy, and that the lack of a single one gives rise to its dissipation" (*BMPHI*, 35). And in an interview he claimed that there have been periods in which there has been "pretty much no or very little politics like at the end of the Roman Empire."[12] Today we seem to be in an exceptional situation, philosophically speaking. One of the conditions seems to have disappeared, namely politics as it became fully identified with the administration of goods and people that are treated in an even less sympathetic way than the objects are; identified with bureaucracy and thus with the state and all this ultimately is but a proof of systemic corruption. But *corruption*—remember that this term appears when there are people who neither want virtue nor terror[13]—as inter alia Varlam Shalamov made clear in his literary writings,[14] has always been the name for the absence of any active collective political project. *Corruption is what appears when politics disappears.*[15]

Today under objective democratic conditions, corruption is what comes out of a democracy of objects, to use this slightly Latourian formula,[16] a democracy which objectivizes and naturalizes what there is. Corruption thus does not only result from the over-presence of reactive or obscure subjects,[17] but their labor as it seems has become much easier, since there has been a saturation of the sequence previously effective in the political condition. The exceptional situation philosophy faces is a *historically specific linkage of saturation, reaction, and obscuration.*[18] Here it is important to proceed step by step. First one needs to understand how a truth procedure can be saturated. Then one can grasp how this very saturation can play in the hands of the reaction and only then one is able to see how all of this generates an exceptional situation for the discipline, for the *endeavour of exceptions*, as one may call philosophy. So why is emancipatory politics today saturated at least with regards to the form that was still active in the twentieth century? And what does saturation of a truth procedure mean? "Saturation" names a concept first developed by Sylvain Lazarus. He developed what he calls the "method of saturation" in his 1996 *Anthropology of the Name* where he defines it in the following way:

> I call "method of saturation" the examination, from the interiority of a work or a thought, which leads to the expiry of one of its fundamental

categories. It thus deals with questioning the work from the point of
the expiry of the category and to re-identify it in this new conjuncture.
(*LAN*, 36)

Saturation names a way of conceiving of the end of the consequences of
a process of thought from a perspective that does not imply any exterior
position of normative evaluation. It is the way to analyze from within the
immanence of a procedure in its own terms, while not taking into account
any other—external—causes. Against this background it is intelligible
that Badiou can apodictically claim in his *Metapolitics*: "a political sequence
does not terminate or come to an end because of external causes, or
contradictions between its essence and its means, but through the strictly
immanent effect of its capacities being exhausted . . . In other word, failure is not relevant here" (*BMP*, 127). In the philosophical analysis of the
end of a truth procedure saturation is hence a counter-category against
the reactionary category of failure—which always tends to too swiftly con-
demn, say, communist politics as simple criminal wrongdoing. It precisely
addresses the question of termination, and more specifically the question
of the termination of "something" which, at least potentially, does not
need to know an end: a generic truth procedure. A termination is conceived of by Lazarus as a transition of what he calls a "political mode," or
what Badiou calls a political truth procedure from its "historicity" (that is
to say historical effectivity, *Wirklichkeit*) to its "intellectuality" (i.e., to the
possibility of offering a balance sheet) (*LAN*, 41). As long as a political
mode is effective and operating, it cannot be adequately and conceptually
comprehended, simply because it still transforms what it will have been.
For Lazarus politics manifests in the material form of actions and organizations performed by subjects and, as he specifies, subjects think, which
implies that actions and organizations are the manifestation of thought.
Politics is a matter of thought and subjects. But what thus immanently has
been thought can again only be apprehended by (philosophical) thought
after the—either abrupt or slow—disappearance of these actions, organizations, and subjects. And as this termination can only be explained as a
consequence of the actions of the thinking subjects involved, it can only
be thoroughly grasped by thinking what they thought.

Here again the famous Hegelian insight holds that that the "owl of
Minerva begins its flight only with the falling of dusk" (*HOP*, 16). Saturation is needed to conceive of what has been thought and what has been
bequeathed to those who want to think what has been thought. For "the
method of saturation distinguishes between what is thought in a thinking
in the moment where it has taken place and on the other hand, between
what has been thought in thought when the mode is closed" (*LAN*, 42). It

thus presents a way of explaining the disappearing, the dis-activation of a truth procedure. This is also why it lies at the heart of, and more precisely, constitutes what the later Badiou calls a "sequence"[19] or in earlier terminology a "period."[20] Any sequence ends with saturation and ultimately this means only saturation makes a sequence into a sequence.

One further way of framing the essential insight behind what Badiou addresses with this concept is that all that exists deserves to perish. This is, although it is rarely taken into account, also valid for truth procedures—since this is why they are sequential—and this even holds if Badiou states that "of no truth can it be said, under the pretext that its historical world has disintegrated, that it is lost forever" (*BLoW*, 66). Truths can never be lost forever but their effectivity, their *generic reality*, as one might put it, can be weakened; it can disappear, disintegrate, because it can become saturated. Saturation names the *termination of a procedure which can never be lost* because it is eternal. The question is hence how to understand this concatenation of eternity and termination, of infinity and finitude. Understanding the exceptional status of philosophy right now, if the "now" depicts a situation of saturation, radically depends on this. If any actions within any procedure of fidelity—be it a political debate, a late night conversation between two lovers, the development of a theorem from scientific axioms, or a stylistic transformation within playwriting—changes the situation in which it takes place, it can be said that one needs to find new means to remain faithful in a changed (which changed precisely due to previous acts of fidelity) situation.

Fidelity always immanently poses the question of how to continue because there can be no law, no rule that could indicate once and for all how to remain faithful under changed circumstances.[21] This is on the one hand why a procedure of fidelity is immanently (potentially) infinite—there is no internal reason why it should terminate—but also on the other this is why it can end. It can end because it can get increasingly difficult to find new means of sustaining fidelity. The failure to renew and invent new means for the continuation of a procedure of fidelity is the cause for saturation. It is what designates a lack of means of fidelity—an immanent failure even with regard to the norms it itself started from. It thus neither refers to a spontaneous rupture nor to a "simple betrayal" but to the progressive difficulty to remain someone (a subject) who remains faithful.

With reference to politics one can clarify this point: there has been, since the mid-1970s, a saturation of revolutionary politics in its traditional framework (of class struggle, political parties, etc.), Badiou even claimed that the word "revolution" itself became saturated, unreadable. This means that it became progressively more and more difficult to find new means to remain faithful to the idea of the revolution after the failure(s) of the Russian and the Chinese Cultural Revolution. It became increasingly difficult as all the means the Russian and the Chinese revolutionaries employed did not hinder certain misdoings with regard to the own universalist norms according to which they tried to act. This is one crucial reason for the violent outcomes that in the last instance led to a transformation of the political procedure into a failed execution of power after taking it in Russia, or to a state-terrorist bureaucracy in China. This was precisely due to central operators of these specific truth procedures (the linkage of politics to power, of power to the state, of the state to the idea of its withering away). On the level of this "first fidelity" of the (Russian or Chinese) collective subject(s) attempting to remain faithful to the idea of emancipatory and revolutionary politics, these procedures became saturated. The saturation that has befallen the two sequences of the "communist hypothesis" materialized in the following way: the first sequence (from the French Revolution, 1792, to the Paris Commune, 1871) combined under the label "communism" mass movements, the idea of overthrowing the state and of taking power. This was what the word "revolution" indicated at this time. But the Paris Commune materialized in its entirely new exercise of power the strictly immanent limitations of this first sequence as it was not able to sustain this exercise against counterrevolutionary tendencies.

The second sequence now (from the Russian Revolution, 1917, to the Cultural Revolution) was occupied with problems the first one was unable to solve: how to organize power after taking it, so that the counterrevolution can be suppressed? Lenin answered this by proposing the form of the revolutionary class-party which organized the newly gained power. Yet, the Communist Party was unable to organize the transition to the dictatorship of the proletariat as it led to a state which became at the same time authoritarian and terrorist by withdrawing from the idea of the decline of the state and hence from the "communist hypothesis" as such. From this perspective, one can understand what happened with the last events of the second sequence—with May 1968 and the Cultural Revolution—that were precisely attempts to overcome these immanent limitations. But all of them internally failed as they proved unable to loosen the knot between party, power, and state. They bear witness to the immanent impossibility to free politics from the frame of the party-state that limited, even imprisoned it. This nonetheless delineates for Badiou the significance of the Cultural Revolution, of the "last revolution" (*BCH*, 101–68): it is still immanent to the party-state model (the Chinese Communist Party) and saturates it. Saturation thus does not only indicate a singular, but unavoidable and saddening outcome of a universalist procedure, rather it also marks something new: since without saturation taking place in the political condition in the 1960s and 1970s, nothing would as yet be thinkable outside the party-state model, outside the classical Marxist framework.[22]

Saturation always marks an irreplaceable experience of immense significance as it conditions the contemporary situation that followed it. This is also why with regard to a saturated sequence one always has a choice. Either one advocates a negative interpretation of saturation (one claims something like: "One cannot but repeat what happened and was experimented in the saturated sequence")—any attempt to be a Leninist today would opt for this stance—a dogmatic interpretation (an attempt to remain faithful in an abstract and nostalgic way to lifeless and obsolete ideas, ignoring the changed historical setting, which is what an "old Marxist"[23] does), or an affirmative interpretation (one claims: "With the help of new events one can find a new fidelity to—the first failed—fidelity"). Here it can be clearly seen that all the reactionaries and even the renegades defend a negative interpretation of the two last sequences of the communist hypothesis. A fidelity to fidelity is neither a simple continuation of the first procedure of fidelity nor is it a break with it. It rather consists in the insistence on the fact that to remain faithful to what has been thought in the saturated sequence, and which will always have been a truth, that is to say by definition eternal, one needs new means and fundamentally renewed and reworked operators of fidelity. The affirmative interpretation thus leads to a renewed concept of what, say, emancipatory politics could be today after a saturated sequence. It can do so by starting ex negatively: the saturation of the last sequence has demonstrated that political emancipation cannot begin with questions of power, the state, or party-like organization (but only "in distance from the state").[24] Saturation is thus not a category that implies pessimism. It rather makes it possible from the proper immanent comprehension of a termination—a singular truth is saturated by its own norms—to an affirmation in the following form: although this saturated procedure will have unfolded eternally valid universal consequences, the situation has changed and one does need new means for a *fidelity to fidelity.*[25] Saturation thus in thinking the end of a truth also implies the important exigency and the affirmation to think the newness (of the condition of art, politics, love, or science).

## Philosophy without Politics? The Barred
## Barred Subject and Philosophical Forcing

Today the dominant ideology of democratic materialism and its reactionary and obscurantist proponents are also feeding on the effects of the saturation of the communist hypothesis within the political realm. And as any effective non-saturated procedure within the condition also presents a means of subjective orientation, it becomes apparent why the saturation of such a procedure immediately produces disorientation. For disorientation is always related to subjective action and thought. This can even be described in a Boltanski–Chiapello-like fashion as an assimilation of the very means that once have been revolutionary and emancipatory: like the party. The party once had been a crucial revolutionary tool, but today it is fully assimilated by the parliamentary system.[26] This is why today it seems completely futile to hope for political emancipation while founding a new party.[27] The fundamental ideological name of this immediate assimilation of former emancipatory means is today the name "democracy." "Democracy" is the hegemonic name, the signifier that today obscures all former emancipatory means.[28] It obscures for example the very idea of a revolutionary party since the contemporary rendering of what democracy is and should be gives any party immediately a capitalist-parliamentary guise. In this way democracy functions in a way such that it presents itself as the only natural and thinkable end of history.[29] Therefore it came as no surprise that in a more or less recent newspaper article on Occupy Wall Street the criticism arose that their display of solidarity with the uprisings in the Arab countries was basically a gesture of Western decadence, since what the Arab people strive for would be nothing but (Western) democracy. Their uprising is an expression of a "desire for the occident" (*BRH*, 76).[30] This is why, as the article continues, within democracy it simply makes no sense to again strive for what one already has. Democracy in this precise sense functions as a name which attempts to naturalize the realm of the given in a way—relying as I elaborated before on the idea of an infinite extension of the possible—which fundamentally abolishes all political desire—as there cannot be anything else to desire than that which the democratic regime has already brought about. Any reactionary subject's position is hence linked to the obscurantist claim that whatever one desires politically, this desire already is satisfied, simply because we are within democracy and democracy is the only thing to desire politically. Any political desire is abolished by the pretension of its constant fulfillment: subjective desire is always already objectively satisfied by the objective installation of democracy, by the democracy of objects, which turns this desire into a something already objectively accomplished.

And this can be done even more easily as one of the means to think what was experienced under the name of communism, namely philosophical thought, is threatened because of its essentially non-democratic nature. Democratic materialism emphasizes the natural, the naturalized realm of the given—be it languages or bodies—and opposes everything non-democratic materialist as being per se non-democratic, even terrorist. This is why what is also attacked in the condemnation of communism is philosophy. As implausible as it may seem: the condemnation of communism is a condemnation of thought *tout court* and hence also of philosophy. Philosophy as a non-democratic endeavor of exceptions and as problematization of the naturalized given is an enemy of democratic materialism; it is therefore treated as any enemy of democratic materialism is treated: it is considered to be useless as long as it does not change its very essence and becomes identical with the university discourse (analytic philosophy is precisely the outcome of this maneuver; a "philosophy" that implies a fake dialectics of a fake two of bodies and languages). This is what philosophy today faces, and this is due to one very fundamental fact: democracy itself became the name of a reactionary regime of the natural, of the fake two of naturalized bodies and always already given, that is, allegedly complete languages.

So philosophy does not know any subjects, but the question can be raised what it can do in times in which one of its conditions seems to be absent, in times of saturation of a previous procedure, in times of disorientation. What I want to suggest is that it is precisely in those times that *philosophy needs to do what it cannot do, it needs to do the impossible and this is absolutely necessary*. This is what I want to refer to under the heading of *philosophical forcing*.[31] Two short remarks on the concept of forcing in general. (1) The method of forcing indicates a transition from truth to knowledge or to be more precise: it names the effects that an effective truth procedure has on a given realm of knowledge within a given historical situation.[32] As soon as any subject starts to develop evental consequences—and a faithful subject is after the forced "yes/no" choice immediately within the realm of consequences—there is also a modification, a transformation of the domain of knowledge. This is why one can claim that "although incomplete, a truth authorizes anticipations of knowledge . . . about *what will have been if the truth reaches completion*" (*BC*, 138). Thus forcing (as a necessary element of any truth procedure) restructures, changes the given realm of knowledge precisely through these anticipations of what will have been consequences of the truth that is in the process of unfolding.[33] This is why it is the hypothesis, the "powerful fiction of a completed truth . . . Starting with such a fiction, I can force new bits of knowledge without even verifying this knowledge" (*BIT*, 65). (2) It can do so because it starts from the powerful hypothesis that a truth procedure (although this is by definition impossible) can be totalized and thus would know an immanent end.[34] By starting from this very hypothesis it can produce new terms within knowledge, it forces them into knowledge. It thus produces something which within the given realm of knowledge did not exist before. But, and this is essential, forcing is an essential feature of any truth procedure, but clearly not of philosophy—because philosophy does not entail any truth procedures. Any truth procedure affects knowledge; philosophy not comprising any truth processes does not entail forcing. So, how and why should philosophy be able to force anything?

I take my cue from a short formulation from Badiou, in which he remarked in passing talking about forcing that: "I have conceived of this power—which Freud perhaps already named with the category of "working through"—under the name of forcing" (*BC*, 138). This is instructive. Forcing is working through, that is, working through the given presentation of elements, working through the situation. Now, if philosophy, as I have shown in the previous chapters, has to work through (dialectics, materialism, etc.) this means: philosophy can force terms into knowledge, but the whole question is, which ones can it force? Any ideology, and also the ideology of democratic materialism, consists in the modification and primarily naturalization of a certain historically and specific knowledge. Thus the democratic materialist modifies and naturalizes the knowledge of the situation that considers anything but the realm of bodies and languages, anything absolute to be unthinkable and impossible. Political events and truths are rendered unthinkable by such a naturalization and this is to say by this obscuration of knowledge.

What I call *philosophical forcing* is a method of counter naturalization. It functions as a *counter-ideology*,[35] as an ideological exception, as an exception to the hegemonic naturalizing ideology. It de-naturalizes. *Philosophical forcing* is a method to reinscribe a certain knowledge into a situation in which it has been lost or rather obscured—for example by negative interpretations of saturated sequences. *Philosophical forcing* is a means of working through knowledge, the knowledge of that which right now seems to be impossible. For—and this is one very precise point of struggle—events have been possible and philosophy affirms this very impossible possibility. This means that *philosophical forcing* implies a transition into or within the domain of knowledge. But as philosophy does not comprise any subjects it has to be rendered differently than the effects a truth procedure has on the knowledge of a given situation. I want to suggest that the transition philosophy produces within knowledge is one *from an objective domain of knowledge into a subjective domain of knowledge*. It forces the obscured knowledge that the new (that which right now seems impossible) already has been converted into a new possibility in a different previous situation.

The concept of "working through" appears for the first time in the famous text by Freud published in 1914 under the title "Remembering, Repeating and Working Through."[36] Working through (as name for philosophical forcing) hence is and should be related to the two other Freudian categories: remembering and repetition. This is what one can get from the reference to Freud's title alone. Here one infers that what the idea of philosophical forcing indicates can only be rendered adequately when one performs a similar move to the one Žižek performed with regards to the Lacanian triad of the imaginary, the symbolic, and the real.[37] All the involved elements should be mutually related to one another. The same goes for the idea of philosophical forcing when considered in terms of working through. Now: what is philosophical forcing? It is a *worked-through form of remembering*, it is a *worked-through way of repetition*—this is why it is creative—and it is a *worked-through manner of working through*. What does this mean?

*Worked-through remembering* means that philosophy in its very operation has to be anamnestic in the old Platonic sense. Philosophy is essentially Platonic. This means that it has to remind the human animal that the impossible possibility of an event became possible before. Philosophy to remain philosophy has to take up this task; philosophy remains philosophy if it reminds the human animal of the possibility of truths.

*Worked-through repetition* means that philosophy constantly—due to historical specificity—has to rearticulate in new ways the very form of how it reminds. All true philosophy is Platonic but there is more than just one way to be a Platonist. This is why philosophy while clarifying the situation does not itself directly or immediately, that is ultimately to say, critically, intervene into it. Philosophy is rather a *meta-critical* endeavor constantly repeating the creative gesture of bringing up and inventing new means for its anamnestic task.

*Worked through working through* is precisely what I call *philosophical forcing*, or to put it differently: working through working through delineates the consequences that the renewed means of philosophical anamnesis produce in the historically specific situation. This is due to the fact that *philosophical forcing* concerns the transition from objective to subjective knowledge. *Philosophical forcing*—working through working-through—consists in the hypothetical assumption, it implies the inscription of the prescription that there always is a choice. This is not directly synonymous with choosing but is rather the *insistence on the very form of a choice*; it is not directly an orientation but it recalls *the very form of subjective orientation* in disoriented times; it is not an anticipation of what will have been the consequences of a truth in a situation, but it clings to the *very form of anticipation*. The operation of philosophical forcing thus can be rendered in one simple formula: there are anticipations, there is orientation, or *there is a choice, always*. In the absence of one of the conditions of philosophy (namely politics) the forcing of the impossible possibility of a choice is what philosophy does. In obscure times it is only philosophy that forces us to think, not by actually forcing thought but by preparing the necessary prerequisites for it. These prerequisites have to be remembered, repeated, worked through. *Philosophical forcing* is a means of philosophy as *meta-critical anamnesis of the impossible*. And this is what philosophy can do in disoriented times.

So, there are no philosophical subjects but there is a philosophical act that today has to take the form of the operation of forcing. One might here add that this does not only split materialism from within but this very act also splits democracy into two: it distinguishes the objective dimension of democracy, the democracy of objects from its subjective dimension, and, obviously, one name of this dimension is communism. Here the reader may counter: without the power of an effective and active truth procedure, without the activity and presence of a subject such an operation of forcing is impossible. And of course, this is obviously correct. No forcing without a subject that unfolds the consequences of a truth within a situation. This is the reason why I want to suggest that from time to time, in exceptional times, but, maybe, always, there needs to be a philosophical subject—that is a *hypothetical subject, an anticipated subject* which holds the place open for a new political subject (but the same goes, as should be clear, for any condition in its absence). The philosophical subject is not a subject forcing knowledge into a situation but it produces a forced shift from the objective domain of knowledge into the subjective, or put differently: it takes the position of the very form of the subject (in the conditions). And as any subject within the conditions is a barred subject, and the philosophical subject is conditioned by the four conditions, the philosophical subject necessarily has to be conceived of as being barred twice.

*The philosophical subject is a barred barred subject*[38]—it is once barred as any subject is in the conditions barred and it has to be barred twice because it does not appear as a subject in the conditions.[39] The philosophical subjects thus would not be some sort of meta-subject (or super-subject) encompassing all others. It rather would be a *subject supposed to remember, repeat, and work through* the thought of loving, militant, artistic, scientific subjects and the impossible actions they already performed. If philosophy needs to think the fidelity to fidelity and has to offer an affirmative interpretation of (even saturated) sequences, philosophy not to become a fully futile intellectual enterprise from time to time has itself to do the impossible. It has to *recall the impossible* as this is one way to render *why we simply should not want to understand ourselves as being nothing but animals*.[40] In such a way, philosophy can intervene, it can be engaged philosophy. It can do so by precisely being a meta-critical anamnesis employing the *necessary but impossible means of philosophical forcing*. And, of course, this raises one question: Does this not lead us back to Hegel?

# 6

# Working Through
# Working Through

## The Immanence of Thought, or Returning
## to Hegel?

> I don't much like hearing that we have *gone beyond* Hegel, the
> way one hears we have *gone beyond* Descartes. We go beyond
> everything and always end up in the same place.
> —J. Lacan

> It is Hegel who is right, as always.
> —*BTS*, 4

## Badiou's Unknown Hegel

Alain Badiou is well known for being a fierce critique of Hegel. And in
the previous chapters I indicated many possible options of why this is.
Badiou once stated with regard to his political position: "there are two
ways of rescuing the idea of communism in philosophy today; either by
abandoning Hegel, not without regret, incidentally and only after repeated considerations of his writings (which is what I do), or by putting
forward a different Hegel, an unknown Hegel" (*BCH*, 237–38). Badiou
opts for an abandonment of Hegel. Another option of how to relate to
Hegel, he suggests, is the rereading of Hegel undertaken by Žižek, a
revamping of a different Hegel that serves the project of a revivification
of communism. However, Badiou makes it clear that he also does take
his distance from the latter path. But the very reasons for his abandonment of Hegel are not that easy to grasp (at least if one assumes that he
avoids the stereotypic cliché-picture of Hegel). Interestingly enough, all

the criticisms of Hegel Badiou formulated are linked to a stage in the development of his own system. Subsequently this will be an attempt to understand his reasons for abandoning Hegel. I take this to be the crucial, complicated, and technical, yet necessary step not only to understand Badiou's own position but also to conceive of any future reading of Hegel. Let me put this more straightforwardly: if Badiou's conception of philosophy can be rendered as what I call meta-critical anamnesis and therefore it essentially implies a renewal of materialism in the sense of an idealism without idealism; if also this philosophical project seeks to be contemporary to our times and hence needs to employ the means of philosophical forcing, the crucial question is, how do we stand with regard to Hegel?

My argument in the following will initially be a very simple one and work like this: Badiou is right in criticizing Hegel for what he criticizes Hegel, and the Hegel Badiou attacks should be abandoned, and yet this is the question I want to raise from a Badiousian perspective: what if there is a Hegel that is unknown to Badiou himself? What if there is a Hegel that can serve as a very useful, maybe even necessary supplement to Badiou's own endeavor? I will in the following demonstrate why Badiou is correct in his critical depiction of Hegel, and thereby also show why if there can be any Hegel after Badiou one needs, this new Hegel is a yet unknown one. What if there is a Hegel who can serve as a very useful, maybe even necessary supplement to Badiou? I will aim to depict why after Badiou's reading of Hegel, one needs a new, another Hegel, one that might be read in complete continuity with Badiou's position. But why should this be the case? Badiou himself compared the contemporary (political) situation to the 1840s, which is to say that we are in the same position as Marx and others were when it comes to the formulation of a new hypothesis of emancipation. Yet, he claimed in his *Pocket Pantheon* à propos Lacan—in a republished text from the 1970s—that "for a French Marxist today Lacan functions like Hegel did for the German revolutionaries of 1840."[1] But if we are again in the same situation as Marx and the German revolutionaries were in the 1840s, it seems not only consistent but logical to suggest that what is of utmost importance today is a return to Hegel. Yet, of course this cannot imply any simple return to orthodox Hegelianism, mindless rationalism, pan-logicism, or even pragmatist neo-Hegelianism, and so on. The very idea of rereading Hegel after Badiou and with Badiou can in the present context rather be linked to the famous anecdote of Lenin who in 1914 withdrew to a lonely place in Switzerland and read Hegel's *Logic*. And in some sense, after the failures of communism, why not repeat this very gesture?[2] This gesture could even be what is needed to remain faithful to Badiou.

Badiou himself thus far seems to have never read anything but Hegel's *Science of Logic*. His very early work addresses the beginning of the *Logic, Theory of the Subject* deals with what follows, namely Being-There; *Being and Event* starts— "crossing swords with Hegel" (*BLoW,* 530)—from the last part of the *Logic* of Being-There, that is, with Hegel's exploration of the dialectics of good and bad infinity. Only *Logics of Worlds* seems to not stand in the line of this diagnosis. Also one can here recall that Badiou claimed that *Being and Event* is his very own *Science of Logic,* and *Logics of Worlds* represents his *Phenomenology of Spirit* (*BLoW,* 8). However, one should never forget that Hegel's *Phenomenology* was the very precondition for his *Science of Logic* (and in Badiou's phenomenology he does solely discuss Hegel's *Logic* and not his *Phenomenology*). In any case it can be stated that each stage of Badiou's intellectual development is accompanied by a reading of yet another part of Hegel's *Logic*.[3] The main or maybe even the sole focus lies on the *Logic*. I take Badiou's working-through of Hegel's *Logic* to offer the coordinates, to formulate the precondition for any re-actualized, that is, contemporary reading of Hegel.

## Beginning With Hegel:
## An Unconscious Materialist

The first text in which Badiou struggles with Hegel (in 1978) addresses a passage which might be considered to be one of the most crucial ones and at the same time one of the most obscure in Hegel, namely the very beginning of his *Science of Logic*. Badiou never resumes this criticism. It is as if he imitates Hegel's own gesture, since Hegel never altered the very beginning of his *Logic,* even when he reworked it in his last years. Badiou never altered his criticism of Hegel's beginning. At the same time Badiou's comments are highly significant, because in Hegel the beginning prefigures and in some sense already entails all that follows; and in some sense Badiou's reading of it will also determine all the following criticisms. So, how does the critique run? Badiou reads the beginning by first acknowledging that Hegel does not begin the beginning with simply one, with one simple term, say with being. Hegel starts in a twofold manner: he begins with being and nothing. "The commencement for Hegel will then be understood as the position of the same term twice" (*BRK,* 51). This is to say, Hegel starts from two terms that, because both of them lack determination, can neither be said to be identical but at the same time cannot be said to be different either. As Hegel puts it wonderfully: "they are not undistinguished" (*HSL,* 83). Badiou continues to state that it is precisely this repeated positing of two terms, this gesture that everything begins with "two names for the void" (*BRK*, 52), which entails a fundamental problem. Why? Because since there is no true difference between them (they are not different, although not simply identical) their relation is "the weakest sort of difference" (*BRK*, 51). A difference that is derived only from the very position the two terms take, that is to say in Hegel's text it is *first* being and *then* nothing. Therefore, the beginning constitutes two terms as being the *two of one* series. Therefore the two dissipate into each other precisely because there is no strong difference between them. Everything seems to begin with a *two*: two terms, two places. However, two positions of a terms do not manifest a proper two, no qualitative difference (to be precise Hegel here runs the risk of being a proponent of a fake two). Being from the very beginning stands in a relation to nothing and nothing is somehow related[4] to being.

There seems to be a strong difference (being and nothing have nothing in common as neither of them has any determination, which they could have in common), but there is none (as what makes them different is precisely what makes them pass over into one another: *being undetermined* they end up *being nothing*—but *the same*). For Badiou at Hegel's beginning one ends up with a quantitative two, a two of one series, a repression of the qualitative Two. Hegel's two embodies a serial movement (Badiou states there is "a certain idea of movement") of *one* thing, of "the same" (*BRK*, 51) posited twice—this double positing is what makes the movement possible. If this were all, Badiou would have demonstrated that Hegel is a philosopher of the one, thus a (substantialist) idealist and doomed to fail. But things are not that simple. For although Hegel seems to repress strong difference, he nonetheless constantly refers to it. As Badiou continues to argue: "suppose that a marking occurs in a space of inscriptions: the commencement—right away, another term is retroactively constituted: the blank on which this mark has just been inscribed. Once a mark is inscribed, it establishes that on which it marks" (*BRK*, 52). There is not only a twofold positing of terms (being and nothing in the same series) but there is with this very act of positing a commencement, an indication of the very space in which this positing takes place. One thus not only ends up with a simple repression of the two, but with two diverging perspectives on the beginning, a proper *parallax*. There is a two that collapses back into the one (being and nothing occurring in one series and implying a movement of the same), which is supplemented by a qualitative two, which amounts to claiming that the second term of the series marks more than just another term of the series: it also and at the same time marks the space where this very series is inscribed, that is, something not-of the series. Thus we have a *repression of the two and a return of the repressed*.

Badiou now argues the problem is that these *two twos*[5] (the quantitative of being and nothing and the qualitative of being and the space where it is posited) are identical, both are decipherable from the name "nothing." There appear to be two Twos but nonetheless there is One. Badiou thereby basically asserts that the very beginning of Hegel's *Logic* is *not dialectical*, but based on iteration and repetition (first of the One, then of the Two as One). As soon as Hegel begins with being, the question where being begins arises, since the very act of positing refers to a locus of its positing. The mark silently refers back to the space of its marking.[6] This "retroactive causality" (*BRK*, 52) generates the necessity to mark the space of the marking itself, which is what the name "nothing" does and this makes it, as Badiou claims, possible for Hegel to continue with the same logic endlessly.[7] Since after "being" is the first mark and "nothing" is marking what this mark is lacking, that is, the space of marking, their very difference (i.e., the difference between two marks) remains unmarked (one only has a mark of the beginning and the marking of the space of the beginning). Hegel will mark the difference between these two marks (of mark and space of marking) via the name "becoming" (that follows "being" and then "nothing"). He thus relies on the idea that "there is always somewhere a void place, an unmarked" and generates infinitely new marks from this very "set of voids" (*BRK*, 53). The *Science of Logic* does thus for Badiou not depict a splitting of one into two (i.e., a "scission of identity"), but rather privileges *repetition over dialectics* and as dialectics is the kernel of any materialist and rational thought, Hegel ends up being an idealist as he cannot account for true change (change is identified with iteration). For the early Badiou what dialectics as true thought of change crucially relies upon, its motor, is contradiction. Thus to counter Badiou's criticism Hegel would have to have a conception of contradiction. But is there one?

Badiou asserts that repetition "is not the only motor here [in the beginning]" (*BRK*, 53) which is what becomes intelligible through the category of becoming. Becoming first is another term generated by repetition, it follows being and nothing; it marks their (non-)difference. Thereby secondly it can be defined as the transition of being into nothing and vice versa (they have no determinate difference distinguishing them, so they collapse into one another). But as they are at the same time not simply identical, but also absolutely different (the mark is not the space of its inscription), "becoming" is not simply a mark marking the yet unmarked difference between two terms in a series (of the same) and it also does not only take the transition of one into the other into account, it rather indicates a "becoming-unity of contraries" (*BRK*, 53). For if one has repression of the qualitative two in the twofold beginning and the return of the repressed, what becoming here marks is the be-coming unity of repression (being and nothing as two elements of one series) and of its return. Again, in "becoming" we have a two but only such that it immediately disappears as soon as it is thought—thinking the two in Hegel amounts to its vanishing, to erasing its traces. This is why: "Hegel makes place for contradiction" (*BRK*, 53), yet: "something of the Hegelian enterprise fails here." What is it that fails? "Nothing less than the attempt to generate the concept (in this case, a concept that in-tegrates the idea of contradiction, namely becoming) in continuity with the one (pure being . . .), the immediate, and the surrender to the life of the object" (*BRK*, 53). Badiou registers that Hegel does not simply assign one function to becoming but again two. This is why, when reading the *Logic* with Badiou and one expects nothing but "the sterile operation of coordinated iteration" there is something "like a clinamen" (*BRK*, 54). The surprise is: Hegel is a cinematic thinker.

For even when there seems to be only one logic—the logic of repeti-tion or iteration generating new terms by marking the yet unmarked—there are actually two. Beginning with Hegel's beginning one constantly oscillates between one splitting into two and two merging into one, and for Badiou this means one oscillates between materialism and idealism. He claims that Hegel saw the danger of fusing everything into the one of iteration: he "saw the constraint of going about this with unsanctioned force" (*BRK*, 53); this is why what appears to be a failure of inference in the presentation of becoming is actually Hegel inscribing something which cannot be derived from repetition, namely contradiction, which is heterogeneous to iteration. Within the continuity of the logic of iteration, as Badiou claims, one thus finds a discontinuity. Thus one seems to arrive at a true Two. But problems reoccur? "To becoming, Hegel assigns the role of being the pivot of this toggling, but the whole contradiction of the project will be re-concentrated upon it" (*BRK*, 53). Why? Because if there is iteration on one side (quantitative two, marking of the yet unmarked), there is contradiction on the other and it is like the effect of a clinamen that these two align under the logic of iteration and not of contradiction. The very maneuver of the beginning is here repeated once again. One seems to have a strong difference, a radical heterogeneity in the deter-mination of "becoming" as marking the unmarked (difference) and as marking that which is neither mark nor unmarked. However, becoming obscures the very strong difference between the two of them, because with becoming one moves from the mark and the yet unmarked to the very operation of marking itself. *Hegel conceives of the operation of marking as being itself markable.* The contradiction thus lies in the fact that Hegel treats this new mark (becoming) as just another mark, yet at the same he sees that this cannot be the case (as it is not yet marked but the very operation of marking that enters the scene).

Which is why for Badiou Hegel assigns two contradictory results to becoming: (1) it results in the stability of a process (i.e., the continuation of iteration); and (2) it results in the vanishing of being and nothing (each dissolve into the other), but also in the vanishing of this very act of vanishing (i.e., instability). Becoming in Hegel is the unification of the contradiction of stability and instability; this is why Badiou claims that the unity of contraries (mark and operation of marking mediating the mark and its space) comes in the form of a new concept which also enters the scene with becoming, namely "sublation." What happens in Hegel is happening like a clinamen, because the very perspective from which one could observe the operation of marking itself that is supposed to provide the ground for the unity of contraries can neither be deduced from the mark nor from the space, with which everything begins. Sublated becoming leads into a depiction of an equilibrium of being and nothing and also into the vanishing of being in nothing and vice versa and therefore into the vanishing of these twofold vanishing movements, which implies that there can be no equilibrium, since vanishing of vanishing and the iteration of stability contradict each other fundamentally. Nonetheless Hegel claims, according to Badiou, that one is here dealing with one and the same thing, namely sublation of being and nothing and one is therefore again knee-deep in the logic of iteration. Thus the criticism: Hegel on one hand claims that the sublation of the logic of iteration is itself derivable from the logic of iteration and on the other he indicates, by affirming discontinuity and instability, that this cannot be the case. He seems to come close to accounting for change (i.e., overcoming iteration via contradiction) but he does not really assert what he is asserting. Thus unconscious contradiction persists; *a contradiction whose precise place is between contradiction and iteration.* Hegel fails for Badiou because he pretends that he can unify and merge the two into one single concept: sublation. It is again akin to the very beginning: a logic of the two and then a repression of it. Hegel for Badiou is thus a philosopher not so much of totality but mostly—at least in what he seeks to attain—a philosopher of "a fundamental identity" (*BRK*, 56), namely of the identity of contradiction and iteration and thereby he forecloses the insight that the distinction between contradiction and iteration cannot be treated neutrally or sublated in one concept without opting for iteration.

There is, for Badiou, no unity of the contraries between iteration and contradiction; simply because the idea of the unity of contraries is an idea that falls on the side of iteration; this is why he affirms contradiction as precondition for materialism (i.e., true thought of change).

*Hegel's greatness for Badiou is to constantly point to that which he represses.* But for him it also holds that necessarily and subjectively one either opts for contradiction or for iteration. In the last instance Hegel gives prevalence, without acknowledging it, maybe even without willing it, to iteration; he does so by assuming that there can be one concept encompassing both sides. The unfolding of his objective logic (of the beginning) is thereby grounded on a repression of this subjective choice, of the qualitative two (between iteration and contradiction). Hegel thus endorses an objective oneness as he seeks for Badiou to do away with the decision between contradiction and iteration to which he constantly hints. Hegel is thus an *unconscious materialist*, by also constantly depicting the defense mechanisms against the return of his own repressed. In reading Hegel one can learn how defense mechanisms against the qualitative two (of the contradiction between contradiction and iteration) work, and therefore reading Hegel is paramount to grasp what needs to be overcome (and abandoned) to think true historical transformation. For the early Badiou, *Hegel is an unconscious materialist as his thought embodies the contradiction between contradiction and the perpetuated defense against it.*

## The Dasein of a Christian Materialist

Very much in line with this critique is what Badiou develops in his second reading of Hegel's *Science of Logic* with which he begins his 1982 *Theory of the Subject.* There everything starts from the claim that "there are two dialectical matrices in Hegel" (*BTS*, 3), such that there can be no "secondary unity" unifying the two. This very assessment of Hegel again amounts to the claim that "Hegel is a materialist!" (*BTS*, 3). But what are these matrices? One of them focuses on alienation, becoming-other, and conceptual sublation, the other on scission and ends with the insight that there is no unity that is not split. What one thus gets is the very schematic between the logic of iteration and its contradictory relation to the logic of contradiction. Badiou does not return to the beginning of the *Logic*, he proceeds to the next chapter, the one on being-there (*Dasein*), on "something." What he elaborates is how Hegel accounts for the idea that "the multiple proceed from the One" (*BTS*, 4)—how in other words quantity can be derived when one begins, as Hegel does, with quality. Badiou's aim is to show how this very question is answered in a manner that makes Hegel into "the modern conjurer of th[e] ecclesiastical question," namely of the question how "God, the absolute form of the One, was able to pulverize a universe of such lasting multiplicity" (*BTS*, 4–5). This is to say that Hegel is a materialist by aligning *two irreconcilable logics*, but he is in his very materialism a Christian thinker.

Why Christian? Because the very logic previously linked to iteration is now conceptually embodied into what Badiou refers to as Christianity: the release of multiplicity from the one and the returning ascent of this very multiplicity to it. The problem remains the same, even if its articulation changes. It is no longer articulated as a question whether Hegel can think change via contradiction, but rather by asking whether he can think actual multiplicity without reducing it to the logic of the one and the same (i.e., iteration), since only from thinking multiplicity can an adequate conception of change and transformation, and subsequently of history, be gained. Hegel does assert the two, yet represses it; does he do the same with multiplicity? Badiou's most crucial claim is that "Hegel is going to study the scission of the something in a movement that is prestructured by a first scission, which is in a way hidden because it is essentially repetitive" (*BTS*, 5). This is what he also refers to as the "structural skeleton" (*BTS*, 6) of the qualitative. One thing—any something—is placed twice (recall: being and nothing). But now this logic somehow changes, since Badiou claims that the very repetition of something as something and something-else (an other) is the constitutive split between what he refers to as "A as such" and "A in another place" (*BTS*, 6). This means that any something (even Hegel) is the split between the something as such and something placed somewhere. This is what follows for being-there from the very beginning of the *Logic*. But we are not dealing here with how things begin, but with precisely how things gain a determination (not with revolution but with the day after, so to speak). Determination [*Bestimmung*] enters via the effect that the place in which something occurs has on the something as such. This is to say we have to start from a determinate something (i.e., something placed) and conceive of it as being the very split between something as such and something according to its place.[8]

Two distributive options can be inferred: the first one is *determination proper* (something gains a determination due to the place where it occurs), and the second one is what Badiou with Hegel calls a *relapse* (something is simply considered as occurring in one place, where the something as such is repressed and thus there is nothing but the place as such; or something as such is conceived without considering the place where it occurs, i.e., in its purity). There is for Badiou a *primordial contradiction* between the space where something is placed[9] and the something as such. This very contradiction never appears; what appears is always only a contradictory unity (something as split between how it is as such and how it is according to its place) that implies determination (derived from the effect the place has on the something) wherefrom a *strict determination* can be derived (the something according to its place gives rise to a determination of the something as such, redetermining the place this time). Badiou continues to analyze this dialectical sequence by stating that after primordial contradiction, constitutive scission, determination and strict determination, there is also what Hegel calls *limitation* and *limit.*

Limitation is the reapplication of the something as such onto itself, which Badiou also calls *force.* This is to say if the space of places can never be said to be all there is (since there is something placed in it), the something can resist the determination it receives from its place and can redetermine itself. This very act of "torsion" (*BTS,* 11 and 148–58) that redetermines the determination the something received from the place where it occurred has a certain and always historically specific limit. This limit is the space of the places. Thus one never gets rid of all determining effects of the space wherein something is placed; there is no absolute purity. So, any being-there implies a scission as the mode of existence of contradiction. This may sound quite materialist. However, for Badiou there is a problem: the very redetermination of the determining effect the something receives from the place, that is the encounter with the limit, is where the very beginning, namely the constitutive scission of the something into itself as such and into itself as being placed, reoccurs, that is, it is repeated. Badiou calls this "Hegelian circularity" (*BTS,* 49). It is what makes Hegel into a Christian and prevents him from thinking historical specificity and also historical transformation proper. For he relies on a dialectic of determination and redetermination that does not allow for true multiplicity, which on the other side for Badiou is the prerequisite to truly account for different historical situations and transformations occurring in them. The multiple is only an "effect of the time required for the concept," an effect of the "self-exposure, through which the absolute arrives at the completely unfolded contemplation of itself" (*BTS,* 5). The circularity—Hegel's theological kernel—lies in the idea of mediating the finite (the space of the places) and the infinite, namely God (something as such placed within it). "God . . . is indexed . . . as specific out-place of the splace" (*BTS,* 15), that is, that which is not finite occurs within the finite world: the something as such is God as father, the something placed is the Son, Christ appearing in the world of the humans. Therefore the infinite (God-father) receives a determination by the very scission into father and son. However the something as such, that is, God, redetermines itself by overcoming the determination of finitude, which names the resurrection of Christ.

The Son—the something according to its place—is resurrected and rejoins the father, which is to say all that we obtain after Christ's advent (the infinite being inscribed into the world of finitude), his death (determination) and resurrection (redetermination of determination) is "only the pure scission of the Father and the Son as integral concept of the redemptive absolute" (*BTS*, 17–18). The problem that Badiou addresses here is also how Hegelian dialectic stands with regard to the question of finitude and infinity and it is related to the crucial question: how does "the dialectical fragment . . . continue?" (*BTS*, 18). Hegel opts for circularity—that is, iteration, which abolishes any type of continuation that is up for truly unforeseeable things—whereas Badiou states "we will oppose (materialist) periodization"—an early version of what he now calls "sequence"[10]— "to (idealist) circularity" (*BTS*, 18). If one opts for circularity one basically claims that what in a dialectical move is attained is nothing but that which will have been there from the very immediate beginning (the split between the finite and the infinite, the constitutive scission). Whereas, what previously was labeled "contradiction" is now articulated by Badiou as "the pure passage from one sequence to the other . . . where the truth of the first stage gives itself to begin with only as the condition of the second as fact without leading back to anything other than the unfolding of this fact" (*BTS*, 19).[11] Hegel's conception of history—Badiou likes to refer to the formula: "time is the being-there of the concept" (*BC*, 97)—therefore ends up not only being circular but actually prevents thought itself from achieving a true historical dimension. What one ends up thinking history in Hegel is for Badiou the insight that *history does not exist*.[12] It does not exist in any other way than as unfolding of the one concept whose history is history. For Badiou Hegel claims: there is one history (of the unfolding of the concept), which implies that there is no true history (all multiplicity that makes up time is part of the same process of unfolding). Badiou's criticism is thus that the conception of history developed by Hegel is (1) not itself historical, (2) that it therefore becomes religious, more precisely: Christian, which implies that (3) Hegel is a thinker of the one, namely the one God (whose existence he necessarily presumes), which then implies (4) that he cannot account for true multiplicity, since he ends up with a circular conception of the relation between infinity and finitude and therefore he (5) again prefers repetition and iteration to true historical transformation. He likes the old (good old Father) more than the new (Sons). A lot of quite devastating charges thus far and up till now Badiou basically has read only the first one and a half chapters of Hegel's *Science of Logic*.[13] He will turn to the second half of the second chapter, to the infamous discussion of bad and good infinity six years later, in his *Being and Event*.

## Beyond Good and Bad: Hegel's De-cision

It took Badiou six more years to turn the pages of the *Logic* again. After criticizing Hegel's conception of beginning (of and in the *Logic*) and his account of being-there (i.e., what follows from the beginning), he now addresses the issue of infinity that Hegel puts forward afterwards. Therefore, it is no surprise that this discussion appears in "Meditation 15" of *Being and Event*[14] under the more general heading of "Being: Nature and Infinity." Badiou is still reading the *Logic* and he is still in the first book, stuck in its second chapter.[15] He frames his debate with Hegel as struggle between Hegel's "generative ontology" and his own "subtractive ontology" (*BBE*, 163). As he claims: "for subtractive ontology, infinity is *a decision* (of ontology), whilst for Hegel it is a *law*" (*BBE*, 163). This formulates the general scope of all the criticisms thus far: *Badiou criticizes Hegel for his disavowed ontological commitment, for his ontology.* For him Hegel endorses the idea that being is linked to a law and any law must be based on a continual repeatability or applicability, otherwise it would not be a law, whereas Badiou himself seeks to establish that any materialist ontology proper acknowledges that one cannot ascribe any form of law to being.

Hegel is thus too *objective* when depicting the logic of being; against this the adequate materialist position consists rather in formalizing the necessity of a *subjective* decision constitutive of any ontology.[16] Yet, in *Being and Event* again the articulation of this point is a very specific one, since Badiou here has to deal with the peculiar problem that for him any conception of infinity encounters when it is grounded on affirming a link between being and an objective law. Badiou offers a complicated account of this problem by reconstructing Hegel's conception of good infinity in five steps that I here resume in an abbreviated manner: (1) Something is something because there is something which it is not. Thereby the something is in a differential relationship to others (other somethings) which makes it possible to conceive of the something as one.[17] Why? Because this means that there *is* one something which is not-all-the-other-somethings. (2) This could simply amount to the claim that the oneness of something can be inferred from its external relations (to other somethings). But to treat the oneness as an intrinsic attribute of the something, Hegel needs to infer that there is a form of totalization of all-the-others which neglects their specificity and particularity and empties them of all qualities.[18] Thereby the oneness of the something is immanent to the something against a "void space" (*BE*, 166), a space which is generated by this totalizing act. Thus there is a voiding totalization which provides the condition of possibility for an immanentization of oneness. (3) The something thereby also immanentized the (voided) non-quality of the other somethings, and thus also internalizes the non-being that is outside of itself. It thereby encounters not only a limit (the emptied-out space of all the other somethings is the limit of the something) but also an (internal) limitation: something internally encounters something-other it sought to overcome.[19] This leads (4) to externalizing the something-other into the voided space wherein the same movement is endlessly repeated. This is what Hegel calls bad infinity. It is bad because it is only potentially infinite, progressing endlessly from the overcoming of one limitation into the overcoming of the next. An endless repetition of the four points delineated above. But then there is (5), the insight into the "presence and the law of repetition" (*BBE*, 166).

This presence is the very alternating movement of positing a limit and overcoming it as a mere limitation (a finite limit that reinscribes a determination and infinite limitation which is related to the void), of the external determination of the something, which is internalized, and then the internally external is overcome. Yet, how can one name this law, this very movement between finitude and infinity, which is bad infinity, "since pure presence as relation to itself is, at this point, the void itself" (*BBE*, 166). The name for this law is for Badiou by Hegel just drawn from the very void that this movement is—a movement of the void, which is the constant emptying out of all fixed determinations (of something). The very name Hegel comes up with—his name for the void—is infinity, good infinity. But: "However heroic the effort, it is *interrupted de facto* by the exteriority itself of the pure multiple" (*BBE*, 169). Hegel makes a shift of perspectives; a shift of names. He tries to cover up the very disjunction which this movement constantly depicts. His distinction of bad and good infinity thus needs to be read as assertion of two different types of infinity that, although Hegel seems to confirm their difference, he treats as though they were identical, by assigning one name "infinity" to the two of them (such that "bad" and "good" are mere names for an internal difference). Badiou's assertion is thus that *Hegel identifies the void and infinity*—its very movement is good infinity—something Badiou challenges by separating the two.[20] The void and infinity both need to be affirmed as existent, yet they are not identical. Badiou therefore thinks "it is at this point that the Hegelian enterprise encounters, as its real, the impossibility of pure disjunction" (*BBE*, 169).

Hegel can think the identity of that which is identical and he can think the identity of that which seems different (the identity of something and something-else); he can also think the difference of that which is different (the something is like the something-else but it is *not* the something-else). But "what Hegel cannot think is the difference between the same and the same, that is, the pure position of two letters" (*BBE*,

169). Hegel for Badiou identifies the identity of that which is different and the difference of that which is different (both he refers to in terms of infinity) and he thereby neglects another, even more consistent option. In pure distributive terms: if one starts from difference and identity: one has the identity of the identical, the identity of the different, the difference of the different and Hegel simply forgets or even worse: obscures the difference of the identical. He can think the immanence of immanence, also the immanence of externality, and the externality of immanence, but he cannot think the externality of externality and thereby he cannot account for how external that is, which even when internalized, remains within the something. He therefore is the thinker of identity. To break the circularity of identity and of the one, one needs to assert the difference within the same as the only thing that makes the same identical to itself. We are hence talking about an identity without identity—this is precisely the position of an idealism without idealism.

Hegel cannot think the otherness of the other, which, as Badiou argues, cannot be derived from one logic but only via a decision: "nothing can save us here from making a decision which, in one go, disjoins the place of the Other from any insistence of same-others" (*BBE*, 169–70). One cannot for Badiou derive actual (good) infinity from the movement of potential (bad) infinity, unless one takes the decision. If one refrains from doing so—or if one represses and obfuscates the very fact that one has already taken a decision—this ends in "a properly Hegelian hallucination" (*BBE*, 169). Hegel's dialectical inference of the dialectics of infinity misses one crucial point: *there is no dialectics of the infinite, the infinite is a decision.* He therefore is now again privileging repetition. But here this is due to the fact the he is by far too rationalist, that is, too objectivist. He is a rationalist who he does not see that even rationalism implies a constitutive decision. The infinity of the rational can only be upheld if it is decided for. Hegel thus falls back into the bad infinity of the (fake) *objective dialectics of good and bad infinity.* Breaking up the dynamics of bad infinity implies a subjective decision (i.e., a real two).[21] The decision of abandoning Hegel is motivated by his own refusal of decision (which implies the obfuscation of decision and thereby an obscuration of its necessity). The decision—the decision that Hegel took and obscured but which nonetheless keeps resurging—is what needs to be repeated. Against pure repetition one needs the repetition of decision.

Badiou moves from criticizing Hegel as proponent of the primacy of iteration over contradiction to a criticism of the circularity of Hegelian dialectics, which neglects history and multiplicity; and in *Being and Event* all of this is rearticulated as a criticism of Hegel's repression of an unavoidable (although *objectively* impossible)[22] *subjective decision.* Therefore it is consistent that the thus far last treatment of Hegel—in *Logics of Worlds*—seeks "to examine the consequences of an axiom so radically opposed to the inaugural axiom of this book" (*BLoW*, 159). Hegel vs. Badiou is a challenge of decisions: repressed decision on one side or a formalization of its (impossible) necessity on the other.

## The End of Hegel Today

Any axiom or decision, even if unacknowledged, produces consequences. The same goes for Hegel according to Badiou. This is why seventeen years after *Being and Event* in *Logics of Worlds* he moves to the very end of the *Science of Logic* (skipping over more than 700 pages) and offers a discussion of the very outcome of the totality of the Hegelian method. Badiou's fundamental assessment reads like this: "Hegel's first word is 'being as concrete totality'" (*BLoW*, 144). Why this statement is fundamental can be seen when he derives from this that in any dialectic there is either "the triple of the Whole: the immediate, or the-thing-according to-its-being; mediation, or the-thing-according-to-its-essence . . . The triple of the non-Whole, which we advocate, is as follows: indifferent multiplicities, or ontological unbinding; worlds of appearing, or the logical link; truth-procedures, or subjective eternity" (*BLoW*, 144). This is what Badiou asserts: one starts with the inexistence of totality. To do so one claims that being is presented as pure multiplicity (externality of externality), that there are worlds in which pure multiplicity appears and that there are furthermore truth-procedures, which provide the very link between the two of them.[23] Badiou can therefore reconstruct the crucial difference between his and Hegel's account as difference between *two ontological axioms*: the whole is vs. the whole is not. This obviously implies a difference that manifests in the *two sets of consequences*. At stake is therefore also a distinction between *two dialectical conceptions*. "Hegel remarks that the complete thinking of the triple of the Whole makes four. This is because the Whole itself, as immediacy-of-the-result, still lies beyond its own dialectical construction. Likewise, so that truths (the third term, thought) may supplement worlds (the second term, logic), whose being is the pure multiple (the first term, ontology), we need a vanishing cause, which is the exact opposite of the Whole: an abolished flash, which we call the event, and which is the fourth term" (*BLoW*, 144).

For Badiou there is—as for Hegel—in the beginning an immediate (an immediate decision), which will have been the result (the event is nothing but its consequences). However, this immediate can neither be identified with a law, nor with being. To have asserted this is Hegel's ultimate failed decision. It is neither negation nor negation of negation. It is *an event, which will have been what it will have been* through the very procedures that it enables and which unfolds its consequences (this is why an event is the *paradoxical entity which belongs to itself*). It is not lawful nor is it being as such. And the very simple reason for this is that something like this does not happen objectively but only happens because of the engagement of subject and hence it happens in extra-philosophical, subjective practices, that is, in love, art, politics, science that condition philosophical thought. The ultimate charge against Hegel is hence that within his framework he denied that philosophy is conditioned. With the shift in the fourth term, everything (in the dialectical conception) changes; it is not being but an *illegal supplement* to it.

Thus, the disagreement Badiou articulates does not only affect the status of the fourth term, but the whole dialectical conception put forth here. Badiou claims Hegel ends up defending a consistent assumption of totality, as he sees that which is unfolded and thus repeated as nothing but the lawful being of being itself. Its law is to appear and what thus needs to be thought is the law of being as entailing its relation to appearance.[24] Against this Badiou asserts that within a different ontological proposal one also has a different conception of thought (thought under the condition of the unlawful event) and thus also a different conception of what and how to conceive of the very logic of appearances. He registers that Hegel's "assertion that being-there is 'essentially being-other' requires a logical arrangement that will lead—via the exemplary dialectic between being-for-another-thing and being-in-itself—towards the concept of reality" (*BLoW*, 145), which is the latter's name for appearance. Badiou does thus on the level of appearance sustain the Hegelian idea "that the moment of the reality of a being is that in which being, locally effectuated as being-there, is in identity with itself and with others, as well as in difference from itself and from others. Hegel proposes a superb formula, which declares that 'Being-there as reality is the differentiation of itself into being-in-itself and being-for-another-thing'" (*BLoW*, 145–46). "The agreement between our thinking and Hegel's is so manifest here" (*BLoW*, 146) because Badiou is also proclaiming that it is being that appears. However, he does challenge Hegel's underlying assumption that appearing *is* a law, an objective implication of being. Why? Because—this results from the definition of the law—there then could only be one way of appearing. If appearing is grounded in being as a quality of the latter, appearing would be *one* quality of the latter. Hegel vs. Badiou when it comes to appearance is another way (for Badiou) of positing that there can only be one world, one logic of appearances against the idea that there are multiple worlds, logics of worlds, for "the essence of the world not to be the totality of existence, and to endure the existence of an infinity of other worlds outside of itself" (*BLoW*, 146–47).

The problem of mediating the transition from being to appearing therefore becomes a problem of negation: "For Hegel, there can neither be a minimal (or nil) determination of the identity between two beings, nor an absolute difference between two beings" (*BLoW*, 147). Because Hegel thinks that "we do not exhibit anything as 'One and the same thing.' It might turn out that in a given world two beings will appear as absolutely unequal. There can be Twos-without-One (. . . this is the great problem of amorous truths)" (*BLoW*, 149). Hegel is guilty of the "axiomatic solution, which puts the negative at the very origin of appearing" that "cannot satisfy us" (*BLoW*, 151), since this is what it means to make appearance itself into a law, the law of the negative inscribed into being. This implies the abandonment not only of contingency (of the transcendental ordering) of any concrete world but also falls short to account for difference proper, for a two without a one, for difference as difference. In Hegel the Law (of the One) and the One (of the Law) prevails.

## Coda: The Immanence of Truth

Hegel is abandoned by Badiou because he is a proponent of a *one-world theory* in which *one being* appears according to *one law* (of the negative) which is grounded in his denial, or rather masking of any form of (true, ontologically classic) decision and he thereby simply cannot account for multiplicity, true difference, history, and anything but repetition. This results from Badiou's reading Hegel's *Logic*. If one assumes Badiou is fully correct, there is no afterlife of Hegel. But what if Hegel's *Logic* is not—as Badiou suggests—depicting the law of being and its outcomes? What if Badiou skipped a crucial bit in his reading of Hegel's *Logic*, which only appeared to be crucial after Badiou performed his reading, namely that which preceded Hegel's actual beginning of the *Logic*? What if the pages Badiou left out, the pages in which Hegel is preoccupied with how to begin after what he developed in the *Phenomenology*? What if taking these pages into account, precisely from a Badiousian perspective, would rather turn Hegel's *Logic* into an account of what Badiou himself would call a truth procedure, a procedure of subjectivization and thought?[25]

Let me be more explicit here: when Badiou states that any forced decision as response to an event has immediate consequences, what I am suggesting is to read Hegel's *Science of Logic* such that it depicts this very immediate realm of consequences, precisely by elaborating how any thought—if it is thought—evolves. This is to say Hegel develops that any evolving thought unfolds from the immediate identity and difference without determination and relation of being and nothing (i.e., with what Badiou calls an event). He then depicts how something (new) is generated from it via a process of becoming (i.e., the becoming of a subject), that is, in a procedure that implies a logic of bad infinity but relies on actual infinity (which Badiou refers to under the heading of "truth") and which ultimately follows a different type of repetition (the new is always the old—this is why truths are eternal—in another form) and generates a new—one new—world of appearances. One could then take Hegel thus to utterly follow Badiou's idea that "thought is the specific mode by which a human animal is traversed and overcome by a truth" (*BIT*, 73). The *Science of Logic* in such a renewed reading would be delineating the very advent and the *very (subjective) immanence of truth*.[26] Badiou can provide the very background against which one should start to read Hegel in a new and unknown way. Badiou is fully justified in his criticism of Hegel's *Logic* as ontological dialectics, but everything changes when one can demonstrate that Hegel does something different from what Badiou thinks he does. A slight shift of perspective that changes everything. Why not read Hegel as theorist of the truth procedure? Why not supplement Badiou with a Hegel not of an objective ontology, but of the truth procedure, of the advent of a singular subject related to an event, *not of law but of truth*. But what prevents this from being just another Hegelian hallucination?

Hegel before the very first lines ("Being, pure being" [*HSL*, 82]) of the *Logic* struggles with the question of how to begin and—to cut a very long story very short—comes up with the following answer: the only thing that can make a beginning is a beginning; one can only begin if one begins and Hegel's name for this is *Entschluss*, "resolve," "decision."[27] This is why Hegel claims that the beginning is both *logically necessary and logically impossible*, that is, how to begin cannot be derived or deduced and remains utterly unanalyzable. The only thing one can rely on when one seeks to begin is for Hegel: "All that is present [*vorhanden*] is simply the resolve, which can also be regarded as arbitrary, that we propose to consider thought as such" (*HSL*, 70). What does this decision decide? It is not deciding anything concretely. It is thus not only a fully immediate but also fully *indeterminate decision*. The decision only decides itself, namely that it has consequences for thought. So in the beginning, before the beginning of being, nothing that Badiou criticized, there stands a decision—an acknowledged and committed decision. If Hegel is reread after Badiou from this point onwards, everything changes—this will bring about a yet completely unknown Hegel.

So, if Badiou's criticism of Hegel's ontology needs to be sustained today—for anyone following Badiou's diagnosis of the contemporary present, for anyone being a committed Badiousian—it is—although it might seem impossible at first—absolutely necessary to supplement Badiou with a yet unknown Hegel. One of true beginnings, of truth procedures. Badiou's ultimate lesson is: it is time to think again. With and for Plato, Descartes, Hegel, and Badiou. With and for philosophy.

# Notes

## Preface

1. David Chalmers, *The Conscious Mind* (Oxford: Oxford University Press, 1996), 101.
2. Immanuel Kant, *Critique of Pure Reason* (London: Everyman's Library, 1988), 264.
3. Ibid., 264–65.
4. Alain Badiou, *Logiques des mondes* (Paris: Editions du Seuil, 2006), 9.

## Introduction

1. Freud 1964.
2. Lacan 2006a, 206.
3. Lacan 2006a, 213.
4. Lacan 2006a, 203.
5. A similar point is made by Lacan when he criticizes American ego analysis, a movement which refused to accept that Freud—a theoretical founding father—had himself an unconscious, something that one needs to accept when reading his texts, although this complicated the manner of how to derive a unified theory from them. Ego analysis thereby also did not accept that even the analyst (and hence anyone) has an unconscious, and by resisting this claim and denying it, it negates itself as a proponent of psychoanalysis. See Lacan 2006b.
6. Freud's own example is that "the patient does not say that he remembers that he used to be defiant and critical towards his parents' authority; instead, he behaves in that way to the doctor" ("FRRW," 150).
7. Hamacher 1996. In the following I follow certain elements of his reading of this passage; I revisit this point in a different context in chapter 6.
8. Freud 1959, 94–95.
9. I leave aside here the intricate question of transference, which one would have to account for to systematically grasp the relation of the elements from a psychoanalytic perspective.
10. See Žižek 2008b.
11. With reference to Lacan, one should note here that this does not refer to an object one can simply find in the world; but it is at the same time not without

an object. Yet the latter is rather what causes the practice and discourse of philosophy.

12. Badiou 1997, 46.

13. See also Badiou and Roudinesco 2012.

14. Lacan 2006b, 337.

15. I here modified the translation. For Hegel, and for Badiou, this implies that "an unreal deed is self-contradictory." Hegel 1979, 433.

16. Lacan 2006c, 73.

17. Hegel 1949, 305.

18. Badiou 2012a, 1.


## Chapter 1

1. See "BSP II."

2. Georg Cantor lived from 1845 to 1918. At one point within his lifetime God and idealism lived through their last moment. One of the most readable, and luckily at the same time not overly simplifying, introductions to his mathematical work is Wallace 2010. See also *SLU*.

3. For a detailed discussion of the conditions of philosophy, see *BC*.

4. For this see also the concise reconstruction in *BBE*, 38–49 and *BLoW*, 153ff.

5. See, for example, one articulation of this claim in "APRW," 7ff.

6. Here one could also be reminded that already Foucault diagnosed in 1970 that any "philosophy of the event"—and Badiou's philosophy fits this description perfectly—"should move in the at first sight paradoxical direction of a materialism of the incorporeal." Foucault 1981, 69. At the same time one should remark here that although a philosophy of the event, or better, of events, has to move into this direction, it needs a separate and distinct theory of incorporation, a theory of the body which describes the (subjective as well as objective) effects an event has on a world. I take Badiou to prove such a materialism of the incorporeal by accounting for what I refer to as "a materialism without matter" (Lacan) and a theory of incorporation. For this see *BLoW*, 449–76. Also it should be noted that Judith Balso used this term of a materialism of the incorporeal in her beautiful book on Pessoa: Balso 2011.

7. Marx 1975, 417. As the specific phrasing of any of the theses on Feuerbach has been the subject of intensive work of interpretation, for the sake of precision I also refer here to the German original: "Die Philosophen haben die Welt nur verschieden *interpretiert*, es kömmt darauf an, sie zu *verändern*."

8. Compare http://www.entretemps.asso.fr/Badiou/seminaire.htm.

9. Labica 1987, 5.

10. Korsch 2009, 120.

11. Haug 1984, 18.

12. Bloch 1986, 278.

13. In this context one should also consult the work of Predrag Vranicki, member of the Yugoslav practice-group. See Vranicki 1985.

14. Engels 1940, 5.

155

NOTES TO PAGES 16–22

15. Bloch 1986, 281.
16. Anders 1980, 5.
17. Adorno 2008, 134 (translation modified).
18. Ibid., 135.
19. Canetti 1983, 68.
20. In one of his weakest (philosophical) moments Heidegger in 1969 presented a reading of the 11th thesis, supposed to be radically criticizing it, which ultimately leads to a different but nonetheless implied articulation of this second reading. Basically Heidegger's claim was that there is no real difference between changing and interpreting the world, which thus is to say that a different interpretation of the (possibilities of a given) world is indistinguishable from changing it, thus, as he claimed, Marx's thesis is inconsistent. For this, see Heidegger 1969 and Heidegger 2005.
21. Žižek 2009a, 90ff.
22. Adorno's own formulation reads: "In psycho-analysis nothing is true except the exaggerations." Adorno 2005, 29.
23. Žižek 2009a, 92.
24. Žižek 2002a, 170
25. This is Rebecca Comay commenting on Hegel's method in her wonderful book. Comay 2011, 96.
26. See *BLoW*, 1–9.
27. In some sense the diagonal construction I am aiming at here follows certain intuitions already implied in the Hegelian notion of "sublation." The only difference is that I am not only trying to overcome two positions due to their internal (and mutually exclusive) one-sidedness, but three. Thus what is at work here is not "sublation" in the "traditional rendering" of the term but rather a construction of something new starting from the old which at the same time does not present an additional option based on the same level. This form of a "worked-through concept of sublation" takes up the idea of eliminating abstractions or hypostatizations, also the idea of solving contradictions on a higher logical level, but also includes the idea to generate something via the subtraction. Put in another way: this diagonal could be conceived of as being a (Hegelian) sublation proper.
28. For this see *BLoW*, 511.
29. *BLoW*, 1–9
30. See "BSP I."
31. See also Badiou 2013a.
32. For this see Badiou 2010d.
33. I will develop this in greater detail throughout the chapters of the present book and give a more concise account of this diagnosis (with reference to Descartes, Kant, Hegel, Marx, and others) in my next book that will be called *Worse Than Error: Indifference and Fatalism*.
34. For this also see "BSP I"–"BSP III."
35. "BSP II."
36. See Badiou et al. 2009e, 56.
37. For an alternative account of human life which I have developed combining Badiou and Marx, see Ruda 2009a.

38. One can clearly see here—maybe even better against the light of subsequent arguments—why this sort of materialism is properly idealist (in the pejorative sense of the word), since it is constitutively based on the attempt to substantialize its own position by totalizing it. Yet, if idealism died with Cantor, one is here dealing with a fake materialism—a pre-Cantorian one—still believing that there is something like a totality in a simple sense of "all there is." Ex negatively it should be clear that a materialist stance refuses such a notion of the "all."

39. That existence is a matter of degree and intensity Badiou develops extensively in *BLoW*, 97–190.

40. The distinction of creatures that have a world (humans), creatures that are poor of world (animals), and that are wordless (stones and alike) was developed by Heidegger. Yet, Badiou here reworks Heidegger by basically stating that animals do not have a *common* world, since they have an environment and environments may be structured by exclusion of certain animals from them.

41. This formula is originally from Lenin. For this see also Lukàcs 2009, 86–98.

42. Compare for the concept of cognitive mapping Jameson 1988.

43. For the theory of points, see *BLoW*, 397–448.

44. Badiou 2005a.

45. Rado Riha has noted a structure comparable to the one I am delineating here in Riha 2005. At the same time the above mentioned quote is directed against a position that Badiou started to analyze in his seminars as the one of the "left," which as he again put it elsewhere emphasizes that one can "change without doing anything" (*BSPQ*, 77). Doing no-thing is *not* not doing anything. Thereby a contemporary materialism does not amount to simple traditional leftism (i.e., parliamentary oppositionism).

46. Badiou comes here very close to what Hegel calls spirit, which he once defined in the following manner: "The fact that what spirit is in accordance with its concept . . . is the Idea which is itself the concept of spirit. As causa sui, i.e., a free causality. . . ." (*HOP* 77). I here refer Badiou's claim back to Hegel, because what the latter has in mind when he speaks of spirit is also a different kind of causality, in which the subject becomes the end in and for itself. Hegel famously calls this "teleology" and harshly distinguishes it from mechanical (whose axiom might be rendered as: all there is are external relations, i.e., forces between objects causing effects on one another) or chemical (whose axiom might be rendered as: all there is are internal causes of objects and/or subjects and they affect their actions) accounts of causality. Whereas the former (by hypostatizing and totalizing externality) cannot properly account for the externality of cause and effect it constantly refers to (since there is nothing external, i.e., no exception to the external relation between objects, which implies that the only thing which was not caused by an object is the mechanical perspective itself), the latter cannot account for the internality it presumes (since an internal cause of, say, a subject always will remain external to the subject, for example when this internal cause determines how long my arm will grow, this internal cause is external to me and my actions). Hegel's attack on mechanism and chemism as accounts of subjective action can be said to subtly resonate in Badiou's immanent criticism of demo-

cratic materialism. I explore the relation between Hegel and Badiou in a more detailed manner subsequently. See also *HSL*, 705–54.

47. Which could be rendered in the following form: "The One is." Or also as: "There is a set of set; there is a consistent all-encompassing totality."

48. In the following chapters I will although to a different extent deal with all three of these thinkers, plus a supernumerary fourth one, namely Marx. Although one should note that the specificity of the contemporary situation makes Marx much more accepted—at least he was a materialist—than Plato, Descartes, or Hegel. Anyone became an anti-capitalist, even the capitalists, retrospectively mourning all the losses of their success stories (which can be read as a universalization of individual morality), thus Marx comes in handy, even for the next-door broker, or for a philosopher defending the present state of things, but not Plato, Descartes, or Hegel. Marx at least was a materialist, thus it might be helpful to return to his insights, even if his—so called—historical predictions proved to be wrong, but who would seriously return to and resurrect Plato (with the exception of Badiou) to rearticulate a materialist position today?

49. See his seminars on Plato: Badiou 2011–2012.

50. That this is fully consistent with Badiou's thought, despite what some defenders of Badiou might claim, becomes clear when one also takes the following statement into account: "There are historical sequences practically void of politics." Badiou and Tarby 2010, 14. Truths, also political ones, can be absent from a world, especially when the world is not a world and the present is thus not a real present.

51. For this see "BSP II," "BSP III."

52. See Macherey 2008; Labica 1987.

53. Engels 1970, 30.

54. It is like one necessarily has to first choose something wrong to make the true thing appear. Without this first move the access to the right thing will forever be blocked.

55. For a detailed analysis of the genesis of early Marxian thought out of Hegel's philosophy of objective spirit, see Ruda 2011a.

56. Macherey 2008, 100.

57. See "BTN."

58. The argument I am developing here does not exclude the possibility that the new dialectical matrix is retroactively already contained in the old (and thus might be precisely what the old will have been). This twist functions comparably to the idea that Kafka created its own predecessors—after Kafka one is able to see some Kafkian elements in authors who (even by centuries) preceded Kafka. In this sense the renewal of the dialectical matrix by Badiou might ultimately prove that through the eyes of Badiou Badiou will have been Hegelian. The whole intricacy consists in delineating which renewal is a proper one that is able to change the past such that the past is that which retroactively will have determined (included) its renewal.

59. For this point see also Žižek 1999, 79–86.

60. Here it should be clear that the present book could have also been called "Hegelianism without Hegelianism" (of course also "Platonism of the Mul-

tiple," i.e., "Platonism without Platonism" or "Cartesianism without Cartesianism"). But I take *Idealism without Idealism* to be the most universal of all these categories.

61. For this see also Althusser 1990.

62. A comradely but nonetheless critical comment by Mladen Dolar concerning this rendering was to point out the danger of an idealism without idealism being nothing but an idealism without the dangerous idealist substance and thus something akin to what Žižek developed with regards to beer without alcohol or coffee without caffeine. For this well-known argument see for example Žižek 2010c. If this danger were what one faces advocating an idealism without idealism, this argument would indeed be devastating. That this cannot be the case should be clear from the argument developed above.

63. Partially, because one sought to realize them in a practical context. One might here just think of Lenin and others, faithful Hegelians, no doubt, yet their endeavors of putting dialectical thought into practice failed in this very practice because they created obstacles to their own enterprise that they have shown themselves unable to overcome. For this also see Ruda 2013b, 137–54.

64. Rado Riha elaborated that any idealism without idealism needs to be supplemented with a materialism without materialism. I without any doubt subscribe to the necessity of having a proper dialectical exposition of what the material appearance of an idea might be. I treat this very problem under a slightly different label and call the logic involved subsequently that of a *dialectics of dialectics and non-dialectics*.

65. One might also in a way say the following: it is comparable to Fichte positing the "I" positing the "Non-I" but only being able to do so by taking into account the being conditioned of the very act of positing.

66. See Lenin 1972.

## Chapter 2

1. This is, of course, already present in Heidegger 2008.

2. See Heidegger 1991.

3. Heidegger 1998, 170.

4. Heidegger 1982.

5. See, for example, Koyré 1968.

6. I am of course very well aware that Badiou is not at all Heideggerian (although to the best of my knowledge there is thus far no detailed investigation of their relationship that would go further than Badiou's own criticism of Heideggerian thought) and I will return to some elements of difference between the two in the points below. For a direct comment of the forgetting of being from Badiou's side, see *BBE*, 443–48.

7. Plato invented philosophy as a form of practice under conditions of other forms of practice. Namely love, politics, art, and science. One can of course argue that there has been love and political forms of organization before Plato

and obviously also art. But what makes philosophy possible is precisely the fourth condition added to the other three, namely science, that is, mathematics. Philosophy is possible when at least four of such conditions are thinkable; three are, as it seems, not enough.

8. In what follows it shall become clear that I limit my remarks only to a specific moment that is implied in Badiou's reference to Plato. For a more detailed study on their relation, see Bartlett 2011.

9. It might be seen nowhere clearer than in the claim by the former French president Sarkozy that it is absolutely necessary to "Forget '68." The simple point to be made here is: if there is nothing more to it, why claim that it has to be forgotten? For this see *BMS*.

10. See *BSMP*, 105–16.

11. To render this in even more simple terms: the claim that there is nothing but democratic materialism is a quite non-dialectical claim.

12. I use this term here in the sense that Badiou introduced. See *BBE*, 265–326.

13. I am here drawing on claims that can be found in "BIV."

14. What is important here is that this creation of new successors functions on the basis of one and the same operation that repeats within the potentially infinite series of numbers generated by it. There is hence something like a *repeated finitude, finitude in and through repetition.*

15. For this see also *SLU*.

16. For this quotation and for a pointed characterization of all the realms that today are governed by this finitized definition of the number, see *BNN*, 1–4. Therefore it helps to counter this very operation by first and foremost comprehending what a number is and on what it constitutively relies.

17. What this is supposed to say is that a politics of administration turns politics into administration and is hence a politics against politics, a politics abolishing politics.

18. As Badiou continues this line of thought: "But we don't know what a number is, so we don't know what we are." *BNN*, 3.

19. This argument can also be traced back to the second existential axiom that Badiou is referring to within the set theoretical setting he moves in. See *BBE*. It also should be remarked that if $\omega$ is not a successor this also implies that it breaks the mechanism of repetition that was fundamental for the natural numbers.

20. I here again refer to *SLU*. One way of rendering it is that the potential infinity is an infinite succession of numbers taking place. But as soon as one claims that there is a number that is not a successor one comes across a different phenomenon, as $\omega$ precisely totalizes the potential infinity.

21. One might say this as all the natural numbers belong in the potentially infinite series of $\omega$ and thus $\omega$ names the very space where their succession can take place (by belonging to $\omega$, i.e., by being smaller than it). See *BNN*, 93–98.

22. Again, this is to say that "the place of succession does not itself succeed." *BNN*, 95.

23. This second succession can of course maximally continue to $\omega + \omega$.

24. This is, to my mind, a risk that anyone denying the constitutive separation of economy and politics has to take into account. This is of course not to say that there could be something like a pure politics (of emancipation) that does not at all care for economic issues. But it is to say that as soon as one forgets or denies this distinction one risks to deduce the very existence of politics from economics (and this is to say one does not at all deduce politics—at least as long as one remains within the democratic materialist framework; things of course stand different with regard to Lenin, although one should even there be careful not to fall into the same trap). The danger here is a problematic form of an objectivism that fetishizes (quantitative) finitude.

25. Mainly in terms of how many things one objectively has in common, how many things one "owns" together and what one is able to achieve by exchanging useful favors (which has become the principle of many so-called dating agencies). For this see Badiou 2012c. Thereby what Kant once said about marriage—it is a contract about the mutual use of the sexual organs of the contractual partners—and what one could even try to convert into a proper criticism of the traditional type of the institution of marriage, has become something like the generalized principle of "love" relationships.

26. This can quite easily be seen in the works of Michael Thompson and others, who try to revamp the idea of a substantial form of (human) life. They usually perform the following maneuver: they first insist on the necessarily holistic constitution of a life form. They then add that what one also needs to admit that all concepts used within such a holistic system can only be made properly intelligible via a constitutive reference to the whole (of the life form), that is, one only understands what "good" means when related to the entirety of human life practices (that themselves can only be accounted for holistically). The allegedly dialectical move from holism to the whole is thus embedded into a second type of holism itself. This is to say that all the life forms are elements of a holistic system through which they gain their determinacy. However, and this is where substantialization comes in, the identities based on the differential holist approach are in terms of life forms nonetheless substantial identities. This is to say that even though everything seems to rely on a differential constitution, this very holism is most basically generating substantial differences, it substantializes the identities once they are constituted and this leads to the fact that for example Thompson can claim something utterly mind boggling: "So it would be with an independently developed Twin English spoken somewhere in the South Seas: it would be a different language. If Captain Cook, overhearing the locals, mistakes them for fellow English speakers—descendants perhaps of earlier shipwrecked Englishmen—he will be wrong. And if he asks (in English), 'Do you know where I can get a shave?' and they answer (in Twin English), 'Go up Mindanao Avenue three blocks, turn left on to Fiji and you'll see it on your right,' and in the end he even gets a shave, still this will not be a conversation; nor, more obviously, will Cook be gaining testamentary knowledge about the places of things. Grammars and dictionaries of the two languages (written, let's suppose, in a third language) will say all the same things, but they will once again say them about different things. This again holds, despite the fact that an individual language is some-

thing universal or general or indefinitely extensible." Does this not recall the same structure at work in claims like: he looks like us; he even talks like us, but be aware he (substantially) is *not* like us? For this see Thompson 2012; the quote is from Thompson 2004, 361.

27. In both cases one might argue that what is forgotten is what thought is. For it is precisely thinking that comes with the peculiar yet unavoidable "obligatory force" (*HOP*, 132) to continue thinking. The oblivion depicted above is first and foremost a forgetting of this very force, that is, of thought itself.

28. Heidegger's rendering of anamnesis is in a paradoxical way far more traditionally Platonic than Badiou's. For a detailed account of Plato anamnesis doctrine, see Huber 1964.

29. This distinction has rarely been taken into account. Yet, I think it is crucial. An idea names the active procedure of unfolding the consequences of an exception; the hypothesis names the very affirmation of the possibility of the existence of an idea. To confuse the two is up to a certain extent to confuse philosophy and politics.

30. Badiou himself argues that there are symbolic, imaginary, and real aspects to what he calls an idea. In a free reformulation one might say: it is the inscription of something real (mass movement, for example) into a historically specific context (symbolic) which at the same time enables the vision to participate in the emancipation of the whole of humanity (imaginary). See *BCH*, 229–60.

31. Metapolitical, as is well known to the reader, names the relation of philosophy to its political condition. Compare *BMP*.

32. As Slavoj Žižek argues: "This . . . is our basic philosophico-political choice (decision) today: either repeat in a materialist vein Plato's assertion of the meta-physical dimension of 'eternal Ideas,' or continue to dwell in the postmodern universe of 'democratic-materialist' historicist relativism, caught in the vicious cycle of the eternal struggle with 'premodern' fundamentalisms." *ZLN*, 41.

33. I here refer to the German version of the text. By now there also exists a French and English translation of this astonishing text, prefaced by Alain Badiou—which may come as no surprise to the reader. See also Pasolini 2013.

34. And also because Badiou himself is currently still working on a movie about the life of Plato; this very gesture is clearly something echoing Pasolini's project.

35. Pasolini alludes to the liturgical saying about the lasting presence of Christ when he claims that "Paul is *here, today amongst us.*" *PPP*, 16.

36. In Pasolini this reads like: "What is clear is that Saint Paul with the simple force of his religious message destroys a society in a revolutionary way, which was based on the violence of class struggle, of imperialism and particularly of slavery." *PPP*, 17.

37. That this is one crucial element of philosophy can be seen in many of Badiou's texts. One can also read this as one element of what in his terms makes a "philosophical institution." See Badiou 2008a, 26–32.

38. See *BMPHI.*

39. For one famous formulation of such a reading see the (hopefully soon to be forgotten) book by Popper: Popper 1966, 68–168.

40. Compare for example how democratic materialists deal with political figures like Mao or Stalin. They are rendered as incarnating evil and thus as representing a complete deprivation of sense or meaning. To transplant Stalin's statements—and I am here of course not defending Stalin—into a contemporary context would not endorse Stalin; it would much rather also invalidate the very gesture of transplanting them.

41. For this see also Ruda 2013a.

42. One might rephrase this by saying that Badiou insists against Heidegger that truth is not the truth of being but rather something emerging in a specific historical situation. This already indicates that there cannot simply be one truth (of being) but there need to be multiple truths. The latter claim can be derived from the following consideration: if anything that is is (for Badiou) a multiple of multiples, the same goes for truth. This claim immediately leads to the dialectical insight that not only are truths composed of multiples of multiples, but one can only have an adequate understanding of truth if truth is essentially also multiple, that is, if there are truths. Thereby no truth can ever be the same (not even as a truth that is constantly present by being absent, as Heidegger would have it).

43. One might here also think of a—today very countercurrent—claim articulated by Hegel. He makes a similar distinction when he writes: "The famous answer: 'I do not see the need for it,' given to the libeler who excused himself with the words: 'But I have to live,' is apposite at this point. Life ceases to be necessary in face of the higher realm of freedom." *HOP*, 125. Life ceases to be necessary, since life as such—life as mere survival—has no value in itself. The only life that is worthy of being lived is a free life.

44. As Badiou claims: "It is reasonable to assume that a philosophy always unfolds its arguments between two imperatives—one negative, the other positive—which define, on the one hand, the vice that destroys true thought, and on the other, the effort, or even the ascesis, which makes true thought possible." Badiou 2006a, 39.

45. For this also see Badiou's definition of a "philosophical situation" in Badiou 2009d.

46. It is thus of quite some importance that one of the chapters is entitled: "What Is an Idea?" See *BRP*, 197–223.

47. Certain contemporary "philosophers" argue that it is enough to make things explicit, that is, to explicitate the conceptually implicit. The difference to Badiou lies in the fact that the latter argues that what is implicit in the idea of the idea is an exception on which the concept is grounded. This means that *that which is implicit* (in the idea, namely its own status, its being) *is not* (implicit) and hence cannot be made explicit.

## Chapter 3

1. Marx 1970a. Translation modified.
2. Lenin 1978, 6.
3. Gans 2005, 204.

4. Cf. also the analysis in Žižek 2009e. The obvious name for the interface of democracy and capitalism is "liberalism." It distinguishes itself today into an *economic liberalism* whose maxim is "pleasure without boundaries" and in a *libertarian liberalism* whose maxim is "one can and therefore one must buy pleasure." Also see "BITP I."

5. See Žižek 1994.

6. See *BCH* and *STF*, 86–157. That the linkage of democracy and capitalism on the level of form and content might lead to the fact that "democracy" might no longer be the name for sustaining such a hypothesis should be clear. See on this also Badiou's remark referring to Rancière: *BCH*, 196. Also see his comments on popular dictatorship in *BRH*, 93ff. Consider also Žižek's polemical statement that today "democracy is not to come, but to go"; Žižek 2009c, 255. One might even add that to which the name communism refers could also simply be called "emancipation." *BSPQ*, 81.

7. Žižek 2005a, 155.

8. Badiou 2002, 14.

9. Lenin 1978, 4.

10. Boltanski and Chiapello 2007, IX.

11. Gould 1982. I owe this reference to Lorenzo Chiesa.

12. One should here bear in mind that the regime determining what is possible and impossible always is for Badiou what he calls the state. Thus, if one follows the line of investigation that I delineate one also has to inquire into what the state of the situation is if one analyzes a concrete situation. As Badiou puts it: "we will say that the State is that which prescribes what, in a given situation, is the impossibility specific to that situation, from the formal prescription of what is possible." *BCH*, 243.

13. A specific contemporary dilemma thus lies in what Badiou calls the "disaster of unlimitedness." "BITP II."

14. For the notion of the transcendental, see *BLoW*, 91–188.

15. This is one Lacanian definition of psychoanalytic cure, taken up in *BMS*, 34. Or as Badiou more recently formulated: "It is important to find a real point [*point reel*] to which we can hold on at whatever cost, an 'impossible' point, uninscribable in the law of the situation. We must hold on to a real point of this type and organize its consequences." "BCP."

16. In Germany this becomes overly apparent since what all parties (left and right, self-declared reformers as much as conservatives) share is the assumption that one cannot change the market dynamic in its entirety and thus has to adapt as well as possible. Political actions that aim at something which challenges this assumption must therefore be considered to be impossible.

17. That "I know very well but nonetheless" is the formula of fetishist disavowal has been elaborated by Mannoni 2003.

18. Anti-capitalism is not only a G20 phenomenon but rather reaches from Angelina Jolie to the German Christian Democrat Heiner Geißler.

19. How much fetishistic disavowal is at work in certain groups that are present at G8 or G20 protests becomes immediately apparent when one gives an even simple phenomenological description of the scenes that one can witness there.

One protests such that, say, the depths of third world countries are annulled. And one addresses the people responsible for the fact that these depths are not annulled. It is completely clear that these very people know what would happen if the depths were annulled and it is also clear that they have no interest whatsoever in doing this. Nonetheless one acts as if it still were possible that these—of course absolutely rational—claims could appear to be convincing, although one knows that they never will be.

20. For the notion of obscurantism, see *BLoW*, 43–78; *BSPU*, 52–54; Badiou 2010c.

21. This formula can be read in a historical materialist way and then one can infer that "it is not enough simply to remain faithful to the communist Idea; one has to locate within historical reality antagonisms which give the Idea a practical urgency" (*ZTF*, 90); or it can be read in a dialectical materialist way so that the content of the political form means that capital itself retroacts in a peculiar way on its own form because "capital is the Real" (Žižek and Daly 2004, 150). Žižek's position comes down to a specific mediation of the two whose formal character I will develop in the following. Since: "yes, once again, the relationship between historical and dialectical materialism is that of a parallax; they are substantially the same, the shift from one to the other is purely a shift of perspective" ("ZPV," 5).

22. Marx 1975b.

23. I have undertaken a reading of early Marx from a Badiousian perspective elsewhere. See Ruda 2009a. See for this also the comradely comments in Chiesa typescript.

24. Marx 1970a.

25. Marx 1858.

26. Žižek 2005a, 36.

27. See *ZTF*, 65.

28. This is what the early Badiou saw in Hegel. See *BRK*.

29. As I argued in the first chapter, there are good reasons for claiming that today materialism is the only option and hence anyone becomes a spontaneous Feuerbachian.

30. See, for example, *BCH*, 66–67.

31. I did present something along these lines in Ruda 2012.

32. This is precisely what the early Badiou claims in *BPP*, 60.

33. This is the position that Badiou claimed to be his in the face of criticisms articulated (by Negri and others) that he is a communist but not a Marxist. *BRH*, 7–15.

34. This is my rendering of what Žižek himself once phrased in the following manner: "From Hegel to Marx . . . and Back." Compare *ZLE*, 213–33.

35. This is of course apparent in Žižek's enterprise nearly from the very beginning till today. See for this Žižek 2011a; *ZLN*. For this one should also refer to the instructive work of Adrian Johnston: Johnston 2008a.

36. For this term see Jameson 1973, 52–89.

37. For this see also Žižek's claim on the post-Hegelian break: *ZLN*, 193–240.

38. Žižek 2009d, 26.

39. One could still render what happened with Cantor in Hegelian terms by stating that if Hegel assumed that it is not enough to not believe in God, God himself has to assert that he does not exist; this is precisely what happened with Cantor. If one assumes that God thinks, he cannot but subscribe to Cantor's demonstration and hence he has to assert and confirm that he does not exist.

40. Badiou 2010c.

41. For this, see also the interview of Peter Hallward with Alain Badiou, in *BE*, 95–144. Also see their self-description and declarations, on http://web.archive.org/web/20071016140303/http://orgapoli.net/spip.php?rubrique14.

42. See http://journalpolitique.blogspot.com. Concerning this name—which in itself contains the most crucial axioms and political stances of the group—let me just briefly quote one of their comments: We have found a new word, an important word, a word which concerns the whole world; everyone can decide if this politics is good, is true, is useful and if it helps, if it allows to think, to act and to be involved."

43. Also articulated in Badiou 2008f.

44. What sort of problematic consequences this conception of political action as expansion of war within the intra-statist realm implied—for example in terms of defining and dealing with the adversary (after the revolution)—can be found in Badiou 2013d.

45. For an impressive history of the Paris Commune, see Lissagaray 2012. An analysis of the Commune can also be found in *BCH*, 168–228.

46. See Badiou 2011e; Althusser and Balibar 1975, 17.

47. This formula can be found in Lenin 1973. It reads in Lenin's words as follows: "It is common knowledge that the masses are divided into classes, that the masses can be contrasted with classes only by contrasting the vast majority in general . . .—classes are led by political parties; that political parties, as a general rule, are run by more or less stable groups composed of the most authoritative, influential and experienced members, who are elected to the most responsible positions, and are called leaders. All this is elementary. All this is clear and simple" (ibid., 38). See also Lazarus 2007.

48. This can also be rendered in the following way. According to the bourgeoisie, the proletariat is the complete negation, that is to say, the abstract negation of all that is defining an ordinary existence in the bourgeois world. It is thus a nonexistence.

49. See also Badiou 2013d; and *BCH*, 101–67.

50. Compare Trotsky 2007.

51. For detailed analyses of the different stages of the Cultural Revolution one cannot but refer to the passionate work of Alessandro Russo.

52. For a more extensive elaboration of this diagnosis, see Ruda 2013a.

53. The best analysis of Stalinist Russia can be found in Getty with Naumov 2010. For a broader contextualization of the Stalinist "perversion" of the Leninist model, see *ZST* and *BMP*, 68–77.

54. For a detailed account of this Hegelian characterization of the French Revolution and its actuality, see the impressive Comay 2011. An abridged analysis can also be found in Ruda 2011a.

55. On the notion of "Saturation," see my entry in Corcoran 2014.

56. See Badiou 2011f.

57. And this is also to say: this repetition, remembering, and working through has to be done by politics *and* philosophy. For the Freudian formula, see Freud 1964.

58. See Marx 1975b.

59. For example, in Žižek and Daly 2004, 61–62.

60. This is, at least, valid starting from his working through of the two matrices of Hegelian dialectics. *BTS*, 1–51.

61. One can easily think of *BTS*, 21–68; *BBE*, 161–172; and *BLoW*, 141–52.

62. The following argument is oriented by *BTN*. The most crucial parts of the subsequent argument I derive from this article, although an elaboration of the following logical distinctions can already be found in *BLoW*, 183–85 and 189–90.

63. See Aristotle 1998, 86ff.

64. Slavoj Žižek has argued in a personal conversation that it is precisely this fourth form of negation which is—contrary to the Badiousian argument—the most powerful and effective. It would describe the operation of negation that is proper to the actions of the proletariat, as the proletariat can only negate the bourgeois world whose product it is, by self-negating itself. One can already see traces of this in the quarrel between Žižek and Badiou over the role of the "negation of negation" in Mao. See Mao 2008. My following remarks attempt to show that the position Žižek rightly aims at pointing out can be articulated in terms that remain faithful to Badiou. I hence do share with Badiou that the fourth type of negation in the above-mentioned schema loses all its force, but a moment of self-negation can nonetheless be thought when the relation between the three forms of negation is properly unfolded.

65. See *BBE*, 37–84.

66. This is precisely what the principle of extensionality means. There is no presumed givenness of the elements that all share a common trait or attribute. It is rather that contingently elements are collected into the unity of a set and sets only differ due to the elements they contain—and not due to attributes all the gathered elements share. The latter presupposition is what defines the intensional conception of set theory. Compare *BBE*, 60–62.

67. For this general claim, compare *BLoW*.

68. *BBE*, 201–54.

69. *BLoW*, 335–380.

70. Jameson 1973.

71. Another way of formulating this would be: an event is that which links the three forms of negation together—the vanishing mediator without which there is simply no relation between them.

72. This is why an event is what Badiou calls a "supplement" to being. Although this might sound Derridean, in Badiou it is clear that this supplement has to be conceived of in a "subtractive way." This simply means the following: if for example in mathematics we subtract something (we write $3 - 2 = X$), we in some sense add something to what is given. But the mode in which we subtractively supplement that which is given implies that the "something" we add to the given is not a positive supplement. In a precise and simple sense, the subtractive

supplement implies a disappearance (the "–2" in the example supplements the "3" but is only qualified by the disappearance—of the "2"—that is indicated by the minus, the very symbol constituting the supplement). Or in Badiou's words: "If a truth cannot come from the given [*une donation*], it is because it originates in a disappearance. This original disappearance, which came, for the time of a flash, to supplement the situation, and which is not localized within the latter except insofar as nothing of it subsists, and which insists *in truth* precisely insofar as it cannot be repeated as presence—this is what I call an 'event.'" *BC*, 132

73. This is in some sense what the early Badiou would have claimed, insisting that change occurs when "something"—a force—is placed in a historical setting and comes to redetermine itself by destroying the determination it received by the space of places it was put in. See *BTS*.

74. Badiou describes this as the logic of parliamentary elections. See *BTN*, 1883. Also see his *BSPQ*. Paraconsistent consequences of an event are thus indistinguishable from no consequences at all. In some sense this indistinguishability of the event and the non-event is a result of the pure—and fetishist—insistence on the possibility of a choice. This insistence is precisely—as Descartes already argued—the lowest form of freedom and leads to irresolution and (a bad form of) indifference.

75. In some sense, this assumption is precisely what defines the essence of *dogmatism*. But to the above-mentioned point one should add another complication: any determinate affirmation with which the process of unfolding of consequences begins needs another supplement, namely subtraction. For with an event there is no (intuitionist and also vulgarized) Hegelian sublation of all contradictions on a higher logical level but rather there is a moment of subtracting all possibilities of differentiating to get to the pure form of a "yes or no." Subtraction then means: to emphasize the primacy of the principle of contradiction before the non-validity of the principle of the excluded middle.

76. This does not only hold for political action. To take a different example: although the elaborated formal conception of the emergence of true change can also render intelligible how to conceive of a love encounter, each love encounter yields radically different appearances of consequences. Any practice of love can be described in these terms, although any concrete love practice appears to be fully different from any other (from the employed terms of endearment to the music the loving couple listens to, etc.).

77. See *BBE*, 201–64.

78. This transition is legitimate, at least heuristically, to properly grasp all dimensions of this dialectical matrix. I here heuristically separate the subjective and objective site to demonstrate their mutual dependence.

79. This is why an event implies three different maneuvers: An operation of intensification, an operation of contraction, and an operation of localization. See *BRH*, 104ff.

80. I cannot dwell on the complex and multilayered concept of clinamen. It might suffice to refer to the brilliant work on this topic by Mladen Dolar. Compare, for example, Dolar typescript 2; Dolar 2013. See also early Badiou's discussion of this concept in *BTS*, 57ff.

81. Throughout this chapter I leave aside one crucial question: where can/ does an event take place? This question of localization is essential to fully develop the concrete levels of the dialectical matrix I am elaborating here. It would imply three things: (1) a detailed reconstruction of what Badiou calls an "evental site" (see *BBE*, 173–90; *BLoW*, 355–96) which would have to lead into a renewed conceptualization of "political places"; (2) a systematic reading of how presentation and representation relate to one another (ontologically), an argument for the fact that *representation is never abolishable*, and an answer to the question of how the presentation and representation relate to the (phenomenological) distinction between existence and inexistence; and (3) a systematic connection of these two layers to the overall dialectical conception I developed here. I leave this aspect aside, but I will subsequently deal with the question of localization in a more extensive manner.

82. I here obviously read Badiou's argument against the background of Hegel's logic of negation. Badiou's worked-through conception of dialectics in my reading thus on the one side attempts to replace the primacy of determinate negation with a complex network of relations between different types of negation and on the other it seeks to replace it with a conception of (subjective) determinate affirmation. Ultimately, I will argue this is completely in line with Hegel.

83. One may say that, for example, an evental encounter in love does not itself produce anything but the possibility of a "yes" (or "no"). Hence only by relating to the choice one draws consequences from the encounter and only the consequences produce something that did not appear before, in this case: a couple.

84. See *BLoW*, 397–424.

85. In some sense one could claim that the paradoxical self-belonging to itself of the event is repeated within the realm of consequences as mutual self-belonging of the objective and subjective side of this dialectical conception.

86. This is my rendering of what Badiou once formulated in the following way: "political decision tears itself away from any dialectic of the subjective and the objective . . . The beginning, under its evental injunction, is pure declaration." Badiou 1993b, 239. I here fully assert what Simon Hajdini remarked in a private communication, namely that "the remainder is only produced as something prior to the process which produces it *because* it is produced as non-dialectizable. Dialectics is a suspension of dialectics (as it produces that which suspends it), while being a process of the suspension of suspension of dialectics."

87. The danger I am referring to here can also be articulated in the following way: hypostatizing one form of negation is hypostatizing the One over the multiple. This is something Badiou's whole oeuvre stands against.

88. One important additional remark: one might here raise the objection that the link between dialectics and the non-dialectical could itself also be rendered as being non-dialectical. Although I do not want to develop a clear-cut systematic answer here, I insist on the following point: if one refrains from articulating the link between these two layers in a dialectical manner, one ends up with a dualist, or in other words: vitalist ontology (dualism and vitalism have more in common than usually perceived). This is why either one claims "there is the

dialectical *and* there is the non-dialectical" and thus posits a two-layer ontology which cannot properly explain their relation (= dualism) or one claims "there is the dialectical and there will have been the non-dialectical prior to the dialectical but only accessible after its emergence" and thus posits—via the logic of retroactivity—a fundamental non-relationality between the two elements involved. My conviction is that the only materialist stance has to start from the latter axiom. I here repeat the very fundamental move of any idealism without idealism—dialectics without dialectical deducibility. Or to put it again differently: if one does not insist on the possibility of thinking that which retroactively precedes thought as that which can only be thought as being unthinkable, one ends up with one or another version of Aristotelianism (= bad and old school idealism).

89. As Hallward put it: "A prescriptive politics presumes a form of classical logic—the confrontation of two contrary positions, to the exclusion of any middle or third." Hallward 2005, 774.

90. I here leave aside the intricate issue that one can find different types of negation in Hegel.

91. Simply put: if the death drive keeps on going no matter what, could one not say that this is only possible as the non-satisfaction and satisfaction of what it desires, of its longing become indistinguishable and this is why it is always persisting being by definition (un)satisfied/(un-)satisfiable?

92. See Mannoni 2003.

93. Here it is indeed still as though Žižek follows early Marx's claim that "criticism of religion" (or ideology in this case) "is the prerequisite of all criticism." See Marx 1970b.

94. It is easy and hence no way out to claim that religion predates capitalism (and which one?).

95. Marx 1970b.

96. That Hegel and his rendering of the dialectics necessarily implies two times two (= 4), the fourth step being the one in which the immediate is repeated as immediate-result, is entirely misunderstood by a whole tradition of thinkers which make the triad into the Hegelian paradigm par excellence. For a recent example of such a misreading, cf. Norrie 2010, 114–15. Against this see Žižek 1999, 79–86.

97. Žižek 2003, 156.

98. See, for example, his Žižek 2000a; Žižek, 2000b; and Žižek 2005c.

99. This point is brilliantly made in Zupančič 2008, 148–82.

100. Nearly all of Žižek's criticisms of Badiou can be summed up by stating that the latter misperceives the precise nature of the death drive, as the death drive is the "name for the uncanny dimension of the human in becoming" (*ZLN*, 410), that is, the proper dimension of subjectivization in Badiou's terms. It shall subsequently become clearer how I conceive of a Badiousian answer with regard to this charge.

101. It should be clear here that the question of what sort of dialectics one develops is inherently linked to the ontology one gets.

102. One might here think of Žižek's famous and ingenious interpretation of the scene in *Fight Club* in which Edward Norton confronting his boss punches

himself in the face. If the act introduces the inscription of the "yes and no" of death drive into the intuitionistically governed world of appearances this also comes with the danger of conceiving of it as the inauguration of an automatism in which ultimately the subject of the act disappears as the agent of this very act (or at least of its continuation or consequences). Although there is a clear line of demarcation between them, if this were to be accurate, Žižek might be closer to Deleuze then one might initially think. For Žižek's powerful criticism of Deleuze (to which I fully subscribe), see Žižek 2003b. As will become apparent after the next chapter, the danger here lies in the following: if one claims at the same time the subject is a process and the subject is the unlocalizable void (it is that which is even lacking lack), this might easily lead to stating that somehow in the beginning there was movement—Eric Santner once in a private conversation referred to this position as *Platonic vitalism*. What thus lies before any world, any discourse as that which can only be grasped retroactively from the world or discourse then would be identical with some form of movement which cannot even be described in terms of movement any longer. I will return to this point when talking about the localization of the void in Badiou's ontology.

103. Another way of rendering it would be the following: As soon as we perform this foursome procedure we arrive at the recognition that a combination of the intuitionistically governed world of appearance (with "yes or no" at its basis) and the paraconsistent ideology bound to it ("yes and no") already will have contained all the necessary elements of the classical logic (a "yes or no" without any third option). With this move one realizes that the choice lies between a "fake" "yes and no" of ideology obfuscating antagonism and a "true" "yes and no" that needs to be discovered: another way of putting it is that the true "yes" or "no" leads to a neither "yes" nor "no"—and this *is* the true "yes" and "no."

104. Badiou made a similar point when praising Žižek in a lecture presented at UCLA. See Badiou 2010e.

105. Here one needs to refer to Alenka Zupančič's brilliant rendering of Badiou's theory of conditions in Zupančič 2004. She proposed an admirable reading, in which the condition of love—because philosophy is philo-sophia, love of wisdom—counts two times (the number of love is the two) and thereby also entails an account of the very relation that philosophy has to all its conditions (namely a loving relation). This rendering makes it possible to account for the singularity of each condition as much as one would have to account for the singularity of someone involved in a love relationship, and at the same time philosophy always changes its own position with regard to the specific condition it relates to (say it is metapolitics with regard to the political condition and inaesthetics with regard to art, etc.). As beautiful as this reading is, it comes with a certain catch, since from my perspective it is not only love that is in this sense reflexively inscribed into philosophy, accounting for its conditionality (engendering a count-as-two with regard to all its conditions), but rather the same goes for the (broken) totality of all the conditions. This means one also has to include a reflexive dimension of politics (namely all conditions are counted as equals and equality is clearly a political category), of science (philosophy has to axiomatically relate to events in its conditions and derive consistent consequences from them), and

art (philosophy under the pressure of certain events has to reshape its form and to reinvent new ones to remain contemporary to what happens in its conditions).

106. It would need to be an at the same time non-contradictory as contradictory notion of contradiction, which would hence be contradictory and thereby be precisely what it is supposed to be. One should bear in mind that, at least for Hegel, contradiction is a principle of all that is living, simply because contradiction generates movement (in multiple possible ways).

107. For this see the enlightening distinction between the "known knowns" (things we know that we know), the "known unknowns" (things we know that we do not know), and the "unknown unknowns" (things we do not know that we do not know) and the "unknown knowns": Žižek 2006b. Žižek rightly also mentions that ideology today functions in a way that "determines, in short, what we have to know but have to pretend we do not know." *ZLE*, 4.

108. A trivial version of this is what is often referred to as neo-Hegelian pragmatism, which in one sense or another—despite the intricacies of the individual positions involved—assumes that the practice of all practices (the proper reflection of all) is philosophy. Astoundingly one may note that this is not an analytically derived result—and not in the slightest correspondence with our everyday language usage—but rather a mere postulate, which is one of the reasons why all the self-proclaimed Hegelians, who Fredric Jameson fittingly called Habermasian Hegelians, are basically Kantians. See Jameson 2010, 54.

109. I know that the easiest way of answering to me would be to assert that what I am framing as a criticism is precisely the point to be affirmed, namely that it is not material practices of concrete individuals that count, as someone like, say, the early Marx would have assumed, but the very assumption of the existence of these practices and individuals is unraveled as an ideological assumption precisely through the very movement of philosophy. Hence, one could then derive from this the very powerful idea that it is first philosophy that counts. I think what is at stake here is if philosophy is what also counts at last; or in different terms: if philosophy is also completely determined by its conditions or if the conditions become what they are due to philosophy, or—of course—both.

110. I am here somehow rephrasing the question that Žižek himself articulated: "After this break, is there not something inherently false in advocating a Hegelian 'absolute Idealism'? . . . when the break we are referring to is not the true break but a false break, the one which obliterates the true break, the true point of impossibility." Žižek 2011b, 203. I here agree with Žižek who considers Schopenhauer's, Marx's, and Kierkegaard's critique of Hegel to represent a false, obliterating break. But the question remains, in Badiousian terms, what if the break was a real break—maybe not with regard to Marx but to the Paris Commune, not with regard to Kierkegaard but Cantor, and so on? I thus fundamentally agree with Žižek that it is nonsensical to attempt to refute Hegel by insisting on the historical relativization of everything that would have been depicted by himself which in the last instance leads to a relativization of his own system ("Anyone who finds such refutations convincing is not to be taken seriously as a reader of Hegel," ibid.). The debate rather revolves around if to be a Hegelian today does not necessarily imply to also be a post-Hegelian, with an emphasis on

both parts of the term. In the last chapter of the present book, I attempt to offer an answer to this question.

111. That it lies prior to the whole constituting process of what the in-itself is for others may generate the impression that one is here dealing with something absolutely other somehow having an effect on us. This is why Žižek is fully justified to distance himself from any position that would substantialize and also de-dialecticize the process of how this point can be reached; paradigmatically such a position can be represented as the one of Levinas. Žižek's powerful critique of Levinas can be found in Žižek 2005b.

112. As Adrian Johnston remarked: "Žižek vacillates between identifying death drive either with the gap in the order of being (i.e., the [meta-]transcendental condition for the genesis of subjectivity) or with the subject itself (i.e., the product of this very same gap)." Johnston 2008a, 109. This indicates not only that one can equate the death drive with the real but with the "real real." For the latter see Žižek 2008b, xii.

113. Readers as different in their theoretical orientation as Adrian Johnston and Robert Pippin have pointed to similar moments and referred to it as the unacknowledged Schellingianism of Žižek's thought. I am not convinced that this point necessarily has to be articulated in Schellingian terms, say of primordial contraction (God cannot not create and hence he is driven to create to be what he is).

## Chapter 4

The third epigraph for this chapter is from Badiou 2008e, 216.

1. Žižek 1999, 1.

2. Žižek 1999, 2.

3. To be more precise: the last meditation is devoted to Descartes and Lacan. It should become clear from my subsequent investigation why Lacan and Descartes, from a Badiousian perspective, share a similar stance with regards to very specific theoretical points.

4. For more detailed information on this, see Badiou's seminars on Plato: Badiou 2011–2012.

5. Badiou 2013b.

6. I already quoted this formula from *Logics of Worlds* ("There are only bodies and languages, except that there are truths" [*BLoW*, 4]). The pun I am putting forward here is on one hand indeed a cheap one as neither Hegel nor Plato can be reduced to the side of bodies or languages (or of individuals and communities, as another version of the formula goes). But at the time it is not as cheap as it might seem on first sight, for one might argue that that which (or better: he who) stands in a position of exception to the two obvious choices offered—Badiou being a Platonist or a refined Hegelian—marks the position where a truth—and this is also to say: a subject—can appear. I will argue that what is needed to fully conceive of Badiou's enterprise is neither only a worked-through dialectical theory nor a renewed theory of what eternal Ideas are. I will claim that one also

needs a renewed contemporary account of the void—of the cogito—and of creation (of truths)—without the Cartesian God.

7. These four points can be mapped onto what Badiou explicitly enlists as
topics in which he considers himself to be indebted to Descartes: the anonym-
ity of exteriority, the category of the subject, the infinite, the will. See "BSP III."

8. A more precise formula is: thought as such is the unity of theory and
practice which materializes itself in a dialectical unfolding of consequences of
an un-dialectical, because not dialectically deducible, emergence of an unprecedented possibility.

9. This also and without a doubt goes for the resistance one faces when
defending the (Platonic) eternity of Ideas or the existence of a (Hegelian) absolute knowledge. Badiou's philosophical trinity is therefore academia's worst of
the worst.

10. The epigraph for this section is from Schürmann 1979, 104.

11. See for example and paradigmatically the dubious reconstruction of
Badiou's meta-ontology in Hair 2006, 267ff. or Hewlett 2007, 40ff. For a more
adequate reconstruction see, for example, Pluth 2010, 33ff. and Hallward 2003,
62ff. Badiou criticized this rendering of his work as an "obscure and objectivist"
reading: Badiou 2011d.

12. For this see also Badiou 2011g.

13. Here one can see that Descartes is (proto-)Badiousian, as he starts from
an axiom (of the equality of anyone with anyone) and attempts to deduce consistent consequences from it. This is also why modern mathematics became paradigmatic for him. Badiou once commented on Descartes's relation to mathematics in
a rather critical manner when comparing Descartes and Lacan: "What Descartes
looks for in mathematics is a paradigm for the *order of reason* . . . their role and
their veritable utility is to conduct the spirit towards 'a different discipline' . . .
In other words, mathematics is treated as a method . . . thanks to which one can
deal with sense. Here, Descartes does not escape the Lacanian criticism, as mathematics cannot be paradigmatic for any other thing than itself . . . But there is another identification of mathematics in Descartes. The mathematical proposition
occupies a particular position with regards to doubt: the 'mathematical truths'
are in fact that which one cannot doubt with the ordinary doubt, for they are
such that, as soon as pronounced, they contain the subject independently of any
reality. To suspend them, one needs the recourse to the 'hyperbolic doubt'; that
is to say, the extreme hypotheses which make it possible that something exterior
to human thought intervenes . . . This is in profound affinity with the Lacanian
figure of Truth." See Badiou 1994–1995. One of the most helpful readings of the
status of science and the role of mathematics in Descartes from a Lacanian perspective can be found in Milner 1998. See also Badiou 2013e.

14. How radical this question is becomes clear when Descartes insists that
we, "because we were all children before being men and because for a long time
it was necessary for us to be governed by our appetites and our teachers" (*DM*,
51), which is to say that there is also an equality of anyone when it comes to our
contingent and accidental upbringing. So, when it is clear that all of us are also
accidentally determined, how can we claim we have more in common than just

our determination by contingency? How to get to a (formally) substantial equality that makes us what we are? How to avoid hypostatizing contingency?

15. Here Žižek's insight applies that all "revolutionary-egalitarian figures from Robespierre to John Brown are (potentially, at least) figures without habit" (*ZID*, 171). One should thus include Descartes in this list.

16. With regard to this passage, one can claim here that Descartes is closer to Beckett than one might think at first sight.

17. Here the reader could intervene and claim that it is precisely Zermelo who in the aftermath of the Russellian antinomy, and from a perspective close to Badiou's, demonstrated that it is more than highly problematic to deduce an existence starting from a concept. There is no way that leads from the conceptual to an existence and this is without a doubt the way Descartes proceeds, yet he depicts a very peculiar kind of existence.

18. One can say that the Cartesian subtraction even of logical deduction marks something akin to the transition from ordinary logic to transcendental logic in Kant's theory of the infinite judgment, as developed by Žižek and others. While (positive and negative) judgments in the ordinary logical framework assign a predicate to a subject ("X is dead") or negate this assignation ("X is not dead"), the infinite judgment takes the form of a prescription of existence via the assertion of a non-predicate to a subject ("X is undead"). From this one can infer that the cogito is precisely this: the undead kernel of any discourse. Although one might also criticize Descartes, as Lacan did, for losing this very (transcendental) indeterminateness of the cogito by introducing further determinations when he claims: "But what then am I? A thing that thinks. What is that? A thing that doubts, understands, affirms, denies, wills, refuses, and that also imagines and senses" (*DMFP*, 110). For an impressive Lacanian reading of Descartes's placing of the cogito, see Dolar 1998. See also Völker 2011.

19. Badiou 2003b, 10.

20. Badiou 1993–1994a. Unfortunately, at least to the best of my knowledge, there is no transcript of the seminar Badiou held in 1983–1984 (in which he briefly after the publication of his *Theory of the Subject* started working on the set theoretical foundation of his meta-ontology) on Descartes, Kant, and Plato and on the question of the One which also is crucial for the argument mentioned above.

21. As Badiou puts it: "The subject affirms nothingness in some sense. Practically you can read the complete history of philosophy as the history of this sort of beginning. What is the possible affirmation of nothingness? You are the affirmation, the rationalist affirmation, of nothingness like in Descartes or Socrates that is the affirmation of the thinking of nothingness." Badiou 2011h.

22. This is why Descartes can argue: "And having noticed that there is nothing at all in this *I think, therefore I am* that assures me that I am speaking the truth, except that I see very clearly that, in order to think, it is necessary to exist" (*DM*, 61). This is to say: it is again *Nothing* in this "I think" that assures me that I am speaking the truth, Nothing, which amounts to me thinking the "I think" thinking nothing.

23. See also the helpful commentary of this claim in Feltham 2008.

24. Thereby Descartes already outlined the central characteristics for the Lacanian project. The void can be located as it is the subject to which any discourse is always already sutured. This is precisely what Badiou will contest in *BBE*, 431–40. For, as Badiou remarks, one central problem with this position: it ends up with a "starting point [which] is the very space of the Cogito, as 'closed' configuration of all possible thoughts, existential point of pure thought. It is claimed (but only the Cogito assures us of this) that something like the set of all my possible thoughts exists." *BNN*, 38.

25. Badiou 1995–1996.

26. For the notion of the "situation," see *BBE*, 81–122. One might refer to one first definition Badiou gave and claim that "the components of a situation are very various, they are neither only individuals nor enunciations. They are all the indications which therein are forged together, discourses, gestures, violences, silences, expressions, gatherings, corpuscles, stars, etc." Badiou 1985a, 39.

27. A helpful comment on this can be found in Badiou 2004, 233.

28. Paradigmatically this difference comes out in Badiou's criticism of Jacques-Alain Miller's reading of Frege (*BNN*, 24–30). That Badiou's reinterpretation of this structure is not only based upon insights put forward by Lacanian psychoanalysis but also inspired by the works of Samuel Beckett can be grasped if one takes into account Badiou's book on Beckett (Badiou 2003b.). This is why his claim that "a post-Cartesian doctrine of the subject is unfolding: its origins can be traced to non-philosophical practices" (*BBE*, 1) does refer to a multiplicity of non-philosophical inventions. For a Lacanian reading of Beckett relating his works to the philosophy of Descartes, see Dolar 2005.

29. This argument follows Descartes's claim that "I never found any [proposition] that was so doubtful that I could not draw from it some quite certain conclusion, even if it had been merely that it contained nothing certain" (*DM*, 59). To know that I know nothing implies that this Nothing is something that I know.

30. This argument bears some similarity with the reasoning via the absurd which is a method Badiou uses in some of his works: see *BBE*, 247–52. One could also claim that it is in this point that Descartes's argument takes a very Platonic turn. For one could easily read this as a rendering of the Platonic idea of anamnesis. I will return to this point.

31. I will return to the question of how to understand the doctrine of the two substances from a Badiousian perspective later in this book. What should be clear is that the "dualism" of Descartes is not as easily done away when one starts with the prescription that any (meta-)ontology has to start from thinking the Two and neither the One nor the Multiple. Countering the bad press it had within the last centuries of philosophical arguments, such a dualism then becomes a necessary materialist prerequisite for any materialist position. This is already what Joan Copjec put forward against any (Foucauldian) historicist position: Copjec 1996. Also see my critique of Foucault in Ruda 2011c.

32. How problematic the commonsense reading of the relationship of the two substances—body and soul—is can be grasped by a systematic reading of how their link has to be conceived. See Nancy 2005.

33. Badiou 1993–1994b.

34. For Descartes's notion of the world, see Descartes 1998.

35. Descartes's greatness precisely lies in the idea that as soon as one ends up with the cogito one is forced to think that which cannot be thought—God. Simply put: Descartes is the proper inventor of the Deleuzian idea that one is forced to think as thinking is to necessarily encounter an impossible limit point of thinking. Thought is thus combining necessity and impossibility. This is where realism originates.

36. As Descartes has it: "I judged from this that being composed of these two natures could not be a perfection in God and that, as a consequence, God was not thus composed; but that, if there are bodies in the world, or even intelligences, or other natures that were not at all entirely perfect, their being had to depend on God's power in such a way that they could not subsist without God for a single moment" (*DM*, 67).

37. This is due to the fact that any thought needs to be discursive and God is that which is not discursively graspable, that is, thinkable. This Cartesian insight is what lies at the ground of any attempt to renew materialist dialectics. There are certain similarities connecting such a renewal with the formerly called "speculative realism" group. Differences between the two positions have been pointed out convincingly in Chiesa 2011.

38. Badiou repeats this claim when he states that "the thesis of dialectical metaphysics claims . . . that any initial gap between the finite and the infinite is to be considered as the place from which thought proceeds, or as the distance it crosses, and not as an obstacle to thought . . . Which means two things. Firstly, that to the extent that the thinkable is thought, it is thought *absolutely*. On this point Hegel carries on the legacy of Plato, Descartes, Spinoza, or Leibniz. Secondly, that everything is thinkable" ("BMPH," 188–89).

39. The reader might notice that I here subtract the supposed Oneness (or one could also say: objectivity, as Oneness is just another name for it) of the Cartesian God. I nonetheless think that this reconstruction remains faithful to the Cartesian letter. Descartes never made it explicit that what he names "God" has to be conceived of as one, or objective (although the notion of "God" seems to necessarily imply this). Or, to play a Hegelian trump card, if Descartes infers the Oneness and existence of God (both determinations that cannot but be discursive), even worse for Descartes, as nothing authorizes this inference.

40. As Badiou states with regard to Descartes: "Only with the proof of the existence of God it is certain that there is anything real." Badiou 2013c, 27.

41. Here it should be clear that I am aiming at a reformulation of what in a different terminology is called the "symbolic real" and the "real real."

42. This point might easily be misunderstood. How can Descartes claim that he demonstrated God's existence if at the same time he needs to claim that God has a being but cannot be linked to any criterion of existence? What I am suggesting here is that Descartes's proof can only be properly understood when read as a proof of (the) being (of God) and not at all of its existence—although Descartes obviously speaks of an existential proof.

43. One might here already anticipate the subsequent argument with regards to Badiou's meta-ontology. As the cogito is in a similar logical position as

the empty set—giving the set theoretical discourse—which at the same time internally "refers" to the void that is the only "element" (without being an element) of the empty set. But the void is also discursively unpresentable as it is nothing but a pure name which sutures the situation to being (that lies retroactively "before" any discourse). The empty set then takes the position of the cogito, the name of being = void the place of God. As Badiou claims: "God is also a void point." See Badiou 1987–1988. But things will get more complex.

44. Badiou calls philosophy meta-ontology in its relation to the condition of mathematics (= ontology), meta-politics in relation to political (emancipatory) practices, inaesthetics in relation to art and, as can be argued, psychoanalysis in relation to the condition of love. These nominations are opposed to any form of political philosophy, aesthetics, or philosophy of mathematics. Why the latter is not the case can be found in Badiou 1995.

45. A different formulation of this is: "The one, being an operation [the count-as-one], is never a presentation" (*BBE*, 24). Badiou distinguishes the one as operation—counting something into ones or unities that thereby become presentable—from the one as result—the one or the unity that is the presented result of the count. See also *BBE*, 23–30.

46. Badiou explicitly asks: "Does this mean that being is not multiple either? Strictly speaking, yes, because being is only multiple inasmuch as it occurs in presentation" (*BE*, 24).

47. For a helpful introduction to the relationship of philosophy and mathematics in the work of Badiou, see Brassier 2005 and also the precise observations regarding the "resistance to mathematics" within the literature on Badiou that is a symptom of a "resistance to nothing" which mathematics enables to think in Clemens 2005.

48. Articulated differently, one might say that there is neither a big "one" (God) which encompasses all multiplicities nor a small "one" (an atom) as that which the multiplicities are made of. There cannot be only one presentation of being as this would be the definition of what God is for pantheism or panpsychism. For Badiou it is rather that there is only one presentation of being as being unpresentable, which is mathematics; this clearly is a Cartesian claim.

49. It should become clear in the following that this "something" which logically lies prior to the count is only accessible and thinkable as that which is retroactively graspable after the count. This is one consequence of the extensional conception of set theory. For a brief reconstruction of the distinction between intensional and extensional conceptions of sets, see Ruda 2011a, 151–55.

50. This is also why Badiou can claim that within set theory there is no representation involved. Presentation relies on the count-as-one and if its operator remains indeterminate—that is, without any definition of what it counts—there cannot be a second count—a count of the count—because it would not be intelligible what this second count would count and it would hence again logically regress to the level of the first count. This is also why set theory—suspending representation—is a presentation of presentation, or of *presentability*.

51. "The multiple from which ontology makes up its situation is composed solely of multiplicities . . . every multiple is a multiple of multiples" (*BBE*, 29).

52. The one as operation (count) and the one as result (consistent presentation) can never be fully mediated due to the fact that what can never be accounted for is the count itself, not even the indeterminate count of set theory. It is precisely in this gap between one as operation and as result that the suturing of ontology to being becomes thinkable. This is the gap between the finite and infinity.

53. This is why Badiou can claim: "What is required is that the operational structure of ontology discerns the multiple without having to make a one out of it, and therefore possessing a definition of the multiple" (BBE, 29).

54. As set theoretical ontology already subtracted the one from its count (it counts-one-minus-one) and consequentially counts pure multiplicity, it is clear that the non-one of the discourse which counts only indeterminate non-ones as one, the immanent non-one, can neither be non-one in the sense of multiplicity nor one. This is what the void is: the (unique) non-one of the *discourse counting non-ones-as-one-minus-one.*

55. Politically one can claim the same with regard to the distinction of democracy and totalitarianism on one side and communism on the other.

56. It should have become clear that the answer to this question also comprises a specification of what I called the dialectics of dialectics and non-dialectics, since dialectics and non-dialectics stand in an analogous relation to the One/Multiple on one side and the void on the other. The only distinctive element is that the non-dialectical element (which is the void) appears eventally and within ontology there is no theory of the event as being itself is precisely not eventual. This is to say: there is no relation between the dialectical part of a dialectics of dialectics and non-dialectics; this is precisely what makes it dialectical.

57. This argument originated in a discussion with Mladen Dolar, to whom I remain deeply indebted for it.

58. This is the precise point where one can grasp why Badiou does not put forward a transcendental argument. It is rather that from the most abstract discourse—ontology—one can learn that any transcendental setting will produce that which will have been constitutively prior to it and there thus just cannot be any transcendental grounding all discourses.

59. It thus makes no sense to speak with reference to the void in terms of movement or stasis. It suspends this very distinction (as it does with regards to the distinction of one/multiple). If anything the void is what I would be tempted to call *meta-stasis*. This is my answer with regard to the debate between Badiou and Žižek I depicted in the last chapter.

60. A different rendering of this point can be given in the following way: The "axiom of extensionality" which governs the realm of set theory states that a set which differs (locally) by one element from another set differs from it globally. But as the void has no elements, it is *indifferent to difference and/or identity*. Being indifferent towards it precisely names why the relationship between the void and the one/multiple is an *un-relation*. As the void is neither identical to any other set nor could it differ from any other (as both would presuppose having an element): the realm of difference and identity is the realm of elements, the void falls out of this realm. This explains the unicity of the void. It is the sole non-extensional and in-different term within set theory.

61. As Badiou has it: "The 'nothing' is what names the unperceivable gap, cancelled then renewed, between presentation as structure and presentation as structured-presentation, between the one as result and the one as operation, between presented consistency and inconsistency as what-will-have-been-presented . . . There is not a-nothing, there is 'nothing', phantom of inconsistency" (*BBE*, 54–55).

62. More precisely: the subject is void but it is not *the* void. As Badiou claims: "The contemporary Subject is void, cleaved, a-substantial, and ir-reflexive. Moreover, one can only suppose its existence in the context of particular processes whose conditions are rigorous" (*BBE*, 3). This means it is "the autonym of an empty idiom." Badiou 1993, 98. To put it in a formula: there is the void and there is a process voidening the situation which is the subject.

63. That the three is nothing but a torsion of the two is very close to what Lorenzo Chiesa calls the Not-Two. See Chiesa forthcoming.

64. I have reconstructed this Badiousian diagnosis in greater detail in Ruda 2009b.

65. Here the word of early Badiou speaking of a "pre-political situation" can be translated into the context of the contemporary ideological situation: because we are under the aegis of democratic materialism and the obstruction of any true conception of the two, we are in a *pre-materialist situation*. A *pre-materialist situation* is a situation after the collapse of idealism, a *post-idealist situation* which nonetheless is not yet materialist enough. In this *pre-materialist situation* the "post-" of post-idealism and the "pre-" of pre-materialism coincide. This is how I understand Badiou's claim that we are today living in an intermediate time; it is the coincidence of a "post" and a "pre." See "BSP I."

66. Why constructability is always a reactionary orientation presupposing a possible totalization—that is, the making-one out—of what "there is" can be grasped in *BBE*, 265–327.

67. Today this can be most evidently seen in the democratic materialist rendering of what love is: it is either the completely objectified register of all the needs of our bodies or it is the fusional becoming One of two individuals. Against this one has to insist that there is a subjective "scene of the Two" (Badiou) which can never be reduced to any fusional One or to something treated by contractual relations, which negotiate objective desires. For this, see Badiou 2012c.

68. One should be more precise here as it is important to even un-totalize non-totalizability once again. This is one of the central differences between any materialist dialectical thought and what Quentin Meillassoux advocated in Meillassoux 2010.

69. In other words: "There is" no "there is."

70. Žižek 2010b, 154.

71. As Badiou has it: "But the Two does not come to being as an ontological couple, it has to be apprehendable from the point of a third position which does not exist in the situation in which only the evental encounter produces the operation of the Two." Badiou 1990–1991.

72. One might even claim that this is precisely the dualism which one needs to uphold: one has to be a materialist *and* a dialectician and one cannot have

one of the sides separately. *No materialism without dialectics, no dialectics without materialism.*

73. This is why one discipline has a very weak stance under democratic materialist regimes, the discipline dealing with the love for wisdom: philosophy.

74. Sex is not abolished within any materialist dialectic but: "As a consequence, sexuality is deposed from its paradigmatic position—without thereby becoming, as in certain religious moralities, a counter-paradigm" (*BLoW*, 34).

75. Badiou: "There is no eternity of the eternal truths. They rise up through a particular act of evental creation and they rise up as eternal. The eternity of a truth is an attribute of truth as such, which is not to say that it is here since forever. It is not a question of duration or preexistence, it is an interior qualification. Eternity thus whatever point of time, it is identifiable as such. This is a Cartesian proposition." "BSP II."

76. Descartes 1824–1826, 6, 109

77. Descartes 1824–1826, 9, 171.

78. Even though the link between truths and subjects is not the most essential distinction, as Badiou asserts: "Of course the link between truth and the subject appears ancient, or in any case to have sealed the destiny of the first philosophical modernity whose inaugural name is Descartes. However, I am claiming to reactivate these terms within an entirely different perspective: . . . a doctrine which is effectively post-Cartesian, or even post-Lacanian . . . and institutes the subject, not as support or origin, but as *fragment* of the process of a truth" (*BBE*, 15).

79. Sartre 1967. See also Badiou 2009e.

80. This contingency of God's free will is crucial to avoid the claim that he cannot but create eternal truths which would limit the freedom involved in the creation of truths. Descartes was the first philosopher to radically insist on the necessity of contingency with regards to truth.

81. And hence we have what Badiou calls a "communication with the infinite." Badiou 2010f, 37.

82. In Badiou—at least taking up the language of *Logics of Worlds*—the contingency refers to more than just the event but also to "the contingency of the worlds, the aleatory character of a site, the efficacy of the organs of a body and the constancy of a subject" (*BLoW*, 513).

83. Descartes claims: "the will is by its nature free in such a way that it can never be constrained." This goes for God's and for anyone's will. Compare Descartes 1989, 41.

84. This is what Badiou once called a "thesis of discontinuity," as there is no necessary link between God and his creation. See "BN."

85. Badiou 1987–1988. At the same time what should become clear here is that even God is not "absolutely perfect" as there never can be a reason why he creates. God has no clue and no reason to create what he creates. He is somehow constituted and thus (logically) "preceded" by the contingency of his own will; he is not creating something out of an already present stuff, matter at hand. He does not simply turn this stuff into a/the world. God emerges through the act of contingently creating truths. *God is not before his act of creation and this very act is contingent* (which is to say: it is God and at the same time not-God who is act-

ing). This is why the very concept of perfection in Descartes—the lack of lack—is somehow the coincidence of perfection and imperfection which fully holds what Žižek once claimed: "if God is to be loved, he must be imperfect, inconsistent in himself; there has to be something 'in him' more than himself.'" *ZST*, 57.

86. As Badiou once put it: "Let us leave God aside." "BSP III."

87. Badiou also claims against Lacan: "What *still* attaches Lacan (but this *still* is the modern perpetuation of sense) to the Cartesian epoch of science is the thought that the subject must be maintained in the pure void of its subtraction if one wishes to save truth" (*BBE*, 432). Concerning the status of the subject in Lacan, see *BRL*, 19–23 and 77ff.

88. This question is a condensation of how to deal with Descartes's methodological monism: there is only one paradigm for truths—the mathematical one—valid for all fields of practice. One might thus deduce that this is also why Descartes can only think one subject as truth and not subjects of truths (which would be a Badiousian formula). This is to my mind a danger of any post-Cartesian (say Lacanian) theory, namely to introduce one monistic conception of the subject/ of truth.

89. And this is an essential exigency after the evental mathematical inventions of Cantor. As he has demonstrated that any "divine infinity in-consists . . ." (*BBE*, 42).

90. One might say it does so by retroactively determining what the evental site will have been. The evental site then is that which will have been the place where the unpresentable will have been named.

91. Hence Badiou does precisely think what some people criticize him for not considering: the subject in its becoming.

92. The possibility of this free choice was not present before the vanishing mediator of the encounter emerged. *The freedom of this free choice is thus no capacity of the individual* (to claim the opposite is what marks any Rousseauist position that relies on an already given capacity of the individual) as such but needs something which is able to produce it. Only retroactively, say, the lovers of a true encounter are able to claim that they voluntarily decided to take it seriously. An evental encounter therefore generates the very capacity which will retroactively have proven to be that which is able to unfold the consequences of the very conditions of possibility of this unfolding. The event creates the God on which it will have relied. This is materialism, idealism without idealism.

93. As Badiou has it, this axiom entails no longer a thesis about the being of God—as it did in Descartes—but about nature. Another rendering of it therefore is: "Nature is infinite" (*BBE*, 150). For his theory of nature and limit ordinals relating to the axiom of infinity, see *BBE*, 150–60. This is why, as I have shown above, the Cartesian God rather takes the place of the void in Badiou's reading of ontology as that which is even lacking lack.

94. "A present is the set of consequences in a world of an evental trace. These consequences only unfold to the extent that a body is capable of holding some points" (*BLoW*, 592).

95. It is potentially infinite because any step within the procedure of fidelity—which Badiou therefore names investigation—investigates a singular

element of a given situation with regard to its connection to the event. It investigates if it is positively or negatively connected to it—for example, can a conversation between lovers include words, sentences that are positively connected with the evental encounter of the loved ones or negatively? Thus by gathering only positively connected singular elements it generates a set of elements which encompasses only singularities. And they are only connected because of the aleatory path of the procedure of fidelity. This is why Badiou can insist on a second moment of infinity within the procedure of unfolding consequences. As he put it: "From an event a certain one-truth is inferred, but also, virtually, an infinity of others in accordance with the hazard and the choice." Badiou 1985, 58.

96. Or as he has it elsewhere: "The paradox for Descartes is that freedom to indifference is coextensive to the will and that this freedom as indifference is the lowest degree of it." Badiou 2002–2003. This distinction between freedom to indifference and freedom as indifference is absolutely crucial; the latter governs democratic materialism, the former is still the most fundamental definition of true freedom as it is based upon a *"decision to decide"* (*ZST*, 162) to be indifferent. The other implies being indifferent without knowing that one is indifferent and thus not knowing that one does not know anything (about the consequences of one's own actions).

97. Badiou takes this up in Badiou 2008b, 72–73.

98. To quote Žižek on this: "It is a well-known fact that the 'Close door' button in most lifts is a totally dysfunctional placebo, put there simply to give individuals the impression that they are somehow participating . . . This the extreme case of fake participation is an appropriate metaphor for individuals' participation in our 'postmodern' political process" (*ZST*, 241).

99. Badiou's diagnosis that we are again in a similar situation as Marx was has a certain surplus insight. Not only are we in the time where what emancipation means is unclear, one also does witness many phenomena that are very akin to Marx's depiction of the functioning of religious belief.

100. For an extensive analysis of elections and why they are essentially "a means to break with the divine violence of the revolutions" see Badiou 2012d, 9.

101. A brilliant rendering of this can be found in Dupuy 2002.

102. But one here should remember the famous French battle call "Tout ce qui bouge n'est pas rouge"—"Not everything that moves is red."

103. One paradigmatic figure representing this "historically enlightened" reactive subjective position is the German "philosopher" Norbert Bolz. Compare Bolz 2009.

104. Alexander Garcia Düttmann analyzed the limitations implied in the category of the possible with regard to Visconti. See Düttmann 2008.

105. See Lazarus 1996l.

106. This is also why, as Alenka Zupančič remarked, starting from the regime of the possible one contemporaneous concrete form of naturalization that eventually occurs is a racism of success: a racism that presents success as a natural category inscribed into our individual bodily capacities and lifestyles. See Zupančič 2008, 5–7.

107. As shall have become clear, this is the task of what I call *meta-critical anamnesis*. The relevant authors for this investigation are precisely Descartes, Hegel,

and Plato. Descartes as first modern theorist for the overcoming of disorienting indifference, Hegel as thinker of the mortifying effects of indifference which philosophy has to tackle, and ultimately Plato, who was the first to attack indifference under the name of the "sophist," one of the oldest enemies of philosophy. And, of course, all three of them clearly have a positive conception of another kind of indifference (God, the absolute, the idea of the Good) that is crucial for countering the ontic indifferences.

108. Badiou 1985, 40.

109. This can easily be learned from a love encounter. No one knows in advance *if* and if so *who* will be hurt if the love relationship does not work out.

110. One might add here that all of these indifferences are implied in what Badiou calls the "political fidelities that are indifferent to the desire for the Occident" (*BRH*, 85). The fetishization of the new is just another version of the fetishization of the youth. Both come with a form of voluntary forgetfulness also with regard to what is eternal in the old. Nothing is per se good, interesting, or relevant about newness or youth as such—one here as always needs conceptual qualifications.

111. In this context one should reread *BCH*.

112. Here one would have to say much more about the different notions of indifference within Badiou (and Descartes). Because it should be clear that being as being—named by the void—is also indifferent to differences. I have to leave this point aside for future investigations.

113. I want to defend the thesis that if philosophy is meta-ontology, meta-politics, and so forth with regards to its conditions, philosophy also has to be a meta-critical discourse.

114. Lacan 1998.

## Chapter 5

The epigraph for this chapter is from Badiou 2008g.

1. This is to say it insists on the split within the concrete historical "there is" that I elaborated on in the previous chapter.

2. See Badiou 1984.

3. Badiou 1993a.

4. For this cf. Badiou 2010d.

5. For this see also Hallward 2005.

6. Badiou 2009d, 13.

7. Badiou 2009d, 21.

8. For this see Badiou 2012e.

9. One rendering of Althusser's famous formula is: "History is a process, and a process without a subject." Althusser 1971a.

10. Marx 1970b, 142.

11. Here one can clearly see why the discussion of Descartes's proof of God in the previous chapter is absolutely crucial.

12. Badiou and Tarby 2010b, 14.

13. See Žižek's commentary of this point in *ZID*, 157–210.

14. The most elaborate interpretation of Shalamov's literary work with regards to his analysis of the absence of politics in terms of corruption was written by Badiou himself in 1985b.

15. Here one should add what Žižek once stated with regard to two different levels of "corruption in democracy: *de facto* empirical corruption, and the corruption that pertains to the very *form* of democracy with its reduction of politics to the negotiation of private interests" (*ZLE*, 55). As should be clear, I am here referring to the latter one.

16. Bruno Latour is the inventor of the charmless idea of what he calls a *parliament of things*. One of the best renderings of his thought—although in an adequately critical manner—can be found in Brassier 2011.

17. See *BLoW*, 43–78.

18. In the general context of Badiou's political thought, the reader obviously should be aware of Bruno Bosteel's work. See, for example, Bosteels 2011.

19. See *BMS*, 97–117.

20. See *BTS*, 13–36.

21. Ex negatively put: as soon as the procedure of fidelity is turned into an exercise of rule following or as soon as within it a law is installed on how to proceed, fidelity already became unfaithful to its own course. Thus one might go as far as claiming that the only way to properly remain faithful (to one's fidelity) is through repeated acts of constant (self-)betrayal—otherwise one establishes something stable and fixed within it. This is also why any true pupil of a master can only be faithful to him or her by utterly betraying him or her at one point.

22. The whole slogan of a "politics in distance from the state" that Badiou and his comrades have been putting forward only makes sense against this background.

23. For this paradigm, see the short polemic text written by Badiou under his early pseudonym: Peyrol 1983.

24. Badiou 2006b. One would have to draw a further line of demarcation here, as this prescription, this slogan, could seem to be another version of what Toni Negri (and others) refer to as "exodus." Hardt and Negri 2011, 150–165. Simply put: politics in distance from the state means acting and organizing as if the state did already perish (without letting oneself be oriented by it in any way), whereas the exodus concept implies an acting out of the very political and social status of those who are included by exclusion. The former position thus leads to actions (and organizations) which already consider the situation from a different perspective (subtracting the state), while the latter leads to affirming the situation as it is (from the very point of view of the situation). Still, this topic remains to be investigated in much greater detail as it also touches on the political dimension of what Heidegger once phrased as letting-things-be (*Seinlassen*).

25. Badiou himself employs this formulation in Badiou 2003c, 95.

26. For a brief but striking analysis of parliamentarism and its "theatralization of the political life," see *BSPQ*, 47ff.

27. This is what in Germany the founding process of the "Linke" demonstrated in an obscenely clear manner.

28. "Democracy" became what Jan Völker and I call a "signifier of disorientation." See Ruda and Völker 2011, 215ff.

29. See *ZID*, 420–62.

30. Although it is quite fashionable to argue that we are criticizing from a quite comfortable position, since there are countries in which things are much worse than in Western democracies, I want to underline the idea that there is precisely no reason why the insight that it is worse somewhere else should justify the present state of things here.

31. For the technical details of this concept, see *BBE*, 391–440; Cohen 2002; Cohen 2008, 129–44. My argument bears certain affinities with what Adrian Johnston developed in Johnston 2008b.

32. To give a simple example: a new mathematical invention does not only produce truth effects in the sense of theoretical consequences (theorems), it also changes what is considered to be the "objective" status of knowledge in the given situation. For example, these effects really materialize when math books in schools will be changed.

33. Badiou himself relates the concept of mathematical forcing to Freud's idea of "working through." *BC*, 138.

34. Here one can see Badiou's dialectical genius. It is not enough to oppose infinite against finitude and it is also not enough to claim that infinity is unfolded by finite agents and hence always in a finite manner. One ultimately also needs to assert that the only possible access to infinity is one that includes the finitude of infinity itself—which is just another way of saying that there are infinitely many infinities. Badiou developed this in greater detail in Badiou 2011d.

35. This is important to note. Philosophy does not counter the democratic materialist ideology by functioning as a science; it does *not* oppose science and ideology. Philosophy operates within the domain of ideology as ideology, or better, as *idea-ology* against any effect of naturalization (the always primary technique of reactionary and obscurantist ideology) by insisting on the necessity of having a conception of eternal ideas. Or put differently: philosophy can only oppose the hegemonic ideological democratic naturalization of the given by insisting on the impossible possibility of an exception.

36. "FRRW." See also Hamacher 1996.

37. See Žižek 2008b, XI–CVII.

38. This is my rendering of Badiou's claim that it is precisely "the mark of castration" that "separates truth from itself and, in the same movement, frees up its power and hypothetical anticipation from the encyclopedic field of forms of knowledge. This power is the power of forcing" (*BC*, 139). Philosophical forcing works by taking the very position of the barring, that is to say of the mark of castration. It is not the position of the bar—as the bar is not one—but in a very precise sense the position of the very operation of the barring, that is to say the very condition for the emergence of a new truth (the split between event and the consequences that it produces). The barred barred subject thus takes the position of the anticipated subject by insisting on the impossible possibility of the place of (any future) barring.

39. This is why the philosophical subject is not a subject in the sense this notion receives in the conditions. It is a subject minus the subject, it takes the posi-

tion of the very minus. It also should be clear that the philosophical subject does not take the position of the event, but of the split between the event and its consequences. Thus it takes the position of the Two, but not of the Two of Love—as Alenka Zupančič has ingeniously suggested (compare Zupančič 2004)—but of the Two of the Two; of the Two in their very form, or put again differently: if any bar produces a split in the twice-barred Two, the split in its form marks the position of the barring (and not of the bar).

40. This formulation I owe to Christoph Menke, who first used it in defining the ethical stance involved in his position. Menke is much closer to Badiou than one would think at first. See his against all appearances not vitalist book: Menke 2012.

Chapter 6

The first epigraph for this chapter is from Lacan 1991, 71.

1. Badiou 2009f, 4.

2. As was already suggested by Žižek in 2002a.

3. This is to say that in *Logic of Worlds* he discusses the overall project of the *Logic*, as I will demonstrate subsequently, starting from its very preconditions and axioms.

4. But to be absolutely precise: *there is no relation* between being and nothing in the beginning of the *Logic*, as Hegel puts it, there is only a "negation devoid of any relation" (*HSL*, 83).

5. One might suspect that one reason for Badiou to insist on the fact that there are four conditions of philosophy can be inferred from a different rendering of how to comprehend the two twos in the beginning of Hegel's *Logic*.

6. This is why Badiou can state that "the mark [is] never equal to itself" (*BRK*, 52).

7. This is the movement which Miller called "stratification." See Miller 2000.

8. This is very close to the split in itself I reconstructed as crucial for Žižek's account of Hegel. Referred to in chapter 4.

9. The space of all possible places where a something can occur is what Badiou with a neologism calls "splace." See *BTS*, 9–10.

10. See *BMS*, 105–17.

11. It shall be clear that Badiou's criticism here implies both (1) Hegel does identify infinity with circularity and hence with oneness and thereby finitize the infinite, and from a different perspective that he (2) is thereby unable to account for the proper finitude of historical sequences. These are basically two sides of one and the same criticism.

12. From a different perspective (materialist periodization) and within a different setting (nonexistence of the one) Badiou subscribes to this claim. History does not exist as totalizable entity. See *BTS*, 92.

13. More precisely the following pages: *HSL*, 82–135.

14. *BBE* 161–72.

15. Yet, one might claim that this is no flaw of Badiou's approach but a very Hegelian handling of Hegel, as everything depends on the very beginning.

16. That Badiou wants to ground his meta-ontological claims on the necessity of a subjective decision—without falling back into relativism or bad subjectivism—is straightforwardly articulated in *Being and Event* from its very meditation onwards. Or as he once put it, his meta-ontology proceeds "by way of axiomatic decisions (*as if* they were contingent) and by way of constraining demonstrations (*as if* they were necessary)." Badiou 2010g, 33.

17. The one something is precisely negatively determined by all the things it is not.

18. Here the fact that the something is negatively determined in an external manner is internalized and presented as a constitutive momentum of the something. But to do so, the external relations cannot count in the same manner they did before. Hence all externalities have to be voided of content, such that the only thing that truly counts is the something; the rest is just empty space around it.

19. One may say the one something encounters the externality within itself.

20. Their separation is what Badiou articulates as the two existential seals of his set theory-based meta-ontological proposal. The first axiomatically affirms the existence of the void (as name of being), the second affirms the existence of proper infinity. See *BBE*, 60–69, 156–57.

21. This point is crucial and implies an inversion of Hegel's schema: there is "good" infinity (i.e., an infinity that is not simple potentially endless repetition) and there is "bad infinity" (i.e., pure multiplicity), yet these two do not coincide; both have to be axiomatically affirmed separately and can never be identified. Another way of rendering Badiou's criticism is: the void is *not* that which grounds the infinite.

22. It is objectively impossible, since there is no objective law that might determine how to decide.

23. This is what I have shown in greater detail in chapter 4.

24. This is, to my mind, Badiou's direct answer to anyone attacking him for not accounting of dialectical mediation—say between being and appearing. Why is there no account of their relation in Badiou? Simply, because there is no relation between them. This is not a flaw of his system but one of the very dialectical points of it. For if you seek to dialecticize everything, that is to say, if you seek to totalize mediation you lose dialectics proper. Badiou in this point is very Hegelian.

25. The following closing remarks are nothing but an abbreviated sketch of a changed perspective on what the Hegelian project seeks to achieve. This will be elaborated extensively in a forthcoming book that I am preparing with Rebecca Comay under the title "The Dash: Vicissitudes of Absolute Knowing."

26. As might be known to the reader, Badiou declared that he is working on the third volume of *Being and Event*, whose title is "Immanence of Truths." This book will be dealing with the question of how to depict what happens to an individual that becomes a (part of a) subject after an evental encounter of a truth procedure from within the individual. What I am suggesting here—fully embracing the logic of the future anterior—is that this very book might already exist: it will have been Hegel's *Science of Logic*. See Badiou 2011i.

27. For this see Ruda 2013c.

# Bibliography

Adorno, Theodor W. 2005. *Minima Moralia: Reflections on Damaged Life.* London: Verso.

———. 2008. *Lectures on Negative Dialectics: Fragments of a Lecture Course 1965/1966.* Cambridge, Eng.: Polity.

Althusser, Louis. 1971a. "Lenin before Hegel." In *Lenin and Philosophy and Other Essays* by Louis Althusser, 107–26. London: Monthly Review Press.

———. 1971b. "Philosophy as Revolutionary Weapon (February 1968)." In *Lenin and Philosophy and other Essays*, 11–12. New York: Monthly Review Press.

———. 1990. *Philosophy and the Spontaneous Philosophy of Scientists and Other Essays.* London: Verso.

Althusser, Louis, and Etienne Balibar. 1975. *Reading Capital.* London: Monthly Review Press.

Anders, Günther. 1980. *Die Antiquiertheit des Menschen. Vol. 2: Über die Zerstörung des Lebens im Zeitalter der dritten industriellen Revolution.* Munich: Fischer.

Aristotle. 1988. *Metaphysics.* London: Penguin.

Badiou, Alain. 1982. "'Théorie du sujet': Entretien avec Alain Badiou." *Le Perroquet* no. 13/14: 10–13.

———. 1984. "Custos quid noctis?" *Critique* 450 (November 1984): 851–63.

———. 1985a. "Six propriétés de la vérité." *Ornicar?* 11, no. 32 (January–March): 39–67.

———. 1985b. *Peut-on penser la politique?* Paris: Seuil.

———. 1987–1988. *"Orientation de pensée transcendante (Cours d'Alain Badiou)."* http://www.entretemps.asso.fr/Badiou/87–88.htm.

———. 1990–1991. *Théorie du mal et de l'amour.* http://www.entretemps.asso.fr/Badiou/90–91.htm.

———. 1991. "On a Finally Objectless Subject." In *What Comes after the Subject?* edited by Eduardo Cadava, Peter Connor, and Jean-Luc Nancy, 93–98. London: Routledge.

———. 1993a. "Nous pouvons redéployer la philosophie." *Le Monde,* August 31, p. 2.

———. 1993b. "Sur le livre de Françoise Proust, *Le ton de l'histoire.*" *Les Temps Modernes* 565/566: 238–48.

———. 1993–1994a. *"Séminaire: Théorie des catégories."* http://www.entretemps.asso.fr/Badiou/seminaire.htm.

———. 1993–1994b. *"Séminaire: L'antiphilosophie de Wittgenstein."* http://www.entretemps.asso.fr/Badiou/93–94.htm.

——. 1994–1995. "*Séminaire sur Lacan.*" http://www.entretemps.asso.fr/Badiou/94–95.htm.

——. 1995. "Platon et/ou Aristote/Leibniz : Théorie des ensembles et théorie des topos sous l'oeil du philosophe." In *L'objectivité mathématique: Platonisme et structures formelles,* edited by Marko Panza and Jean-Michel Salanskis, 61–83. Paris: Masson.

——. 1995–1996. "*Séminaire: Topos ou logiques de l'onto-logique.*" http://www.entretemps.asso.fr/Badiou/95–96.htm.

——. 1997. "Lacans Herausforderung der Philosophie." In *Politik der Wahrheit,* edited by Rado Riha, 46–54. Vienna: Turia + Kant.

——. 1999. *Manifesto for Philosophy.* Albany: SUNY Press.

——. 2000. "Metaphysics and the Critique of Metaphysics." *Pli* 10: 174–90.

——. 2000–2001. "*La nature: Cours d'agrégation (ENS).*" http://www.entretemps.asso.fr/Badiou/00–01.Nature.htm.

——. 2001. *Ethics: An Essay on the Understanding of Evil.* London: Verso.

——. 2001–2002. "*Séminaire: Image du temps présent I.*" http://www.entretemps.asso.fr/Badiou/01–02.3.htm.

——. 2002. *Metapolitica.* Napels: Cronopio.

——. 2002–2003. "*La volonté": Cours d'agrégation d'Alain Badiou.*" http://www.entretemps.asso.fr/Badiou/02–03.2.htm.

——. 2002–2003a. "*Séminaire : Image du temps présent II.*" http://www.entretemps.asso.fr/Badiou/02–03.3.htm.

——. 2003a. *Infinite Thought: Truth and the Return of Philosophy.* London: Continuum.

——. 2003b. *On Beckett.* Manchester: Clinamen.

——. 2003c. *Saint Paul: The Foundation of Universalism.* Stanford, Calif.: Stanford University Press.

——. 2004. "Some Replies to a Demanding Friend." In *Think Again: Alain Badiou and the Future of Philosophy,* edited by Peter Hallward, 232–37. London: Continuum.

——. 2004–2005. "*Séminaire: S'orienter dans la pensée, s'orienter dans l'existence I.*" http://www.entretemps.asso.fr/Badiou/04–05.2.htm.

——. 2005a. "Manifesto of Affirmationism." *Lacanian Ink* 24/25: 92–109.

——. 2005b. *Being and Event.* London: Continuum.

——. 2005c. *Metapolitics.* London: Verso.

——. 2005–2006. "*Séminaire : S'orienter dans la pensée, s'orienter dans l'existence II.*" http://www.entretemps.asso.fr/Badiou/05–06.2.htm.

——. 2006a. "Plato, Our Dear Plato!" *Angelaki: Journal for the Theoretical Humanities* 2, no. 3 (December): 39–45.

——. 2006b. "Politique et vérité." *Contretemps* no. 15 (February): 47–66.

——. 2006–2007. "*Séminaire : S'orienter dans la pensée, s'orienter dans l'existence III.*" http://www.entretemps.asso.fr/Badiou/06–07.2.htm.

——. 2007a. "Philosophy as Creative Repetition." *The Symptom: Online Journal for Lacan.com* 8 (Winter). http://www.lacan.com/badrepeat.html.

——. 2007b. *The Century.* Cambridge, Eng.: Polity.

——. 2008a. *Conditions.* London: Continuum.

——. 2008b. *The Meaning of Sarkozy.* London: Verso.

———. 2008c. *Number and Numbers*. Cambridge, Eng.: Polity.

———. 2008d. "The Three Negations." *Cardozo Law Review* 29, no. 5: 1877–83.

———. 2008e. "Rhapsody for the Theater." *Theater Survey* 49, no. 2 (November): 187–238.

———. 2008f. "Le 21e siècle: Entretien avec Elie During." http://www.ciepfc.fr/spip.php?article57.

———. 2008g. "Philosophy as Biography." *The Symptom: Online Journal for Lacan.com* 9 (Winter). http://www.lacan.com/symptom9_articles/badiou19.html.

———. 2009a. *Logics of Worlds: Being and Event, 2*. London: Continuum.

———. 2009b. *Of an Obscure Disaster/On the End of State-Truth*. Maastricht: Jan van Eyck.

———. 2009c. *Theory of the Subject*. London: Continuum.

———. 2009d "Thinking the Event." In *Philosophy in the Present*, by Alain Badiou and Slavoj Žižek, 1–48. Cambridge, Eng.: Polity.

———. 2009e. "Jean-Paul Sartre." In *Pocket Pantheon: Figures of Postwar Philosophy*, by Alain Badiou, 14–35. London: Verso.

———. 2009f. "Jacques Lacan." In *Pocket Pantheon: Figures of Postwar Philosophy*, by Alain Badiou, 1–4. London: Verso.

———. 2010a. *The Communist Hypothesis*. London: Continuum.

———. 2010b. *Le fini et l'infini*. Montrouge: Bayard.

———. 2010c. "De l'obscurantisme contemporain." *Le Monde* May 7. http://www.lemonde.fr/retrospective/article/2010/05/07/de-l-obscurantisme-contemporain-par-alain-badiou_1348095_1453557.html.

———. 2010d. "Beyond Positivism and Nihilism." http://www.egs.edu/faculty/alain-badiou/videos/beyond-positivism-and-nihilism/.

———. 2010e. "Lacan and Philosophy." http://www.youtube.com/watch?v=-GY8a3DYV0U.

———. 2010f. "The Courage of the Present." http://www.scribd.com/doc/52646249/Badiou-The-Courage-of-the-Present.

———. 2010g. "Commitment, Detachment, Fidelity." In *The Adventure of French Philosophy*, by Alain Badiou, 27–37. London: Verso.

———. 2010–2011. *"Séminaire: Que signifie 'changer le monde'"*? http://www.entretemps.asso.fr/Badiou/10-11.htm.

———. 2011a. *Le réveil de l'histoire: Circonstances, 6*. Paris: Lignes.

——— et al. 2011b. *The Rational Kernal of the Hegelian Dialectic*. Melbourne: re.press.

———. 2011c. *Second Manifesto for Philosophy*. Cambridge, Eng.: Polity.

———. 2011d. "Towards a Contemporary Conception of the Absolute." http://vimeo.com/28417395.

———. 2011e. "Politics: A Non-Expressive Dialectics." In *Beyond Potentialities? Politics between the Possible and the Impossible*, edited by Mark Potocnik, Frank Ruda, and Jan Völker, 13–22. Zurich: Diaphanes.

———. 2011f. "The Crisis of Negation: An Interview with Alain Badiou." http://continentcontinent.cc/index.php/continent/article/viewArticle/65.

———. 2011g. "A History of Finitude and Infinity: Classicism." http://www.egs.edu/faculty/alain-badiou/articles/a-history-of-finitude-and-infinity/.

———. 2011h. "Infinity and Set Theory: How to Begin with the Void." http://www.egs.edu/faculty/alain-badiou/articles/infinity-and-set-theory/.

———. 2011i. "Conférence de Ljubljana." *Filozofski vestnik* 32, no. 2: 7–24.

———. 2011–2012. *"Séminaire pour aujourd'hui: Platon!"* http://www.entretemps .asso.fr/Badiou/07–08.htm.

———. 2012a. "The Current Situation on the Philosophical Front." In *The Adventure of French Philosophy*, by Alain Badiou, 1–18. London: Verso.

———. 2012b. "Logology Against Ontology." In *The Adventure of French Philosophy*, by Alain Badiou, 309–20. London: Verso.

———. 2012c. *In Praise of Love*. New York: New.

———. 2012d. *Sarkozy: Pire que prévu, les autres: Prévoir le pire: Circonstances, 7.* Paris: Lignes.

———. 2012e. "The Enigmatic Relationship between Philosophy and Politics." In *Philosophy for Militants*, by Alain Badiou, 1–40. London: Verso.

———. 2012f. *The Rebirth of History: Times of Riots and Uprisings*. London: Verso.

———. 2012–2013. *"Séminaire: L'immanence des vérités."* http://www.entretemps .asso.fr/Badiou/12–13.htm.

———. 2013a. *La pornographie du temps présent*. Paris: Fayard.

———. 2013b. *Plato's Republic: A Dialogue in 16 Chapters*. Cambridge, Eng.: Polity.

———. 2013c. *Philosophie und die Idee des Kommunismus: Im Gespräch mit Peter Engelmann*. Vienna: Passagen.

———. 2013d. "The Communist Idea and the Question of Terror." In *The Idea of Communism 2: The New York Conference*, edited by Alain Badiou and Slavoj Žižek, 1–12. London: Verso.

———. 2013e. *Le séminaire: Lacan: L'antiphilosophie 3, 1994–1995*. Paris: Fayard.

Badiou, Alain, Frank Ruda, and Jan Völker. 2009. "Wir müssen das affirmative Begehren hüten." In *Dritter Entwurf eines Manifests für den Affirmationismus*, by Alain Badiou, 37–54. Berlin: Merve.

Badiou, Alain, and Fabien Tarby. 2010b. *La philosophie de l'événément: Entretiens*. Paris: Germina

Badiou, Alain, Joel Bellassen, and Louis Mossot. 2011. *The Rational Kernel of the Hegelian Dialectic*. Melbourne: re.press.

Badiou, Alain, and Élisabeth Roudinesco. 2012. *Lacan, passé present: Dialogue*. Paris: Seuil.

Balso, Judith. 2011. *Pessao, The Metaphysical Courier*. New York: Atropos.

Bartlett, A. J. 2011. *Badiou and Plato: An Education by Truths*. Edinburgh: Edinburgh University Press.

Bloch, Ernst. 1986. *The Principle of Hope, vol. 1*. Massachusetts: MIT Press.

Boltanski, Luc, and Eve Chiapello. 2007. *The New Spirit of Capitalism*. London: Verso.

Bolz, Norbert. 2009. *Diskurs über die Ungleichheit: Ein Anti-Rousseau*. Munich: Fink.

Bosteels, Bruno. 2011. *Badiou and Politics*. Durham, N.C.: Duke University Press.

Brassier, Ray. 2005. "Badiou's Materialist Epistemology of Mathematics." *Angelaki: Journal of the Theoretical Humanities* 10, no. 2: 135–50.

———. 2011. "Concepts and Objects." In *The Speculative Turn: Continental Materialism and Realism*, edited by Levy Bryant, Nick Srnicek, and Graham Harman, 51–54. Melbourne: re.press.

Canetti, Elias. "Realismus und neue Wirklichkeit." In *Das Gewissen der Worte: Essays*, by Elias Canetti, 66–72. Munich: Hanser.

Chiesa, Lorenzo. 2011. "Notes Towards a Manifesto for Metacritical Realism." In *Beyond Potentialities? Politics between the Possible and the Impossible*, edited by Mark Potocnik, Frank Ruda, and Jan Völker, 23–38. Zurich: Diaphanes.

———. Typescript. "The Body of the Structural Dialectic, or the Partisan and the 'Human Animal.'"

———. forthcoming. *The Not-Two: Logic, Love and God in Lacan.*

Clemens Justin. 2005. "Doubles of Nothing: The Problem of Binding Truth to Being in the Work of Alain Badiou." *Filozofski Vestnik* 26, no. 2: 97–111.

Cohen, Paul. 2001. "The Discovery of Forcing." *Rocky Mountain Journal of Mathematics* 32, no. 4 (Winter): 1071–1100.

———. 2008. *Set Theory and Continuum Hypothesis.* New York: Dover Books.

Comay, Rebecca. 2011. *Mourning Sickness: Hegel and the French Revolution.* Stanford, Calif.: Stanford University Press.

Copjec, Joan. 1996. *Read My Desire: Lacan against the Historicists.* Massachusetts: MIT Press.

Corcoran, Steve. 2014. *The Badiou Dictionary.* Edinburgh: Edinburgh University Press.

Descartes, René. 1824–1826. *Oeuvres de Descartes,* edited by Victor Cousin. 11 vols. Paris: Levraut (quoted as Descartes 1824–1826 followed by volume number and page rank).

———. 1989. *The Passions of the Soul.* Indianapolis, Ind.: Hackett.

———. 1998. *The World and Other Writings.* Cambridge, Eng.: Cambridge University Press.

———. 2000a. *Meditations on First Philosophy (1641).* In *Philosophical Essays and Correspondence,* by René Descartes, 97–142. Indianapolis, Ind.: Hackett.

———. 2000b. *Discourse on the Method for Conducting One's Reason Well and for Seeking the Truth in the Sciences (1637).* In *Philosophical Essays and Correspondence,* by René Descartes, 46–83. Indianapolis, Ind.: Hackett.

Dolar, Mladen. Typescript 1. "Tyche, clinamen, den."

———. Typescript 2. "Clinamen."

———. 1998. "Cogito as Subject of the Unconscious." In *Cogito and the Unconscious,* edited by Slavoj Žižek, 11–40. Durham, N.C.: Duke University Press.

———. 2005. "Nothing Has Changed." *Filozosfki vestnik* 26, no. 2: 147–60.

———. 2013. "The Atom and the Void—from Democritus to Lacan." *Filozosfki vestnik* 34, no. 2: 11–26.

Dupuy, Jean-Pierre. 2002. *Pour un catastrophisme éclairé: Quand l'impossible est certain.* Paris: Seuil.

Düttmann, Alexander Garcia. 2008. *Visconti: Insights into Flesh and Blood.* Stanford, Calif.: Stanford University Press.

Engels, Friedrich. 1940. *Dialectics of Nature.* Translated by C. P. Dutt. New York: International.

———. 1970. *Ludwig Feuerbach and the Outcome of Classical German Philosophy.* New York: International.

Feltham, Oliver. 2008. *Alain Badiou: Live Theory.* London: Continuum.

Foucault, Michel. 1981. "The Order of Discourse." In *Untying the Text: A Post-Structuralist Reader,* edited by Robert Young. Boston: Routledge.

Freud, Sigmund. 1959. *Inhibition, Symptom, Anxiety.* In *The Standard Edition of the Psychological Works of Sigmund Freud, vol.* 20, 77–175. New York: Norton and Norton.

———. 1964. "Remembering, Repeating, Working Through. (Further Recommendations on the Technique of Psycho-Analysis II)." In *The Standard Edition of the Psychological Works of Sigmund Freud,* vol. 12, 145–56. New York: Norton and Norton.

Gans, Eduard. 2005. *Naturrecht und Universalgeschichte: Vorlesungen nach G.W.F. Hegel.* Tübingen: Klett-Cotta.

Getty, J. Arch, and Oleg V. Naumov. 2010. *The Road to Terror: Stalin and the Self-Destruction of the Bolsheviks, 1932–1939.* New Haven, Conn.: Yale University Press.

Gould, Stephen Jay. 1982. "A Crucial Tool for Evolutionary Biology." *Journal of Social Issues* 47: 43–65.

Hair, Lindsey. 2006. "Ontology and Appearing: Documentary Realism as a Mathematical Thought." In *The Practice of Alain Badiou,* edited by Paul Ashton, A. J. Bartlett, and Justin Clemens, 265–90. Melbourne: re.press.

Hallward, Peter. 2003. *Badiou: A Subject to Truth.* Minneapolis: University of Minnesota Press.

———. 2005. "The Politics of Prescription." *The South Atlantic Quarterly* 104, no. 4 (Fall): 769–89.

Hamacher, Werner. 1996. "Working Through Working: Notes on the Concept of Work under National Socialism." *Modernism/Modernity* 3, no. 1 (Spring): 23–55.

Hardt, Michael, and Toni Negri. 2011. *Commonwealth.* Cambridge, Mass.: Belknap Press of Harvard University.

Haug, Wolfgang Fritz. 1984. "Die Camera obscura des Bewusstseins." In *Die Camera obscura der Ideologie,* edited by Projekt Ideologie-Theorie, 9–95. Berlin: Argument Verlag.

Hegel, G. W. F. 1969. *Science of Logic.* New York: Humanity Books.

———.1971. *Early Theological Writings.* Chicago: University of Pennsylvania Press.

———. 1979. *Phenomenology of Spirit.* Oxford: Oxford University Press.

———. 2004. *Philosophy of Nature: Part Two of the Encyclopedia of Philosophical Sciences (1830).* Oxford: Oxford University Press.

———. 2008. *Outlines of the Philosophy of Right.* Oxford: Oxford University Press.

Heidegger, Martin. 1969. "On Marx." http://www.youtube.com/watch?v=Oxmz GTlw_kk.

———. 1982. "The Question Concerning Technology." In *The Question Concerning Technology and Other Essays* by Martin Heidegger, 3–35. New York: Harper.

———. 1991. *Nietzsche.* New York: Harper and Row.

———. 1998. "Plato's Doctrine of Truth (1931/32, 1940)." In *Pathmarks,* by Martin Heidegger, 155–83. Cambridge, Eng.: Cambridge University Press.

———. 2005. *Seminar in Le Thor 1969.* In *Gesamtausgabe.* Vol. 15. Tübingen: Klostermann.

———. 2008. *Being and Time.* New York: Harper and Row.

Hewlett, Nick. *Badiou, Balibar, Rancière: Re-thinking Emancipation.* London: Continuum.

Huber, Carlo Ernst. 1964. *Anamnesis bei Plato.* Munich: Hueber.

Jameson, Fredric. 1973. "The Vanishing Mediator: Narrative Structure in Max Weber." *New German Critique* no. 1 (Winter): 52–89

———. 1988. "Cognitive Mapping." In *Marxism and the Interpretation of Culture,* edited by Cary Nelson and Lawrence Grossberg, 347–60. Champaign: University of Illinois Press.

———. 2010. *The Hegel Variations: On the "Phenomenology of Spirit."* London: Verso.

Johnston, Adrian. 2008a. *Žižek's Ontology: A Transcendental Materialist Theory of Subjectivity.* Evanston, Ill.: Northwestern University Press.

———. 2008b. "Courage before the Event: The Force of Affects." *Filozofski vestnik* 29, no. 2: 101–33.

Korsch, Karl. 2009. *Marxism and Philosophy.* New York: Monthly Review.

Koyré, Alexandre. 1968. *Discovering Plato.* New York: Columbia University Press.

Labica, Georges. 1987. *Karl Marx: Les thèses sur Feuerbach.* Paris: Presses Universitaires de France.

Lacan, Jacques. 1991. *The Seminar: Book II: The Ego in Freud's Theory and in the Technique of Psychoanalysis.* New York: Norton and Norton.

———. 1992. *The Seminar: Book VII: The Ethics of Psychoanalysis, 1959–60.* London: Routledge.

———. 1998. *Le séminaire 5: Les formations de l'inconscient.* Paris: Seuil.

———. 2006a. "The Function and Field of Speech and Language in Psychoanalysis." In *Écrits,* by Jacques Lacan, 197–268. New York: Norton and Norton.

———. 2006b. "The Freudian Thing, or the Meaning of the Return to Freud." In *Écrits,* by Jacques Lacan, 334–63. New York: Norton and Norton.

———. 2006c. "Beyond the "Reality Principle." In *Écrits,* by Jacques Lacan, 58–74. New York: Norton and Norton.

Lavine, Shaughan. 1998. *Understanding the Infinite.* Cambridge, Mass.: Harvard University Press.

Lazarus, Sylvain. 1996. *Anthropologie du nom.* Paris: Seuil.

———. 2007. "Lenin and the Party, 1902—November 1917." In *Lenin Reloaded: Toward a Politics of Truth,* edited by Sebastian Budgen, Stathis Kouvelakis, and Slavoj Žižek, 255–68. Durham, N.C.: Duke University Press.

Lenin, V. I. 1972. "On the Significance of Militant Materialism." In *Collected Works,* vol. 33, 227–36. Moscow: Progress.

———. 1973. "Left-Wing Communism: An Infantile Disorder." In *Collected Works,* vol. 31, 17–118. Moscow: Progress.

———. 1978. *The State and Revolution: The Marxist Teaching on the State and the Tasks of the Proletariat in the Revolution.* Peking: International.

Lissagaray, Prosper Olivier. 2012. *The History of the Paris Commune of 1871.* London: Verso.

Lukàcs, György. 2009. *Lenin: A Study on the Unity of his Thought.* London: Verso.

Macherey, Pierre. 2008. *Marx 1845: Les "theses" sur Feuerbach.* Paris: Amsterdam.

Manonni, Octave. 2003. "I Know Very Well, But All the Same." In *Perversion and Social Relation,* edited by Molly Anne Rothenberg, Dennis Foster, and Slavoj Žižek, 68–92. Durham, N.C.: Duke University Press.

Mao Zedong. 2008. *De la pratique et de la contradiction: Avec une lettre d'Alain Badiou et la réponse de Slavoj Žižek.* Paris: La Fabrique.

Marx, Karl. 1858. "Letter to F. Lassalle." http://www.cddc.vt.edu/marxists/archive/marx/works/1858/letters/58_02_22.htm.

———. 1970a. *Critique of Hegel's "Philosophy of Right."* Cambridge, Eng.: Cambridge University Press.

———. 1970b. "A Contribution to the Critique of Hegel's *Philosophy of Right.* Introduction." In *Critique of Hegel's "Philosophy of Right,"* by Karl Marx, 129–42. Cambridge, Eng.: Cambridge University Press.

———. 1975. "Concerning Feuerbach." In *Early Writings*, by Karl Marx, 421–23. London: Penguin.

———. 1975b. "Economic and Philosophical Manuscripts (1844)." In *Early Writings*, by Karl Marx, 279–400. London: Penguin.

Meillassoux, Quentin. 2010. *After Finitude: An Essay on Contingency and Necessity.* London: Continuum.

Menke, Christoph. 2012. *Force: A Fundamental Concept of Aesthetic Anthropology.* New York: Fordham University Press.

Miller, Jacques-Alain. 2000. "Matrix." http://www.lacan.com/symptom13/?p=127.

Milner, Jean-Claude. 1998. *L'oeuvre Claire: Lacan, la science, la philosophie.* Paris: Seuil.

Nancy, Jean-Luc. 2005. *L'extension de l'âme.* Paris: Fabrique.

Norrie, Alan. 2009. *Dialectic and Difference: Dialectical Critical Realism and the Grounds of Justice.* Oxon., Eng.: Routledge.

Pasolini, Pier Paolo. 2007. *Der heilige Paulus.* Schüren: Marburg.

———. 2013. *Saint Paul.* Paris: Fayard.

Peyrol, Georges (Badiou, Alain). 1983. "30 moyens de reconnaitre à coup sûr un vieux-marxiste." *Le Perroquet* 29–30: 5–6.

Pluth, Ed. 2010. *Badiou: A Philosophy of the New.* Cambridge, Eng.: Polity.

Popper, Karl Raimund. 1966. *The Open Society and Its Enemies, vol. 1: The Spell of Plato.* Princeton, N.J.: Princeton University Press.

Riha, Rado. 2005. "Handeln, 'ob ich gleich nichts anderes wollte': Kants praktische Philosophie als Theorie subjektivierenden Handelns." *Filozofski vestnik* 26, no. 2: 37–50.

Ruda, Frank. 2009a. "Humanism Reconsidered, or Life Living Life." *Filozosfki Vestnik* 30, no. 2: 175–93.

———. 2009b. "Zmoremo, torej moramo." *Filozosfki Vestnik* 30, no. 2: 175–97.

———. 2011a. *Hegel's Rabble: An Investigation into Hegel's Philosophy of Right.* London: Continuum.

———. 2011c. "Back to the Factory: A Plea for a Renewal of Concrete Analysis of Concrete Situations." In *Beyond Potentialities? Politics between the Possible and the Impossible*, edited by Mark Potocnik, Frank Ruda, and Jan Völker, 39–54. Zurich: Diaphanes.

———. 2012. "The Speculative Family, or Critique of the Critical Critique of Critique." *Filozofski vestnik* 33, no. 2: 53–76.

———. 2013a. "Remembering the Impossible: For a Meta-Critical Anamnesis of Communism." In *The Idea of Communism, Vol. 2*, edited by Alain Badiou and Slavoj Žižek, 137–68. London: Verso.

————. 2013b. "Thinking Politics Concretely: Negation, Affirmation and the Dialectics of Dialectics and Non-Dialectics." In *Thinking—Resisting—Reading the Political*, edited by Anneka-Esch-can-Kan, Stephen Packard, and Philip Schulte, 137–54. Zurich: Diaphanes.

————. 2013c. "Heglove prve besede." *Problemi* 3–4: 29–82.

————. 2014. "Saturation." In *The Badiou Dictionary*, edited by Steve Corcoran. Edinburgh: Edinburgh University Press.

Ruda, Frank, and Jan Völker. 2011. "Thèses pour une morale provisoire communiste." In *L'idée du communisme, vol. 2, Berlin 2010*, edited by Alain Badiou and Slavoj Žižek, 215–38. Paris: Lignes.

Ruda, Frank, and Rebecca Comay. forthcoming. *The Dash: Vicissitudes of Absolutes Knowing*. Cambridge, Mass.: MIT Press.

Sartre, Jean-Paul. 1967. "Cartesian Freedom." In *Literary Philosophical Essays*, by Jean-Paul Sartre, 180–97. Vancouver, Can.: Collier Books.

Schürmann, Rainer. 1979. "The Ontological Difference and Political Philosophy." *Philosophy and Phenomenological Research* 40, no. 1 (September): 99–122.

Thompson, Michael. 2004. "What Is It to Wrong Someone? A Puzzle about Justice." In *Reason and Value*, edited by R. Wallace, Philippe Petit, Samuel Scheffler, and Michael Smith, 333–84. Oxford: Oxford University Press.

————. 2012. *Life and Action: Elementary Structures of Practice and Practical Thought*. Cambridge, Mass.: Harvard University Press.

Trotsky, Leon. 2007. *Terrorism and Communism: A Reply to Karl Kautsky*. London: Verso.

Völker, Jan. 2011. *Ästhetik der Lebendigkeit: Kants dritte Kritik*. Munich: Fink.

Vranicki, Predrag. 1985. *Marxismus und Sozialismus*. Frankfurt am Main: Suhrkamp.

Wallace, David Foster. 2010. *Everything and More: A Compact History of Infinity*. New York: W. W. Norton.

Žižek, Slavoj. 1994. "The Specter of Ideology." In *Mapping Ideology*, edited by Slavoj Žižek, 1–33. London: Verso.

————. 1999. *The Ticklish Subject: The Absent Centre of Political Ontology*. London: Verso.

————. 2000a. "Melancholy and the Act." *Critical Inquiry* 26, no. 4 (Summer): 657–81.

————. 2000b. "From Proto-Reality to the Act: A Reply to Peter Dews." *Angelaki: Journal of the Theoretical Humanities* 5, no. 3 (December): 141–48.

————. 2001. *Did Somebody Say Totalitarianism? Five Interventions on the (Mis)Use of a Notion*. London: Verso.

————. 2002a. *Revolution at the Gates: Žižek on Lenin: The 1917 Writings*. London: Verso.

————. 2002b. *Die Revolution steht bevor: Dreizehn Versuche über Lenin*. Frankfurt am Main: Suhrkamp.

————. 2003a. *Die Puppe und der Zwerg*. Frankfurt am Main: Suhrkamp.

————. 2003b. *Organs without Bodies: Deleuze and Consequences*. Oxon.: Routledge.

————. 2005a. *Die politische Suspension des Ethischen*. Frankfurt am Main: Suhrkamp.

————. 2005b. "Neighbors and Other Monsters." In *The Neighbor: Three Inquiries into Political Theology*, edited by Kenneth Reinhard, Eric Santner, and Slavoj Žižek, 134–90. Chicago: University of Chicago Press.

———. 2005c. "The Act and Its Vicissitudes." *The Symptom: Online Journal for Lacan .com*, issue 6. http://www.lacan.com/symptom6_articles/zizek.html.

———. 2006a. *The Parallax View.* Cambridge, Mass.: MIT Press.

———. 2006b. "Philosophy, the 'Unknown Knowns,' and the Public Use of Reason." *Topoi* 2: 137–42.

———. 2008. *In Defense of Lost Causes.* London: Verso.

———. 2008a. *Violence: Six Sideways Reflections.* New York: Picador.

———. 2008b. *For They Know Not What They Do: Enjoyment as Political Factor.* London: Verso.

———. 2009a. *The Plague of Fantasies.* London: Verso.

———. 2009b. *First as Tragedy, Then as Farce.* London: Verso.

———. 2009c. "Dialectical Clarity versus the Misty Conceit of Parody." In *The Monstrosity of Christ: Paradox or Dialectic?* edited by Slavoj Žižek and John Milbank, 234–306. Cambridge, Mass.: MIT Press.

———. 2009d. "The Fear of Four Words: A Modest Plea for the Hegelian Reading of Christianity." In *The Monstrosity of Christ: Paradox or Dialectic?* edited by Slavoj Žižek and John Milbank, 24–109. Cambridge, Mass.: MIT Press.

———. 2009e. "The Liberal Utopia." http://www.egs.edu/faculty/slavoj-zizek/articles/denial-the-liberal-utopia/.

———. 2010a. *Living in the End Times.* London: Verso.

———. 2010b. "Plagiarizing from the Future." *Lacanian Ink* 36 (Spring): 148–61.

———. 2010c. "A Cup of Decaf Reality." http://www.lacan.com/zizekdecaf.htm.

———. 2011a. *Le plus sublime des hystériques.* Paris: Presses Universitaires de France.

———. 2011b. "Is It Still Possible to Be a Hegelian Today?" In *The Speculative Turn: Continental Materialism and Realism,* edited by Levy Bryant, Nick Srnicek, and Graham Harman, 202–23. Melbourne: re.press.

———. 2012. *Less Than Nothing: Hegel and the Shadow of Dialectical Materialism.* London: Verso.

Žižek, Slavoj, and Glyn Daly. 2004. *Conversations with Žižek.* Cambridge, Eng.: Polity.

Zupančič, Alenka. 2004. "The Fifth Conditions." In *Think Again: Alain Badiou and the Future of Philosophy,* edited by Peter Hallward, 191–201. London: Continuum.

———. 2008. *The Odd One In.* Cambridge, Mass.: MIT Press.

# Index